In My House

In My House

A Memoir Noel Charles

To Dr Peter Thanks

Harpese, Noel

Foreword by
Julian Lennon

Afterword by
Cynthia Lennon

Disco Daddy Publishing

To Cynthia and Julian

for their unwavering faith and love,
and for their constant support
in my life's journey

For my beautiful daughters:
Lisa, Penelope, Chloe
and Rosanna – with love

Also for the memory of my dear
departed brother, Courtenay

First published in 2012
by Disco Daddy Publishing

All photographs are from the author's personal collection.

1

Cataloguing in Publication Data is available from the
British Library.

ISBN 978-0-9571365-0-2

Designed by Craig Stevens
Edited by Julian Flanders
Typeset in Bodoni

Printed and bound in the UK by the MPG Books Group,
Bodmin and King's Lynn

Disco Daddy Publishing Limited
20 Bulstrode Street
London W1U 2JW

Contents

Foreword

by Julian Lennon

Noel Charles is the older brother I never had and also, in many ways, the father I always wanted. Today he remains one of my dearest friends. I am so pleased to be able to write a brief introduction to this book, a book which has been many years in the making, and which has been eagerly awaited by many around the world. It is a remarkable story about an extraordinary man, which, unsurprisingly, is always honest, always generous and always entertaining.

As Noel recounts in these pages, our first meeting was at a nightclub in London not long after my father's death. I was in my late teens. During that evening, Noel extended what I thought was a casual invitation to visit him in Barbados. Shortly afterwards, I was actually taken to Barbados by a friend of mine, whose family were also friends of Noel's. It was my first real trip away from the UK as a young man, so it was a very exciting time.

Noel was then perhaps the most influential player on the island's social scene. There wasn't anyone who didn't recognise him as the head honcho when it came to clubs, and in particular his club, Alexandra's. It was the most elegant, trendy, cool nightspot in Barbados – and possibly the entire Caribbean. All the other bars and clubs at that time were predictably 'tropical', built of driftwood logs and palm tree leaves, with sand floors. However, Alexandra's was in a league of its own. Catering to the wealthy elite of the island, Europe and North America, it boasted 30-foot high ceilings, beautiful polished wood floors; served superb champagnes and fine wines to accompany its delectable menu of haute cuisine. Noel was as gracious as they came: always well dressed, always ready with a charming smile and always welcoming. I was fortunate that he liked me and took me under his protective wing, as there were plenty of destructive influences rattling around. The last thing he wanted was for something bad to happen to me. I trusted him and, looking back years later, I appreciate his discreet care. While I certainly enjoyed myself as a young man on my heady adventure, it would have been very easy for me to lose control and to lose sight of myself. Noel made sure that didn't happen.

Over the years, the tide changed in Barbados. The brilliant elegance of Alexandra's was eclipsed, and only the beach clubs were surviving. The very popularity of the island seemed to have provoked a kind of identity crisis, a revolt against its own best interests. As a result, Noel found himself at a loss. His early success had naturally provoked jealousy among some, and he had his share of enemies. His many hopeful new projects just couldn't quite come to fruition. Eventually, he found himself on hard times.

We always spent time together whenever I came to the island, our friendship grew and matured, but the past was gone. I felt sorry for him after all he had accomplished. He was a huge personality, a distinguished man, who had been reduced to working inside a rough and tumble bar hut. Of course, there were still many who remembered the good old days and who bought him a round or two on occasion. Happily, there was also a solid core of grateful friends who always stood by Noel back in England, New York and Canada, as well as on Barbados and his native Trinidad. I was never in any doubt that Noel would prevail over life's hard knocks, but there were times I could not help worrying about him. My worries ended years ago.

In essence I introduced mum and Noel. I thought that they'd both been through the mill and had so many similar experiences, so much history, that surely they'd be a perfect match for each other. At the time, they both seemed at a loss for meaningful love and friendship. Sadly, their first experiences together were far from warm or compassionate. In truth, they were like chalk and cheese, oil and water. But fast forward one year and something clicked. Suddenly, nobody could separate the buggers! They became like naughty children. They still are! Watching them together, I often think they seem to share a secret, one that nobody else should know, and one that they're not going to tell the rest of us. Needless to say, I was overjoyed when they fell in love and eventually married.

This is a book which I am sure will interest (and inspire) thousands of readers who lacked an opportunity to know Noel Charles in person, as I am fortunate to know him, but who will never forget the remarkable man who comes to life in these pages.

Part One

Trinidad

It is Sunday afternoon when I hear the roar. I am in the garden, playing marbles on my knees in the dirt circle. My brother kneels beside me, our eyes fixed on the brightly coloured cat's eye spheres that we flick with our thumbs. We carved this circle out of the lush tropical vegetation behind our tin roofed house on a hillside overlooking Port of Spain. I am seven years old. I have lived on the island of Trinidad all my life.

We are back from that morning's church service, where my father preached his sermon, where we prayed and sang the ancient English and Scottish hymns of the Brethren. My father and mother are very religious, and my brother and I live according to our parents' strict rules and the Brethren's high principles. My father is also the owner of a successful shoemaking and shoe repair business. His handmade shoes are of the finest quality, also made according to strict rules and high standards.

The roar is coming from the sky.

I worship my father, a very formal and dignified man who loves my brother, my sister and me deeply, even if he rarely touches us. After church, we returned to our house in Belmont and my mother served us the lunch she had cooked earlier that morning. My brother and I are always careful to use the very best table manners, to bow our heads deeply as our father says grace, to eat our soup out of the correct side of the bowl. We can feel our mother's fierce eyes watching every move we make at the table. We know that if we make a mistake, we will get the painful strap later, when she is alone with us, when we are lying helpless in our beds. But never in front of Father. Our sister, however, is far less concerned, chatting happily away at the lunch table. She is older than us, and is our mother's favourite child, even though she was adopted eight years before I was born. My sister Dorothy never gets the strap.

'What is it?' my brother asks. We both stare up into the sky. The roar grows louder and louder, but we cannot see anything unusual in the vast blue Caribbean sky.

'There!' I shout. It's just come over the green crest of the hill above us. Is it an enormous bird? Is it a flying cross? I have never before seen an aeroplane.

'Father!' shouts my brother Courtenay.

'Father, please come here!' I shout beside him.

We can both hear sudden movements inside the wooden house 50 feet away from our marble circle. Our eyes are wide open in terror as we watch this monster fly directly above us, several thousand feet up, gleaming silver, deafening us. Is this a true flight of the imagination – or is it real?

Still dressed in his best Sunday suit and tie, my father appears in the doorway of our house, six feet six inches tall, one of his religious books in his hand. He stares down at us in the circle with stern eyes, at our bare arms pointing up at the sky. Then he allows his head to rise and his eyes take in the object of our concern. I watch his face carefully, knowing that his response will tell me everything I need to know. Should we start running, try to throw ourselves beneath the house? Should we drop on our bellies and crawl under the green leaves of the garden?

My father's smile is rare, but when it comes it makes me feel better than anything else in the world. Now I watch his mouth shape the grin that I love so much. He laughs out loud.

'You two silly boys, haven't you ever seen an aeroplane before?'

We shake our heads. This is Trinidad in 1946. We have never seen an airplane above our heads until this moment.

'Don't be afraid now,' he says, coming down the step and into the garden. He walks to where we stand. 'Don't you know that an aeroplane is one of man's greatest creations? It can carry dozens of people all the way to New York City, Paris or London. It can lift you up above the clouds and bring you to a place in a few hours that would take weeks to reach on a ship.'

Together we stand and watch the aeroplane as it heads out of sight beyond the mango trees in our neighbour's yard. The roar is softer now, diminishing with each second. The aeroplane is heading out across the ocean.

At that very serious moment, I suddenly know that one day I will be inside an aeroplane, crossing an ocean, alone but happy, living my own dream, and remembering the warmth of my father's smile on this Sunday afternoon in the garden.

My father was born on another island, with a different name. In 1892, Henry Joseph Braithwaite was born on Barbados, in the east coast parish of St John.

One of seven brothers, he left the island in his teens to go and work on the Panama Canal. The men worked in shifts of a month's duration out in the wretched mosquito-infested swamps of the isthmus, and then returned to the base camp where they and their families lived. After a few weeks' break, the men would return to the swamp.

In the base camp, my father met and fell in love with a pretty girl named Matilda, who eventually became his common-law wife. His life was not easy, but he was relatively content until he fell ill with fever out in the swamps. He was sent back to base camp to recuperate. Walking in the door, unexpected, he discovered Matilda in bed with another man. Devastated, he fled and went to a friend's shack to wait until he was well enough to travel. Back on his feet, but heartsick at Matilda's betrayal, he decided to leave Panama. When he went to the harbour, the next departing ship was bound for Jamaica. He booked his passage. Once there, he found a position as a shoemaker's apprentice. His good sense told him that cobblers could always make a decent living.

Time passed quickly. Henry learned his trade well, and eventually saved enough money to open his own shop. But, using the ship's manifest, Matilda had traced him to Jamaica and one day she appeared on his doorstep. Begging for forgiveness, she tried to embrace him. 'It's too late for that. The only thing I want is to see the back of you.'

Matilda refused to leave him alone. She rented a room nearby and began to follow him day and night, constantly begging for his forgiveness or attempting to seduce him. The best he could do was to stall for time. He told her that, if she would leave him alone for one week, he would think hard about her pleas for reconciliation.

Without telling her, he packed his clothes and left for Grenada.

Within months, he had fallen in love with a local beauty – a petite, well-spoken girl named Drucilla, whose appearance reflected her partially Spanish ancestry. She possessed a natural sense of style and the best manners of any person he had ever met. He was convinced that she would never betray him. In turn, Drucilla adored her dignified Bajan craftsman who was never arrogant or reckless, who shared her devout faith in God, and who was the gentlest man she had ever known.

But when Matilda, again having found his name on a ship's passenger manifest, appeared on Grenada, Henry knew he would have to flee once more. He asked Drucilla to elope with him, to Trinidad. Determined never to be traced again, he changed his name to Henry Joseph Charles. As soon as they arrived in Port of Spain, he and Drucilla were married at the Christian Brethren church.

In Trinidad he launched his career as a shoemaker. Business was good from the start in Port of Spain. He opened the first heel repair bar on the island, as well as his own line of made-to-order shoes. Equally industrious, Drucilla began to design stylish dresses and hats, and to bake fancy cakes, which she gave to their neighbours and to their church. She became pregnant, but when the child died at birth, Henry convinced her they should adopt a one-year-old orphan named Dorothy.

This girl child became everything to Drucilla, a cherub to be spoiled in all ways, dressed in the finest little dresses and shoes, with hours spent brushing her hair and pampering in every way. As the cobbling business prospered, the Charles family would move into a succession of larger and more comfortable houses. Along the way, they acquired Ruth – nanny, cook and maid to the household.

Eight years after the death of their first child, I was born. Four more years passed and my brother Courtenay came into the world. While my father was overjoyed to have sons, my mother was strangely resentful. I have no memories whatsoever of maternal affection, only memories of her anger, suspicion and beatings. In her house, little boys were never to be trusted. Little boys were to be beaten into good behaviour.

Ruth, our housekeeper, was encouraged to punish us severely whenever she deemed it necessary, and even our neighbours were told to beat us when they felt it was appropriate. My sister Dorothy, of course, was never scolded, let alone beaten. God help anyone who dared to upset little Dorothy.

'Noel, where is your brother?' my mother would ask.

'I don't know, Mother.'

'You are lying. I know what you two get up to. As soon as I leave for town, you both go to play with those filthy ruffians down the street. Ruth, where is that naughty boy?'

'I call him in the road, but he jus run away.'

'Go fetch him for me, Ruth. Wait until I get my hands on him. And you, Noel, are going to be truly sorry you lied to me today.'

How I admired my younger brother Courtenay for his independence and his courage. Although smaller than me, he was more confident, soft-spoken but tough, loyal and uncompromising when it came to our mother's attempts to curb his freedom. Often his independent ways cost me dearly, as I would be hit for Courtenay's misconduct simply because I was there while he had slipped away. Indeed, I could be whipped simply for the expression on my face.

Hence I learned to keep an expressionless poker face from a very early age. At my mother's knee, as they say. Later in life this would pay me handsome rewards. Perhaps I should be grateful to her for that lesson in life. Still, it cost me enough.

My very first home is the flat above my father's shop in the heart of Port of Spain, on the busy corner of Henry Street and Prince Street. Upstairs is the large attic, which my father uses as a storage space for his lasts, leathers and other materials. Downstairs on the street is the constant flow of humanity that makes Trinidad one of the most cosmopolitan places on earth. The faces I see as a young child reflect a social mixture of African, Indian, Spanish, Arab, French, Chinese, English and Hindi ancestry. I grow up in a world that is so multiracial, multicultural and multi-religious that, years later, when I first arrive in London, I will be shocked to see so many white faces. I grow up without racial prejudice on an island that, to my mind, is very close to paradise. A prosperous island, Trinidad is rich in both agriculture – cocoa, sugar cane, rice, coffee, citrus fruit and in mineral wealth, with the abundant oil reserves you would expect due to its close proximity to Venezuela.

From a very early age, I am thrilled when the streets of Port of Spain explode with the sounds, costumes and dances of Carnival week. The melodious 'panning' of the steel bands goes on all night and the dancers – calypso was actually invented on the island – whirl and shimmy with sensual abandon. Everyone is equal at Carnival. All ages, classes, races lose their inhibitions to revel in the raucous streets. It is the culmination of the Trinidadian year, the ultimate island experience. In addition to Carnival, the island celebrates several major Hindu festivals. Most important, Diwali in October is another national holiday, when outside Indian homes, shops and temples coconut oil flames burn into the night in rows of small ceramic *deya* lamps to mark this 'festival of lights'. There is also the Holi festival, when buildings, even whole villages, are draped in red cloth and the people chant devotional songs to the beating of drums.

These holidays are very much part of my world, but a part that is always forbidden territory for my brother Courtenay and me. Our mother will not allow us to dress in costumes or to dance in the streets. That does not stop Courtenay, however, who early on develops a passion for steel pan drumming. This, too, originated on the island of Trinidad, and Courtenay will sneak off to learn the secrets of 'panning' from an early age, eventually becoming a member of one of the legendary bands – the Invaders – and embarking on a life's journey as a musician.

But our normal day begins in our father's bedroom. Already dressed in one of his tailored suits, he sits in his chair and we perch on the edge of his bed. He reads to us from the Bible. Then we bow our heads and say prayers. Only then can we clamber to the breakfast table, where blessings are said before we touch a bit of food. Another prayer after we finish eating, then hurry to collect our books so that we can leave on time for the walk to school.

At the catholic Rosary Boys' School, in downtown Port of Spain, we start our mornings in the school hall. The teachers say prayers, and heaven won't protect you from their wrath if you are late. This is one of the best schools on the island, and it is ruled with iron discipline. I can never relax here, always afraid of the stern teachers and, most of all, the headmaster, a large man who wields a cane that can leave scars on your legs – and on your mind – that will last the rest of your life. I study mathematics, history, English, Latin, Spanish, religion and literature.

As my father's business prospers, he moves our family out of the centre of Port of Spain and up the slope to Belmont, to our own house, with its lush garden and proximity to Queen's Park Savannah.

One of our favourite games in Belmont is playing 'Cowboys and Indians'. Some of the boys have air rifles, so we shoot small birds. Sometimes we each take something from our parents' kitchens – a potato, some rice, garlic, spices, vegetables – and we build a fire and cook up our own feasts using the fish or game we have captured. I love to cook, and I have carefully studied what goes on in my own kitchen when Ruth or my mother is at the stove. My friends soon let me try out various combinations, and this is the beginning of what will become a lifetime's pastime of cooking for family and friends. Few things in life make me happier.

At the bottom of the garden in Belmont is a one-bedroom bungalow. This is occupied by a Trinidadian Hindu couple – Jit and Moon are their names – who have converted the balcony into a little shop where they sell vegetables, flour, coal pots, toys and home baked rotis, doubles, alloo pies, pholourie and tomato choka. Having this pastry shop on my doorstep is a delightful part of childhood. Exposure to the different aromas and flavours of my mother's West Indian cooking, Ruth's Trinidadian specialties and Moon's Trinidadian Indian delicacies will give me an adventurous palate that will last the rest of my life.

Jit is a tall, lanky man who loves his rum, although it doesn't always love him. Moon is just the opposite, short and plump, with a face that evokes her name. I am her favourite among the Charles kids and she is my stalwart defender when it comes to Ruth's strict harassment. I am sorry that many nights I hear her soft sobbing across the yard while Jit shouts drunken insults at her.

'Ruth, why yuh don't leave that boy alone? He's a good boy.'

'Mind yuh own business woman!'

'Yuh always beatin dat boy. Leave him be.'

'Yur man Jit he beats on you. Tell him to leave yuh alone, nuh?'

'You must be crazy mean, Ruth, nuh?'

The only time I ever see my father in a true rage comes the afternoon a panic-stricken Moon bursts into our kitchen. She is clutching a towel around her naked body, and fleeing a drunken Jit, shouting, 'Please help me. He's gonna kill me today.' She rushes straight into my room. I am stunned to see her cower in the corner, but can't help peeking out through the door.

My father has been sound asleep, napping in his chair in the drawing room. One thing he has always taught us is not to wake him – or anyone – abruptly, with loud noises. Now Moon's screams have woken him from a well-deserved nap and I hear the anger in his voice when he shouts, 'What is going on here? What's all this noise?'

I hear Jit's drunken, enraged voice outside in the yard, shouting, 'Woman, come heah now! Get out heah!'

'You get off my back steps and out of my yard,' says my father.

'Where is she at?' demands Jit, daring to step into the kitchen.

'Out of my house!' Then I see my father reach for a wood saw that happens to be in the kitchen, left there after some recent repairs. He raises it like a sabre and advances on the drunken Hindu, 'You're going to be very sorry Jit if you don't get back to your own house this instant. Go now!'

I hear the slurred mumblings and clattering footsteps of Jit's hasty retreat. Soon my father is back in the house, telling my mother to look after Moon. 'Get her something to wear and give her a cup of tea, please will you,' he orders. I have never seen my father angry like this before. I know that waking him suddenly from his sleep is a very bad thing.

Later that evening I ask, 'What were you going to do to Jit with that saw, Father?'

'Saw him in half, the fool. How can a man behave like that to his own dear wife? Respect the ladies, Noel. You must always respect the ladies.' I listen to his advice very carefully, but in my heart I suspect that my father would never saw anyone in half, or truly hurt them, even if he was woken from the deepest sleep.

The slipway in Port of Spain juts its two concrete arms out into the sea. It is where boats used to be launched, but now it is abandoned. As well as a good fishing spot, it is a place for us boys to swim, joke around, and toss each other into the water. In fact, this is where I learn to swim shortly after we move to Belmont. Some boys toss me into the water, and I have to fight to keep my head clear, my arms and legs moving, until I reach the other side. It's terrifying, but I feel a rush of pride. I can't wait to make that swim again. I throw myself right back into the sea.

It is a perfect spring day. I am sitting with my friends on the edge of the playing field behind the school. We have just finished eating our lunches and the bell will ring in a few minutes to call us back for afternoon classes. 'It's so fine and hot. Sure would like a swim,' says one guy.

'Love to jump in the water down at the "Hot Pot",' says another guy. Strange how we all decide to take the risk without even a half-hearted debate. I suppose that's what happens to boys when spring arrives.

We slip back through the trees and gardens, across the road, and down through the narrow streets, towards our favourite swimming hole. This is outside the Trinidad Electric Company's power plant, and is actually a canal full of hot water that has been used inside the plant. You can jump off the edge and into the rushing water, feeling like you are flying naked for a second, then pulled along in a hot gush. It's a fantasy of freedom and daring. All too brief, of course.

The two truant officers who arrive at the Hot Pot have ferocious scowls on their faces. They shout at us to get out of the water immediately, make us put on our clothes although we're still soaking wet, slap our heads and pull our ears to herd us back up the hillside.

In front of the whole school, the headmaster takes the cane to each of us in turn. Six strokes apiece and the pain is terrible. No mercy is shown. 'Now each of you back to your classrooms. I am going to write to your families and tell them one more wicked escapade like this and you will each be expelled.'

I spend the next few days looking out for the post but the letter comes while I am at school. When I arrive home, any thought of racing out to play is quickly banished by the sight of my mother at the kitchen table, the strap already in her hand. She swings it at my face, but I duck away. She hits me across the backside, and then on my neck, my arms, my bare legs, already marked by the headmaster's cane and unbearably tender.

'What do we send you to that school for? So you can go swimming? You little ruffian, I will beat respect into you if it's the last thing I do.'

'Please stop, Mother.' I say this in a calm voice. I never beg my mother.

'You just wait till I tell your father. He's going to throw you out of his house. You are going to be an orphan, begging on the streets. Then you see, Noel, how sorry you will be.'

Of course, my father, disappointed as he might be with my misbehaviour, will never throw me out of his house. He loves his two sons with a love that, I believe, makes my mother jealous. Just as we are jealous of Dorothy and all the fancy dresses, special shoes, adorable hats that she receives from my mother. On the surface, our father treats all three of his children with equality. Yet I believe – though perhaps it is only wishful thinking – he secretly favours his two boys. I would never confess to it, but I want it to be so.

On Saturdays my father takes me to his shop in the centre of Port of Spain. He gives me a bowl full of brown pennies and I stand just inside the doorway. The line of poor beggars stretches around the corner. My job is to hand each man a penny. I am amazed how many poor men there are, and wonder where they all come from. I know that this charity is important to my father. It makes me feel important too, putting a coin into each of those outstretched, unwashed palms.

'Father!'

'What is it, Noel?'

'That man who just left. I think it was his third time in the line today.'

My father frowns and says sternly. 'Maybe it's because he *needs* it.'

These few words hit me harder than my mother's strap ever does. I feel my cheeks flush hot with shame and I lower my eyes. I feel my father can read my thoughts. I cannot hide anything from him, and I do not want to do so. The next man steps forward and, without looking at his face, I take two pennies out of the bowl and press them into his hand.

I am always in a hurry to drop off my books, change my clothes and grab my fishing gear. I head down the hill to the slipway, which juts out into the turquoise blue water. Sitting on the end, I bait my hook and cast it out as far as I can. I am not alone, and share the slipway with the regular fishermen, mostly men far older than me, and the swimmers. It varies, but usually the water here is teeming with fish. Still it is rare to catch one big enough to take home. How proud I am on the evenings I arrive home with a fish that will make Ruth smile in the kitchen. 'I fry it up for you suppa, Noel. You a good fishermun, sure you is.'

My mother resents even this harmless escape from her control. 'Boy, we don't need any more fish in this house. Your father provides all we need for our table,' she says one night. 'I don't like you fishing at night.'

We are in the drawing room. My father is reading his newspaper, but he lowers it now and stares at his wife, then at his small son, who is looking at the floor. 'What's wrong with the boy fishing?' he asks. 'If he wants to fish, let him fish.' It is a rare intervention, but his decision is always final.

The time comes when my father is doing so well in his business that he decides to move us again. He buys a lovely three-bedroom house in the middle-class suburb of Woodbrook, not far from the sea. In the back garden, he turns a shed into a two-storey house for Ruth and her daughter.

In Woodbrook, I learn how to roller skate. Skating becomes the 'in' thing with all my friends. We go to the outdoor basketball court where the asphalt is very smooth and clip our skates onto our shoes and boots. I design my own skating boots and learn to make them in my father's shop – white, with a lightning bolt down the side. Like skateboarders today, we practice doing stunts for hours after school. I see a film in which Sonja Hennie stars and I fall in love with her, and the whole enchanting world of ice skating. Of course, on a tropical island, the closest I can get to gliding over the ice is on a pair of metal skates that traverse a flat expanse of asphalt. But that does not stop my imagination from casting me in films where I skate in tandem with Sonja, defying gravity in romantic leaps and whirling together in endless graceful circles.

A man named Defreitas, an excellent skater, takes a real interest in us, shows us how to waltz with girl partners and choreograph our own performances. With his help, we decide to put on a show. I am so excited by this – and so inspired by my waltzing partner – that I can't sleep at night for all the thoughts I have in my head about costumes and new skating moves and how we can decorate the basketball court for the night of the performance. Looking back I believe this was a turning point in my life: the moment when I started to care passionately about all the elements of design and decoration that would one day, when I was designing my nightclubs, be such an essential part of my success. For me, roller skating is more than just moving fast, it is actually the first step on a road that will lead me to care passionately about elegance, about crystal chandeliers, velvet curtains, gilded mirrors and all the other refined elements that composed the unique – and much copied – atmosphere of my nightclubs.

My sister Dorothy is married not long after our move to Woodbrook. Her husband is a Trinidadian man, a member of our church, who has moved to New York City. Dorothy will leave and accompany him back to America. My father gives his approval, but my mother is very upset. For my part, I think this just may be my chance. I feel a new hope. My mother could now dote on me for a change, stop berating and beating me.

It is a vain hope. Within a week of Dorothy's departure, a very dark-skinned, handsome young woman named Selma, 18 years old and an orphan member of our church, is brought to live with us. She is my mother's replacement for Dorothy, and immediately she begins to receive the same pampering, the same lengthy hair combing and plaiting sessions, same fancy dresses and special shoes. She is determined to 'polish' her new 'daughter' until she shines like a rare jewel.

Selma towers above both my brother and I. She has a voluptuous figure, and I find it difficult not to gawp at her. My brother Courtenay finds her extremely annoying and becomes even more resentful of this stranger who receives so much love from his mother, love he knows should be his. But I notice something in Selma that Courtenay does not see, a look in her eyes when they meet mine.

Time passes and my body begins to change. One night Selma passes me in the corridor and her breast pushes softly against my arm. I don't know what gives me the courage but, after an hour of feigning sleep, I rise from my bed and leave my room. I can hear the sound of my father's snores, my mother's regular breathing. Very carefully, I enter the drawing room where Selma sleeps on the sofa bed. She stirs and I go to stand beside her. Without saying a word, she reaches up and takes my hand. She brings it to her bosom outside the sheet. I sit down on the edge of the bed and feel my fingers clasp the firmness of her curving breast. Then I slip my hand under the linen and onto the cotton nightdress, and inside to the heat of her bare flesh. As I move my fingers to the hard bud of her nipple, Selma takes a sharp intake of breath. She allows me to touch her for a few minutes, first one breast, then the other. My heart beats like thunder.

Suddenly her hands grab my wrist and hold it tight. She pulls my hand out. 'Go now,' she whispers. 'Don't tell nobody.'

'I won't tell. Don't you tell either.'

'Goodnight, Noel.'

I stand and cross the floor as quietly as possible, then slip out of her room and make my way back to my own. It is the first of many nights with Selma, nights of touching and, in my case, nights of sweet revenge.

I am 13 years old when my father says, 'Things must be as they will. Noel, you are ready to learn the trade, to use the materials. From now on, you can come to the shop after school on Fridays and all day on Saturday. You can use my materials and machines, and keep the money you earn from what you make, same as the other men here. Time you earned your own money.'

I have grown up inside the shoe shop and, from an early age, had been encouraged to mend my own shoes. Now my father has instructed his workers to teach me how to cobble. These are the best years of my young life, working in the shop.

'No, no, not like that,' Theo would say.

'What did I do wrong?'

'You haven't done anything wrong yet. But you going too fast. Slow down your hands. Take it careful. This is how to pack the last.'

Theo is my father's foreman – a short, stocky man in his 40s, with a crooked neck that bends so far to the left sometimes I think it is in danger of falling right off. He never smiles, but he is very kind. Today he is working the darning machine when he says, 'Noel, can you take over here?'

'Sure, Theo.'

I have been watching him work this machine for years, so now I slip right into the rhythm, darning the leather pieces together, thinking about the tidy sum I am earning, until I run the needle right through my thumb just as my father enters the shop.

'Noel, what did you do to yourself?'

'It's nothing, Father. I missed the bone.'

'It's bleeding badly.'

'No, it's fine.'

I can see my father's pride in me as he goes to the cupboard where the first aid kit is stored. He comes back and takes my hand, cleans the little wound with alcohol, and wraps a bandage around it.

'OK, you get back to work now. But be careful, son. That machine is not a toy. Not a little fishhook either.'

'Yes, Father.'

Saturdays at the shop bring a dramatic increase in my income. I still get an allowance, but now I am earning my own money as well. Now I can treat my friends to rotis and soft drinks. I buy a new cricket bat, new pads, even a new bicycle. I feel much freer with this new money in my pocket. And so begins another lifelong passion – gambling. I believe that the discovery of luck combined with skill is one of the most important moments of every boy's life. Certainly it was for me. From a very early age, I was thrilled by the act of winning. Whether it was playing marbles as a small child or racing to the finish in a long-distance race in Woodbrook, I loved the feeling of winning. And I would continue to seek out this feeling – luck combined with skill, the ability to use your 'third eye' to see a winning opportunity – for the rest of my life: in casinos, at poker tables and at the racetrack.

Selby, Kirby and Wally are three brothers who have a wealthy father, Mr Thomson, who owns and races horses. One day when I am at their house, I overhear a conservation between Mr Thomson and his trainer, jockey and the groom. I listen carefully as they discuss the card for that coming Saturday's races at the Savannah track in Port of Spain.

I ask my father if I can take Saturday afternoon off to go to Savannah Park with my friends the Thomsons. I don't mention horse racing, for he would surely disapprove, but the Savannah is where the racetrack is located. He gives me his permission. At the track, remembering what names had been mentioned, I place a winning bet on the first race. Then Selby Thomson explains about forecasting and multiple bets, and seems to know just what horses we should pick. By the end of the day, I have won big, what seems like a small fortune to me.

When I reach home that evening, my mother is sitting at the dining room table reading her Bible. I cannot help myself and empty out my pockets on the table in front of her.

'Noel, wherever you get that money from, I want you to take it back right this minute.'

'Can't take it back. I won all this at the races today.'

'You did what? Wait until your father hears this!'

'It's all mine. And Father gave me the permission to go to Savannah with the Thomsons.'

She removes her spectacles, her mouth dropping open, then tightening in rage. I feel as if I have been punched in the stomach as she shouts, 'You fool! You sinner! Surely you didn't mention gambling on horses to your father.'

'Why am I a fool? Look how much I won.'

'You are a sinful fool and not worth beating.'

'Mother, please, what did I do wrong?'

She stands up and turns to leave the room. 'I cannot bear the sight of you. You are not my child. You are somebody else's fool.'

I stand there looking at the bills spread out on the table and feeling more confused than ever. What would it take to earn my mother's respect, her love? I have no idea, none whatsoever, as I gather the money and stuff it back in my pockets.

Of all the adults, apart from my father, my favourite is Uncle Harry. Whether he is an uncle by blood or simply an honorary one I will never know, but a bond has been forged between me and this dark-skinned older man – gentle, decent, straightforward – who always takes a keen interest in me on his rare visits to the city.

Uncle Harry lives on a hillside in Trinidad's deep country, beside the dense rainforest of Guayaguayare in the south-easternmost part of the island. Although rich oil deposits were found there as far back as 1870, much of the territory is still virgin rainforest. From an early age, Harry entertains me with stories about his bucolic life. When Uncle Harry is in our house, he seems to bring out the best in everyone, even in my mother, who loves to listen to his stories and who seems to soften when in his presence.

Uncle Harry has built his own house from trees that he felled when clearing the site. This fact alone awes me, gives me a vision of natural balance and perfection. Uncle Harry lives off the land, hunts game in the forest, gathers wild fruit and edible roots. He tells stories about hunting agouti, Lapp, iguana and deer. About the big snakes that must be avoided when crossing the jungle floor.

Uncle Harry has often invited me to come and visit his home, but my mother always forbids it. Until one Sunday lunch early in my summer holiday when Uncle Harry repeats his invitation and my father says, 'That seems like a good idea for Noel. He could do with some new experiences to help his confidence.'

My mother bites her lip and says nothing, while Uncle Harry reaches across the table, claps me on the shoulder and says, 'We gonna give him some new experiences that's for sure.'

After Uncle Harry departs for his home, all during the next few weeks before my own departure, my mother wears a vacant look on her face, refusing to acknowledge my presence, humming old hymns softly to herself, staring into space from the kitchen door.

I take a train south to San Fernando. I have been looking forward to this part of the journey especially. Train rides are a delicious rarity in my young life, usually limited to the annual Sunday school excursion to Aranguez in St Juan, not far from home at all. As I sit on that train, I feel the delicious excitement of freedom. Uncle Harry meets me at the station. He has come along with a friend who owns a car. On the long drive across country towards the village of Guayaguayare, Harry chats away and I ask many questions, but he never loses his patience, always explains things in vivid detail.

Once we reach the village, we have a trek up into the hills ahead of us. This is a revelation. We follow a stream with many cascades and crystal pools where you can see the iridescent flashes of darting fish and crustaceans. We step along a path over the snaggled roots of golden apple, kymit and mango trees. Overhead the canopy is alive with different birdsongs. The rainforest is beyond my wildest imaginings, so beautiful after the city life I have grown up in that I feel tears forming in my eyes as I watch the vibrant ginger lilies, the explosion of a bird of paradise, the wild hibiscus. A woodpecker drills alone and echoes endlessly. Hummingbirds float from flower to flower. I see an occasional monkey staring down at us from a high branch, munching on a piece of fruit, tossing it away casually. This is a magical journey.

I see the house above us. Rising on wooden stilts, it is encircled by a spacious deck. As we approach, a woman comes out to stare at us. Softly rounded, jet-black, she flashes the brightest smile and gleaming white teeth. It's Uncle Harry's Venezuelan common-law wife Tilda. He's often mentioned her, telling stories of how he met her on a trip to Maracaibo.

'So is this Mr Noel himself, of whom I have heard so much?' she says.

'Pleased to meet you, Tilda,' I say and extend my hand. She ignores this and engulfs me in a huge padded embrace. Then she insists I tell her how each of my family is faring back in Port of Spain. From this moment, I feel completely at home. Inside, all the rooms are large, high ceilinged, cool with the breezes up here above the forest. The furniture is hand-made from various rare woods. The water, explains Tilda, is pure and fresh from a natural spring higher up the hill. Born and raised in the city, this is my dream of Swiss Family Robinson, of Wild West adventure, of perfect freedom.

The days pass and Uncle Harry teaches me many secrets of a self-sufficient natural lifestyle. I am so grateful for every detail. And let myself sink into the warm affection of Tilda, who mothers me as I have never been mothered before.

Uncle Harry teaches me how to fire his rifle and I practice for hours. After practice, he takes me on long walks to pick wild fruit. He knows I love to fish, so one morning he announces we are going down to fish in a pool on the river where he knows the fish are 'big as your arm, Noel, and delicious to eat the way Tilda cook them.'

The time comes when he trusts me enough to take me hunting. We rise early in the morning and set out on a walk deep into the forest. I feel completely lost, but Uncle Harry assures me he knows exactly where we are going. When he signals for me to keep quiet, I follow behind him on my tiptoes as he eases himself into thick brush. He stops and points. I see the iguana ahead, two of them, in a sun-dappled clearing. Large, ferocious-looking reptiles, they make delicious eating. He hands me the shotgun and positions me in front of him. He taps the part of his body that he wants me to aim for on the lizard. I feel my arm shaking but force it steady as I sight along the barrel. The pulled trigger releases an explosion in the jungle that seems to echo for minutes, while the two iguanas bolt. Except one of them only takes two strides before tumbling on its shoulder. It's down and it's my first kill.

I stare at this animal with a mixture of pride and fear as Uncle Harry turns it so I can see the surprisingly small wound where my bullet entered the side of its head. He hefts it up and slings it across his shoulders. 'Good eating here for two days, Noel. You shot like you been shootin all your life.'

Soon after this, Uncle Harry encourages me to take the rifle out hunting on my own. I am too much of a city boy to stalk with his skill, so rarely find anything to shoot at. Then I step on a log across a narrow path only to have it twitch and then slink away. It is a sleeping boa constrictor. Another day I lift a rock near the house, only to discover what looks at first like a beautiful beaded bracelet. My mother's voice suddenly enters my head, and I recall a story she told me about how, when she was a girl, she picked up a coral snake without knowing what it was. Very small, with bands of bright colour on their soft bodies, coral snakes are lethal if they bite you. Fortunately, she was not bitten. Now I resist the urge to touch this creature and slowly back away from it. So pretty and so deadly, I feel my heart racing.

Day by day, with Uncle Harry's guidance and Tilda's love, I learn more about facing my fears than I have ever learned before. When the three weeks come to an end and it is time for me to return to the city, I walk down the hill beside the river with a new confidence. I must be a man now, I think. But as soon as I walk into the door of my parents' house, later that evening, I know I'm far from a man. Still, I am determined to become a man as soon as I possibly can.

I still visit Selma late at night, from time to time. We never go all the way, but we do kiss and explore one another. Then the day comes when she says, 'Noel, you get out of here right now. Don't you know I am going to get married?'

'No, nobody told me that.'

'Well, why should they tell you, boy? It's true. All arranged. He's a nice man and I can't be doing something foolish like this anymore.'

'You won't tell him, will you?'

'Don't be a fool. Get out, Noel.'

So I go away, and soon Selma goes away too. And I am happy to see her go.

I am at my best friend Bash's house a block from my home. We often play here in the large laundry room on the ground floor. We are kicking a small rubber ball back and forth across the linoleum floor today, confident that neither of his parents is likely to venture downstairs to check on us. But we are not alone.

Franka is the family maid. She is in her early thirties, East Indian, with slender hips and wide seductive lips on her attractive face. Both Bash and I are very conscious of her long pointed nipples clearly visible through her white cotton blouse. She follows our eyes and laughs at us. 'What you looking at, you boys? What you thinking?'

'Not looking at nothing,' Bash says.

'Oh yeah? Let me see then?' she says, and makes a grab for his crotch. She gets a firm hand on it as a startled Bash tries to jump backwards. I laugh.

'What you laughin at? I know you lookin too!' Suddenly her hand is between my legs, finding my penis and giving it a firm squeeze. 'Boy, dat ting small. Too small,' she teases. Then she laughs loudly, grabs the basket full of folded sheets and is gone from the room.

Bash and I look at each other and shake our heads. Words are beyond us. We've been lusting after Franka for months, ever since we turned 13. Bash has already had a wet dream. I am envious, and curious, and long to experience this myself. And this is not the first time Franka has touched us. She loves to tease us both, unmercifully.

A few weeks pass. Bash and I walk to buy sweets together. 'My mum and dad are going to India on Friday. They are going to make a pilgrimage up into the Himalayas and will be gone for six months,' says Bash. 'So this morning Franka whispers to me, "I gonna teach you and your friend a thing or two when they gone."'

'You're kidding? Do you think she means…?'

'You know Franka. I think she means it. She's going to give us her pussy, yes.'

That night I cannot sleep with my head exploding with Franka fantasies. I think of her breasts and her hips and my hand moves up and down. I almost never masturbate, and I feel self-conscious doing so, but I am too excited to stop. My heart is beating very hard and my hand going faster and faster. Suddenly, everything goes over the edge, like flying on soft white clouds, not just my body but my whole being. My breath comes in gasps, but gradually I recover. The image of my mother and her rage if she ever discovered me cancels the bliss. In the dead of night, I creep out to the bathroom and rinse the evidence from the sheet. Then I re-make the bed and sleep on the only dry part for the rest of the night.

On Friday, the instant his parents drive away in the car, Bash telephones me at home and says to come right over. I find them waiting for me in Franka's bedroom next to the laundry. Sparsely furnished with a single bed, dresser and straight-backed chair, the room is spotlessly clean. At the sight of them sitting there on the edge of her bed, awaiting my arrival, my eyes fall in embarrassment to the green and yellow linoleum floor, with its suddenly fascinating blue and black specks…

Franka smiles and pulls her blouse right up over her head, exposing her sharp little breasts. It is late afternoon, very hot, and I see a few drops of perspiration on her cleavage. 'Noel, go get a towel out of that basket in the wash room.'

'Yes, Franka.'

By the time I return, Bash is already on top of her, with her hands hastily pulling down his shorts, her legs cradling him, her bare feet in the air. I stand and watch them, afraid to move another inch. I listen to them make strange growling noises. I see the sweat begin to pour off Franka's face, her eyes shut tight, her mouth making sounds that frighten me. I have never been so excited, and so scared, absolutely dumbstruck. Do my parents do this? Is this normal? Is this really happening? Then Bash cries out as if he has been mortally wounded. The deed is done. Almost immediately, he rolls off and smiles at me.

'You next,' she says, staring at me with her long black hair fanned over the pillow. She beckons me towards her open legs. I stare at that dark thatch and wonder if I will do this correctly. I am in a trance now. I drop my trousers and cross to the bed, fall upon her. With her hand guiding me, I am barely inside long enough to remember any first impressions. I spurt and it's all over. She laughs but kisses me on the cheek, pats my bottom and ousts me from her embrace.

'That's you first lessons,' she says. 'Tomorrow we gonna improve yourselves. Lots of teaching we got to do.'

We are back in Franka's room the next afternoon. So begins the longest erotic dream of my adolescence, one that persists for week after week, month after month. We are learning our lessons, and we are improving ourselves. Franka – in retrospect, a classic paedophile – is having the time of her life, grooming us to keep her pleasured for months to come. We are sleepwalking awake most of the time. I am both ashamed and proud, overwhelmed by my new status, engulfed by images of sensuality, thinking of being a man one moment, the next of what punishment I would suffer if my parents ever knew. It's almost impossible to concentrate on homework or my father's Bible readings or anything that happens outside of Franka's room until…

Bash calls me on the telephone. 'My parents just came back, so don't come over here now. Franka told me you should come later, very late. Maybe two o'clock in the morning.'

'Why did they come back? They know something?'

'No, don't know nothing. It's been three months and they decided to come home early, that's all. You just sneak over about two this morning. See ya then.'

In the dark, I slip across the front of Bash's yard. Clumsily, I let the door click gently behind me as I enter the ground floor corridor. It doesn't matter.

I hear a gruff voice. It's Bash's father, holding a shotgun, dressed in his white cotton pyjamas and standing inside Franka's room. He doesn't hear or see me, and I press myself back against the shadows. I can't see anything, but I can hear.

'What in hell have you been playing at?' demands his father.

'Nothing, Father.'

'Don't tell me this rubbish, Bash. You stupid boy! What if she's pregnant? You'll have to marry her. So how long has this filthy behaviour been going on? Ever since we left, I suppose... '

I pull the door open and slip outside into the dark night. Three quiet steps past the closed garage, then I begin to race across the yard and down the block, my heart screaming with shame and disappointment and the fear. Above all, the fear. I do not sleep for a moment that night, and for months afterwards I walk long extra blocks out of the way to avoid going past Bash's house. Later, I learn that Franka was thrown out of the house that very night, and Bash was grounded, then sent away to school. We are never close friends again. But at least my parents do not learn about any of this. Losing my virginity is just another illusory step on the real journey to becoming a man.

I'm hanging out with some friends in the neighbourhood when Courtenay comes walking up the road. I see immediately – his shoulders are up and his eyes are burning into mine – that he's not right. 'Hey, brother, what's the problem?' I ask.

'Come here, Noel. I need to talk with you.'

I nod and follow him. We pause 30 yards away from the other boys. 'So what's up, Court?'

'I hit her, Noel.'

'Who?'

'Mother. I did some accidental thing – knock one of her picture frames loose – and she goes all crazy and starts with the strap. She beat me like she want to kill me. All up my head. I just lost control and turned and punched her. Right in the stomach. She drop the strap and screams, and run out of the room.'

'Oh, brother, you didn't hit her? She maybe going to kill you now.'

'She was trying to kill me then. I couldn't help myself.'

I feel joy to hear of Courtenay's revenge, and great fear for his welfare. She just might kill us both now. But I am wrong. After this day, my mother will never hit either one of us again. That doesn't stop her tongue from lashing out, doesn't change her attitude towards us one bit.

I wonder what had made her like she was. Never once did she speak of her own childhood. Had she been unloved, or worse, abused? I decided that something terrible must have happened to shape her into such a cruel mother for her sons. When she pours out her vicious poison now, I don't let it burn me, but ask myself where in her life is this coming from. All my life I will wonder.

My father can read my thoughts, and he sees that I am changing fast as I grow taller, and that I need something more than what he can give to me now. Home does not make me happy. Home is where my heart aches. One day my father calls me into his room and says, 'How would you like to go study in America? You could live with my brother Albert?' His eldest brother Albert, whom we have met only a few times, is a successful businessman in America, with his own petrol station and a happy family.

'New York City? Yes, that would be great.'

'Not in New York City. Albert lives in Philadelphia.'

'Oh, where is that in America?'

'Not so far from New York, but not so close either. I will write to Albert to see if he is willing to board you. If he is, then he will help to find you a school there.'

My uncle Albert writes back saying he has a spare room and would be pleased to welcome his nephew into his family. However, I must apply for a visa to enter and live in the United States, he says, and this can take a long time. I go to the US Embassy and eventually I send off my visa application, and wait impatiently for an answer. And wait, and wait. I write again asking if they have received it, but no answer comes. What I did not understand is that in 1952 the US Congress has passed the McCarran-Walter Act, which limited Caribbean immigrants to just eight hundred a year. My wait was likely to be endless.

However, while I am not in any particular hurry to leave my father, who I believe is a saint, so generous and wise, and strong, one day I say, 'Father, why am I going to study in America when all my books have been from England?'

He stares at me for a long time. 'You have a point there, Noel. Would you prefer to study in England? We can all have British passports. No visa is necessary.'

'Yes, that is true.'

'Going to England makes good sense, although I have no brothers there. Let me think about this situation.'

Six weeks later, he comes into the parlour and says, 'Noel, I have made all the arrangements. Meet me at the shop after school tomorrow and we'll go pick up your ticket to England. And buy you some warm clothing.'

I am on cloud nine the next day walking along Prince Street towards Independence Square. This is where Eric Williams had delivered the blistering freedom speech 'Massa Day Done' that won him the election as the first prime minister of an independent Trinidad and Tobago. My father had supported Williams, had given money to the movement, and refused any land or compensation in return. He said he did not want 'to be involved' but he acted from his heart. Now my father is beside me, and we pause to look at the statue.

'Noel, beware of politicians,' he says.

'Why do you say that? What do you mean, Father?'

'Just remember, beware of politicians.'

Decades later, I will recall this moment and think this was the one piece of my father's wise advice that I should never have forgotten. By then, of course, it will be much too late.

On the day of my departure, I say goodbye to my brother Courtenay outside our house in Woodbrook, then make the drive to the quayside with my father and mother. My mother does not talk. She just stares out the window, off into space, and I wonder what is running through her mind. I am bound for London, for manhood. Words cannot express the excitement, the hope that I feel in these last hours on my island.

I can see the single tall smokestack of the *Ascania* from a distance, leaking a thin ribbon of white steam into the blue sky. We join a traffic jam of other families making their way to the ship. This year, 1958, will see almost 25,000 West Indians emigrate to the United Kingdom. It has been this way since 1954, this tidal wave of people crossing the Atlantic towards our 'motherland'. I have no inkling yet of the reaction this will provoke in England amongst some white racists who fear being 'engulfed' by black faces. In fact, while Trinidad has been allowed to govern itself since 1956, it is still a British colony, and will not achieve full independence until 1962. We have every right to travel to England.

In Trinidad, I already know that many of my fellow islanders are bound for a part of London called Notting Hill. Later I will learn that the favoured London district for Jamaicans is Brixton. But my own destination will be somewhere called Finsbury Park, where my father has arranged for me to stay with a Greek couple who are members of the Brethren church.

The *Ascania* impresses me at first sight. Built on the Tyne in England, the Cunard liner is 520 feet long and weighs 14,000 tonnes. It is one of the largest ships I have ever seen in Port of Spain harbour. We are scheduled to stop at many ports in the Caribbean – including Grenada, Jamaica and Port au Prince – before heading out into the Atlantic, a stop in Madeira, then finally Southampton, many weeks after departure.

I have a large case full of 'warm clothes' that needs to be wrestled up the gangplank, after showing my ticket and passport to the uniformed ship's officer. I know that I must find the cabin I will share with three other men. I lug the heavy case up the sloping ramp, then pause to look back and wave at my parents. I am shocked by what I see.

She is weeping, staring at me, looking so small and helpless, and so sad. My father stands tall beside her. I wave at them both. Why, I wonder, is my mother crying? I will see this image in my memory for the rest of my life, and I will always wonder why, at this moment, my mother is showing me the depth of her love, just as I am leaving.

I turn back to the ship and continue up the ramp amidst the crowd. It seems like a large part of Trinidad is getting aboard, and many are carrying huge bundles and trunks full of precious belongings. I do not feel alone. I feel like a significant part of my island is coming along on this journey. I feel part of something that, much later, I will understand is History.

For the first time in my life, I am free.

London

When I disembark on the wharf in Southampton, I am part of a crowd of familiar faces – faces of every shade of Caribbean humanity. We have all lived together for weeks crossing the Atlantic. My first taste of freedom on the ship has been unforgettable, and already I feel far away from my childhood in Trinidad. Now most passengers are heading for the trains to London. Fresh off the boat, our multiracial Caribbean world, our varying shades of skin, we still take these for granted – but not for long.

The shock hits me when I step off the train in London. I am suddenly alone in a vast sea of white faces. Fortunately, when I reach Maria and Constantine's boarding house in Finsbury Park, they go out of their way to make me feel welcome. These two kindly Greeks are members of the Christian Brethren Church in London, and my father has arranged for me to lodge with them through the church network they share. Their house is located at the bottom of a cobblestone lane that is lined with cherry trees and old-fashioned gas lamps. From my very first evening in London, I love to watch the lamplighter move from post to post, igniting the glass-covered boxes.

'What a big and handsome boy you are,' says Maria, my new maternal guardian. We are standing in the kitchen as she makes me my first cup of tea on English soil.

'Yes, look at him,' says Constantine. 'Tell us, Noel, did you enjoy yourself on your long journey?'

I feel my face blush with embarrassment. 'Yes, it was… interesting,' I stammer. 'It did seem to take forever. I never realised how big the Atlantic Ocean really is.'

What I cannot mention are all the incredible experiences I had on board the *Ascania*. Not a word about the missionary's wife who had virtually overpowered me, and pulled me into her cabin. Or about the sweet black Chinese girl from Jamaica who received me every evening. Or about the Trinidadian woman en route to join her husband in London who had kissed me suddenly on the upper deck under a full moon. These were experiences that I could not confess.

Such stories would undoubtedly shock Maria and Constantine, with whom I will be attending the local Brethren church every Sunday. One word of such experiences and I fear that I will be packed off back to Trinidad.

Not long after I arrive, an old chum from Woodbrook named Sidney Bacchus also comes to study in London. Sidney and his family are members of our church on Trinidad. His parents own and operate the Bacchus Taxi Service. I arrange for him to rent a room across the hall from mine in Maria and Constantine's boarding house. Together we two begin to explore the delights of London.

One of our favourite discoveries is located at the corner of Tottenham Court Road and Oxford Street. On Wednesday evenings, we take the Underground into the centre of town, to the Astoria Ballroom where we lose ourselves in dancing the bolero, cha-cha, tango, rumba and quickstep. With our backgrounds firmly rooted in the land of calypso, just off the coast of South America, we show-off our Latin dancing skills, not to mention our flirting skills with the many young ladies who flock to the ballroom each week.

I am studying economics at the North-West Polytechnic, which is located in Kentish Town, together with students from all over Great Britain and the Commonwealth. I feel very shy the first time I enter the student common room, where a ping-pong table is the centre of attraction. It's around this table that I begin to make my first friends, including Peter, Babis and a tall and handsome young African, with exquisite tribal marks carved into his dark cheeks named Zihute. He is from Ghana, a tribal prince, and soon becomes one of my best friends at school. His royal blood, I think, is evident in the way he stands, talks, in all of his bearing. His father, the king, has sent Zihute to receive an English education just as he had once received years before. Zihute studies economics all day and works as an attaché at the Ghanaian embassy the rest of the time. Indeed, he is often called to perform extraordinary diplomatic missions for his country, flying off to exotic places at a moment's notice.

It's the late 1950s and the civil rights movement in the US and UK are only in their infancy. At the Poly, the African students often look down on the Caribbean students. There is no 'black unity' on campus.

The Africans accuse West Indians of being 'descendants of slaves' – and my Caribbean peers take great offence at these remarks. Zihute, however, is far too noble and refined to ever make such insulting remarks. In any case, when these accusations are said in heated moments, I find myself saying, 'But it's true, we are descendents of slaves.'

This irks my fellow Caribbeans, but I don't care. I am my father's son, and honesty is far more important to me than politics. However, to my great surprise, I am popular at school. In fact, one day I arrive late at the campus and the whole class begins clapping and cheering. I think they are putting me on until I see a banner strung across the wall: 'Vote for Charles and Zihute' with a picture of Charles Atlas holding the world on his shoulders. Without our knowledge, the economics faculty and students have selected us to represent them in the Student Union elections. And we win!

I am elected Social Secretary. At first, I don't have a clue what to do. And I am hesitant about taking on any more responsibilities on top of my considerable academic workload. However, I soon see that this position of Social Secretary opens some interesting new opportunities. One of the perks of the job, for example, is an office next to the Student Common Room.

My first official duty is to organise entertainment for the prom. I get lucky and hire an upcoming band led by clarinettist Acker Bilk. They are just beginning a rise to fame that will, in the end, produce 11 number one hits in the UK. Tickets are so popular I end up selling them for triple the usual rate. The evening turns out to be a smashing success, both socially and financially. We take in more money that night than the Student Union earned the entire previous year. The general consensus is that it's all my doing. In a way, from that moment forward, the balance of power on campus shifts from the faculty's hands to ours.

To make ends meet, I have found a part-time job washing dishes at the American Officer's Club in Bayswater. It pays very well and I am able to get jobs for friends and fellow students. Then I get an offer. The Social Secretary's office is empty most of the time, so I agree to rent it to a couple of my classmates who want to hold a poker game there every afternoon. Suddenly, I have my allowance, my wages from the bar and now the poker rent. I begin to live the lifestyle of a student from a rich family – taking taxis to and from campus, wearing bespoke suits and shirts. And I make my first entrance into the world of 'professional' gambling – a world that I will come to know and love in the years ahead.

One day I am approached by two of my new friends, a charming young Englishman named Peter and Babis, a rambunctious but brilliant Greek. The three of us have become almost inseparable during the spring term, and together we have embarked on a number of successful money-making schemes.

'Noel,' Babis says, 'Peter and I have decided we can afford a proper summer holiday. We're thinking of Russia, with a few detours along the way: Paris, Berlin, Prague. What do you say, want to join us?'

'I'd love to, but I'll have to write for my father's permission first. I think he had some plans for me this summer.' In fact, he had mentioned something about working for the Brethren Church, which certainly had not sounded very exciting to me. So I write him a long letter in which I make the trip to Russia sound almost a requirement for a serious young economics student. Lo and behold, several weeks pass before my father's letter of permission arrives – including a hefty money order to finance the excursion. So Peter, Babis and I apply for our visas at the Soviet embassy and spend hours with maps planning our route across Europe to Moscow. We are going to travel in Babis's car. Moreover, through my position at the student union, I contact a young Frenchman named Jean Claude who is my counterpart at a school in Paris. We speak on the phone and he enthusiastically promises to ensure that we will have a marvellous and 'very educational' visit to Paris.

On arriving in Paris, we head straight to the café where Jean Claude has promised to meet us at six o'clock. There he sits, with two extremely attractive, young Gallic women: Nicole and Babette. They are art students, and keen to practice their English. After a quick round of beers, they take us to a cheap hotel where they arrange student discounts for our rooms, then we are off on a two-day whirlwind visit to all the celebrated sites – the Eiffel Tower, Arc de

Triumph, the Louvre and Notre Dame – and a number of less famous, but far more fun, nightclubs and bars. By the end of two days, just when I am in danger of falling in love with Nicole and announcing my intention to stay in Paris for the rest of my life, Peter and Babis drag me out of our hotel and into the waiting car.

Leaving Paris is a nightmare unless you know exactly how to fight the ferocious traffic and get through the right 'porte' and onto the correct road. Babis doesn't have a clue. We end up on a road that we hope is heading north-west, away from the city. Suddenly Babis slams on the brakes. 'Check them out,' he says. We turn and look back at two redheads with their thumbs out, whom we've just passed. 'Don't you think we need a couple of guides?'

'Definitely,' says Peter.

'I'm not sure,' I say. In the first place, my head is still brimming with visions of Nicole from the previous night. Secondly, I don't exactly like the slightly raffish look of these two hitchhiking girls.

'What's the problem?' says Peter. 'They're stunning slappers.'

In another second, the girls are leaning down to smile at us through the open car windows. 'We go to St Tropez. You take us, yes?'

'How far is St Tropez?' Babis asks. 'The least we can do is take you to the next town.'

'OK, great,' says the girl as she opens the door.

'Hold on a minute,' I say, as she slides in next to me in the backseat. 'We're going to Russia, not the Riviera.'

'Be nice, Noel,' Babis says.

The girls introduce themselves: Janna and Natasha. They are both sexy, but hardly students. I suspect they are in their late twenties, a good deal older than us. They are from Prague. 'We grow up together,' says Natasha. 'Janna is my best friend, you know?' She already has her hand on my thigh as she says this. Still, I cannot get rid of a feeling in the pit of my stomach warning me off these girls. This caution doesn't seem to be shared by Babis and Peter who are already launched into flirtatious monologues with our two passengers. This carries on for the next several hours, as the girls assure us that we are on the correct road south to Lyon, and the Riviera beyond.

In mid-afternoon, we leave the main road looking for a place to eat. I am starving, since the last thing I ate was a croissant with a strong cup of coffee back in Paris. We quickly find a rural restaurant that fronts a campsite. Bottles of wine are put on the table even before we order food. It's going to be a long, very liquid lunch, with Babis and Peter laughing, flirting and touching the two Czech girls at every opportunity. I feel isolated and grumpy. The numbers don't work, and I am still caught up in my memories of Nicole. Peter keeps ordering bottles of wine. Eventually, Natasha says, 'We too drunk to drive now. We stay here tonight, yes?'

'Why not?' Babis slurs.

At seven in the evening, the bill arrives on the table. Quite reasonable considering all we had to drink. Peter volunteers to go out to the car and get some cash from our pooled stash of funds locked in the glovebox. Janna insists on paying their share of the lunch. Then we all go to the campsite office where we fork out enough for a couple of tents furnished with cots. The plan is to drive into the nearest town, where the restaurant staff had told us there was a lively brasserie and bar. But suddenly, rather tipsy, I don't notice one of the tent pegs and trip onto the ground. Damn, I've twisted my ankle. Instantly, I feel very sober, tired and fed up with the whole scene. What happened to our plans?

'Listen, I feel like hell. You guys go on without me. I am going to find the showers and then go to sleep. I'm not feeling very sociable.'

'Oh come on, Noel,' Babis says. 'The night is young!'

'Yes, come with us. We cheer you up,' Janna says.

'No. I'm finished drinking and my ankle is killing me. I need to put my feet up,' I insist. So off they go, leaving me alone in the tent. I undress and take my towel out and limp off to the communal men's showers with it wrapped around my waist. A long hot rinse, and I limp back to the tent. There is Janna lying on one of the cots, her hands behind her head, her full breasts very evident even in this pose, with her legs splayed apart and her skirt above her knees.

'I thought you went with the others?'

'I want to make you feel better,' she says, and sits up. 'You come lie here and I will give you massage.' I shrug and do as she says.

She kneels beside the cot and begins to gently massage my foot and swollen ankle. I close my eyes and have to stifle my grin as I feel one of her hands sneak away from my ankle and up under the towel. I feel conflicted. Am I cheating on Nicole already? Have I let down one of my friends, who is clearly hoping to score with Janna? Her hand fails to arouse me, so she brushes the towel aside. Soon her lips are achieving what her hand could not and I feel the length of me swallowed to the hilt. She is very good at this and it does not take me long to have an orgasm. Almost immediately, I fall asleep.

I awake the next morning and sit up to examine the empty tent. My ankle is even more inflamed, but I limp painfully over to the other tent. It's empty. Eventually I dress and go out to the little restaurant and have an omelette. Still no sign of them. I lie around in the tent, then go back and have a couple of beers, then eat some delicious stew for lunch. Since I have no money, I appreciate the owner of the restaurant putting everything on a tab. Where the hell are they?

At two in the afternoon, I hear Babis's car pull into the campsite. I rise and look at the quartet, who appear sober but sheepish. 'Where have you been? You left me here stranded, and with no money!'

'We had a night on the town, and stayed over in a hotel. Too drunk to drive back here. Sorry, Noel, but what a night it was!' says Peter.

'Well, let's hit the road. And the right road this time. Remember Russia? Our plans? The big adventure?'

'We've promised the girls a lift as far as Grenoble. There we can cut up to Geneva and then across to Germany,' says Babis, his arm casually draped around Janna's waist.

'You have a nice night, Janna?' I ask sarcastically.

She cannot meet my eyes. 'Very nice, thank you, Noel.'

So we drive south for many hours until, in the middle of the night, we park at another campsite on the outskirts of Grenoble. We all retire to our rented tents, and I listen to the sounds of lovemaking through canvas walls until I fall asleep. I am awakened by a loud curse from Peter the next morning.

'They're gone! And they stole all our money! Those whores!'

It is true. In the middle of the night, the two Prague girls had taken the car keys and emptied the glovebox. There is no sign of them now. All they've left behind are the keys to Babis's car on the front seat. No sign of our stash, hundreds of francs and pounds missing! All our money for the whole summer adventure!

I am outraged. My gut feeling was one hundred per cent correct. The girls were crooked from the start. In fact, they were professionals. Peter cannot stop cursing. Only Babis, who spent two nights with Janna, reacts without anger. Instead he is doubled over with hysterical laughter. Some kind of weird defence mechanism, all he can do is laugh and shake his head, his arms hugging his chest. Crazy Greek.

'That's it,' I say. 'We've got no choice now. Either we find summer jobs right away, or we are going to be stuck here forever. I think I had better call Jean Claude in Paris and ask his advice.' Secretly, I am thinking – hoping – that Jean Claude will suggest that we return to Paris – and Nicole – with a plan for us to make some money there.

Jean Claude does indeed have a suggestion for us, but it doesn't involve Paris. After some quick research, he calls me back and gives me the name and address of a large fruit farm in Provence where students from all over Europe are being hired. We borrow some money for petrol – promising to send it back as soon as possible – from friends in the campsite restaurant, and proceed to drive south for the rest of the day. The sky is blazing red at twilight, with a new crescent moon low in the sky, when we arrive at the farm. The first person we meet is a friendly Aussie who welcomes us enthusiastically and guides us to the main camp. About 35 students like us are lighting a huge bonfire and cooking up a communal supper. We are welcomed warmly, the songs begin and the feeling of fellowship overwhelms all our gloom from that morning's misfortune.

So it goes for the next ten days. The work in the hot sunshine is hard, but almost fun, since we are sharing it with interesting new friends. Every night is another party with cheap wine, good cheese and grilled meat. Lots of singing, plenty of flirtatious laughter. The pay isn't great, but we work long hours and spend almost nothing. By the time we are ready to leave, the three of us have put together another stash that ought to see us clear to St Tropez. (We have hatched a plan to go in search of Janna and Natasha and try to recover our money.)

In fact, several of the students at the farm have been to St Tropez and regale us with anecdotes about the nude beaches and the glamorous life to be found there. I have my doubts about the three of us being comfortable stripping off on a public beach, but Babis trumpets his enthusiasm for the idea. 'I have nothing to hide,' he tells Peter and me. 'Maybe you, Noel, are afraid to unleash the monster, but not me.'

When we stop to buy bread and cheese in a roadside café later that first day, the smell of something delicious changes our resolve to travel as cheaply as possible. We ask the counter man what is cooking and he says, 'That is my wife's bouillabaisse, monsieur. Feesh in wine, and oser good things. You want to try?'

We instantly agree, and he sets the table for us by the road outside along with an icy bottle of white wine. While we are waiting, an attractive young backpacker comes over to our table. Her name is Lena. It turns out that she, too, is heading for St Tropez. Despite our recent lesson of the dangers of picking up beautiful hitchhikers, Babis quickly invites her to ride along with us. Smiling, she slips off her rucksack and sits down with us. She is from Malmo, Sweden, but has visited France many times. It's hard to believe she is Scandinavian, with her black hair and almost oriental eyes. She explains that her family is originally from Lapland, far to the north. We introduce ourselves. The fish stew arrives and we all eat with ecstatic expressions of approval. I vow to make the most of French cooking for the rest of our stay.

'You see that picture on the wall inside,' Lena says. We turn and look at a watercolour painting of the café where we are sitting. 'My ex-boyfriend painted that two years ago when we were here. We had little money and it paid for our food. Unfortunately, this place has new owners and they don't know me, or maybe we could all get this meal free too.'

'Have you been to Tahiti and Pampelonne beaches?' asks Babis.

'I practically lived on them,' says Lena.

'What're they like?'

'Oh, I think you will like them a lot, you boys.'

It turns out that Lena's father owns three restaurants in Sweden and started taking his family on French holidays every summer when she was very young. She speaks perfect French, and as the meal continues, I feel less and less wary. Indeed Lena Olsson is a breath of fresh air after the two redheaded bandits: natural, direct, honest. She offers to be our guide to the South of France, starting immediately with a suggested detour.

'Two friends of my family – Swedish men who are, you know, homosexual – have a chateau an hour from here. I would suggest we all pay them a visit. What do you feel about this, boys?'

'Why not?' Babis says.

'I am sure they will welcome you. And they are good cooks too.'

Later that day, we arrive at 'Chateau Svensk' in deepest Provence, surrounded by orchards and beautiful gardens. The classic Provencal house has yellow walls and white-painted shutters. Torsten and Bent are both successful scriptwriters, with another house in Los Angeles. They have worked with some of the most famous directors and actors in Hollywood.

As I have met very few openly gay men in my life, at first I feel rather uneasy. The men are handsome and masculine, not at all stereotypical 'queers'. Gradually, my nervousness subsides and I see there is nothing to fear from them. Their affection for Lena is very obvious and, I feel, any friend of this gracious young woman can be a friend of mine. They greet us as if we were old friends of theirs too.

'Lena, so good to see you. Will you and your friends spend the night? We have a new cook who is marvellous.'

Lena looks to us and we agree that another delay on our journey to St Tropez (whatever happened to Russia, I think) is more than possible. Of course we will accept their hospitality.

'Come on then, let me show you to your rooms,' says Torsten. 'Then you can all have a swim in the pool. Perhaps later you will want to have siestas? We don't dine until nine.'

At dinner, which is served by an older butler from Papua New Guinea named Pierre, our two hosts do most of the talking, and I am spellbound by their tales of working with Ingmar Bergman, Ingrid Bergman, of Grace, Sophia, and even Greta. The wine is delicious and flows endlessly. The Hollywood gossip is even more intoxicating than the wine. The food is, of course, fantastic. The whole atmosphere is pure fantasy. Our hosts are outrageously outspoken and very funny. And very much a loving couple, which is a kind of revelation for me. By the time we stagger up to our comfortable beds, I am so over-excited that I toss and turn for another hour before I can sleep. Finally, I sink into the soft feather pillows and hours of vivid dreams.

My first thought upon awakening, with the sunlight streaming through the brightly coloured curtains, is that I never want to leave such luxury. Downstairs, breakfast is just as sumptuous as dinner: wet scrambled eggs, smoked salmon, fresh croissants and freshly squeezed orange juice with champagne for those who want it. Although I find the relationship between Torsten and Bent almost incomprehensible, and wonder what my parents would say about such a thing, I also find it easy to accept now that I have seen it with my own eyes.

'So you are heading to Tahiti Beach, you four?' Bent says. 'Well, if you're not careful, you might get laid... I mean lucky!'

We all laugh at this, just as Pierre comes into the room to announce that he has packed our luggage and placed it in Babis's car. We say our goodbyes. As we drive away from that magical house, Torsten stands on top of the steps and blows kisses. I look around me, for I am sitting in the front seat today. I may be wrong, but my impression is that Lena and Babis are acting even friendlier than yesterday. Has Babis engaged in some corridor creeping last night? I would bet money on it.

Our arrival at the famous Tahiti Beach, much later that day, is clouded by the fact that we get a flat tyre. The spare tyre is also kaput. This all takes some sorting out, but Lena comes through for us by asking a Swedish couple in a red Volvo for help. They promise to send someone from the nearest garage.

By the time we hit the beach, it's very hot and crowded on the golden sand. Behind the strand are several restaurants with bright umbrellas and loud music, scurrying waiters and laughing regulars. People are naked, or dressed in the tiniest scraps of cloth, which barely hide their most intimate parts. Immediately, Lena strips off all her clothes. I have to stare at the sand. She has young breasts with perfect pink nipples, a carefully trimmed pubic triangle, and firm, well-rounded buttocks. Erotic fantasies race through my head. Babis is a very lucky Greek, I think.

'We must swim!' Lena orders, and races towards the sea, where the near horizon is studded with bobbing yachts that have come out of St Tropez for the day.

'I'm coming,' shouts Babis, who is suddenly wearing nothing but a smug grim. He catches up with her and they wade into the water holding hands. Peter and I are left – in our swimming trunks – lying on the sand and watching in silence. After about 20 minutes, I stand up and say, 'Fuck modesty. When in Rome…' I shuck off my trunks.

'I suppose you're right,' says Peter, and does the same.

When Lena and Babis return from their swim, they laugh and point at the two of us. I notice Lena staring openly at my crotch and feel like digging a hole in the sand. The sight of her sprawling on the sand with her legs wide open is almost like a dirty joke that I don't want to hear. We munch delicious snacks that the cook at Torsten and Bent's has prepared for us from a hamper the butler stashed in the car.

And then a sudden thunderstorm arrives with no warning. We race towards one of the restaurants, and Babis suddenly spots the tow-truck arriving in the parking lot back in the dunes. He pulls on his trunks and runs off to deal with it. Watching the rain pour down, a heavy tropical storm under a thick black sky, we stand with dozens of other soaking wet, naked people beneath the dripping umbrellas on the restaurant terrace. 'This doesn't look like it's going to end very soon,' says Peter with concern. 'Where are we intending to spend the night? A hotel?'

'Hotels are all very expensive around here, but I know a good campsite near St Maxime,' Lena says. 'They are friends and, once the car is fixed, we can go there for the night.'

It takes more than an hour for the mechanic to remove the flat tyre from Babis's car and, together with the spare tyre, return to the garage, patch them and bring them back to the beach. While we wait, Babis and Lena talk together at one end of the covered terrace, their heads touching, their hands clasped. 'He's really fallen for her,' Peter says to me.

'Who wouldn't fall for her? She's sexy and smart and…'

'Pure magic? Yes, I am jealous too,' Peter says.

When Babis suggests that Lena sits behind the wheel and drive us to the campsite in St Maxime, it confirms just how madly in love he is, since he is fiercely protective of his car. He's never allowed Peter or me to drive it so much as three feet. Luckily, Lena turns out to be an expert driver. Is there anything she can't do?

It's almost dark when we reach the campsite, off the main road next to a small petrol station with its own café, directly in front of a dense pine forest. The couple who run the place remember Lena immediately and are quick to get us all out of the rain, give us coffees, suggest a quiet corner of the property where there are some basic rooms with cots. There is something about the owner and his wife that reminds me of my Uncle Harry and his wife back in the Trinidad rainforest. They kindly make us some omelettes and then take us to our rooms. Once again, it is Peter and I who share a space, while Lena and Babis are next door. Mercifully, I fall into a deep sleep immediately.

The next morning we are eating breakfast in the petrol station café when a huge white Cadillac pulls up to the pumps. An elegant older woman emerges, dressed in a white trouser suit with a large-brimmed matching white hat complete with a long purple ribbon. She says something to the attendant, hands him her keys, then takes another outdoor table. Her seat faces where I am sitting and it's not long before Lena leans over and whispers, 'She's looking at you, Noel.'

'And here's looking at you, kid.'

'Nahh, she's looking at me,' teases Babis.

'Oh yes? Well, I'll go find out for sure then,' announces Lena, rising from the table. Without any self-consciousness, she engages the lady in conversation. In a few moments, they are laughing together. Then Lena turns and says, 'Noel, please come here. Madame Jeremy would like to meet you!'

When I sheepishly do as I am told, Madame Jeremy extends her hand and says, 'Please do sit down, Monsieur. I understand that you are from Trinidad. Which part of the island?'

'Port of Spain.'

'I know it well. I've been there to Carnival. So extraordinary!'

'Yes, it's the best carnival in the world, they say.'

'Better than Rio? Well, perhaps. Next time I go, and I will go again, I want to dress up in costume like the people there and dance all day and all night.'

I look at her full crimson lips, sipping a milky *pastis* delicately, staring at me through flared dark glasses under the brim of her amazing hat. She dips her head and I catch a flash of eyes so green they remind me of the brilliant marbles I had played with back in our garden on Trinidad. 'Tell me, what are your plans? Are you and your friends staying here for a long time?'

'Probably not. We're kind of touring the area. Not sure we have many plans. Lena is our guide...'

'Well, if you are going to be here another day, would you be my guest for dinner? I have a restaurant located not too far from here – Le Maison de Toulouse. And there's someone I would like you to meet there.'

I turn and call to Lena. 'Are we staying here another night?'

'Of course, Noel. Don't you think we ought to check out more beaches in St Tropez than just Tahiti?'

'Yes, it looks like we will be staying another night,' I say to Madame Jeremy.

'Then I will be back at seven o'clock this evening to pick you up. I will flash my headlights three times, OK? Now I must go. See you later, Noel.' She rises and then surprises me by leaning down and giving me a kiss on each cheek. The exotic scent of her perfume gets me going. I watch as she takes the keys from the attendant and walks on very high heels across the forecourt to the waiting Cadillac. Her figure is voluptuous and her walk as provocative as any I have ever seen.

Back at the table, everyone wants to know all about the conversation I have just had with this mysterious vamp who drives onto the road with a spray of gravel and a roar of V-8. All I can do is grin, ear to ear, and say, 'Far out'.

Far out? If only I had known just how far out. While I am no virgin, the woman who has just driven away will soon introduce me to a world I have not known before. She is a woman who will make me understand truly what it is to be a man.

Needless to say, I am all dressed in my best and cleanest clothes and waiting in the petrol station long before the appointed hour of her arrival. When I see the white Caddy enter the forecourt, I am on my feet and opening the door before the third flash of her headlights. She laughs at my exuberance and leans across and plants a kiss lightly on my lips. And with that, I suddenly feel my stomach fall into an abyss.

Frankly, I am frightened by her. She's far more experienced than I am, far more sophisticated. What have I got myself into here? My thoughts immediately race back to the demanding older missionary's wife on the *Ascania*, of how intimidated she had made me feel. Clearly my own relationship with my mother has something to do with the panic and unease that I now feel sitting beside this older woman, heading up the road to somewhere unknown. Although she chats away, and asks me lots of questions – about my life, my studies, my girlfriends – I can do little more than smile. I tell myself to relax. This is going to be one – another one – of these enchanted evenings that are making this my first summer of pure freedom.

'Are you all right, Noel?' she asks, patting my leg gently.

'Yes, I'm fine,' I lie.

'We're nearly there. I am sorry the drive is so long.'

When we pull into the white gravel drive in front of the nineteenth-century manor house that is La Maison de Toulouse, I see a uniformed doorman rushing down the stairs at the sight of his boss's Cadillac. He throws open the driver's door as soon as we stop and says, '*Bon nuit, Madame Jeremy*'

'*Bon nuit, Pierre.*' She turns around and looks into the back seat. 'Angelique, wake up, my darling. *Arrivee!*'

I whirl around to see a rather lovely young woman rubbing the sleep from her eyes as she arises from her 'bed' on the back seat of the car. We greet each other, me with raised eyebrows, she with a yawn. I look at my hostess with some confusion. Was this her 'chaperone' for the drive?

'This is Angelique, my niece. This is Noel, Angelique. She is afraid of car travel, so she likes to lie down facing the other way when we drive. And she usually falls asleep, which is good for her, because she needs her Sleeping Beauty rest,' Madame Jeremy says. 'Now come along, you two, our table is ready.'

The table is in the prime corner of the ornately decorated main dining room, sparkling with crystal and porcelain, with a gorgeous bouquet of flowers at its centre. The maître d' and all the waiters flock to welcome us, while Angelique goes off to freshen up. Madame Jeremy says, 'That poor girl lost her parents – my sister and her husband – in a car accident outside Paris two years ago. Ever since then, I have looked after her in the holidays, for she, like you, is a student. Now we won't have menus because I have already ordered our dinner. In fact,' and she looks up at the beaming maître d' and says, 'Claude, will you ask Kelvin to come to our table for a moment please. This, Noel, is the reason why I brought you here tonight… to meet him.'

In a few moments, a tall, very dark man dressed in immaculate white chef's coat and gray trousers enters the dining room. By now, Angelique has re-joined us. 'Noel, this is Kelvin,' she says. 'Kelvin, meet your fellow countryman Noel. You are both from Trinidad.'

'No way?' I blurt, and then rise to shake Kelvin's hand. 'Good to meet you, man. We're both a long way from home tonight.'

'Coming here is de best move I ever made, mon,' Kelvin says. 'Madame Jeremy, she a beautiful person, dis lady. I gonna make you some good food here tonight, mon. I hope you like it.'

'I am sure I will, Kelvin.'

'I stole him away from the Hilton.'

'Good for you,' I say.

The rest of the dinner is far more relaxed than the drive to the restaurant. Kelvin sends out a series of French Creole dishes that contain some of the most delicious food I have ever tasted, culminating in a lemon tart with a blueberry sauce and Chantilly cream that is undoubtedly the best dessert I have eaten in my relatively short life. Angelique and I get along very well, and chat about her life at the Sorbonne in Paris. There is a sadness in her eyes that touches me, makes me feel protective, and also makes me feel gratitude towards Madame Jeremy for everything she is doing for her orphaned niece. Madame Jeremy explains that she inherited this restaurant from her father, who had trained as a chef in Biarritz before coming here to the Riviera and buying this place when she was in her late teens. Although I can feel the heat from her eyes as they examine me from across the table, Madame Jeremy is very correct during dinner. I sense that she has plans for me, but I am blissfully unaware of how this will affect me. In fact, I am very blasé when she suggests that, following our coffee and Armagnac, we all go to her house a short drive away for 'nightcaps'.

Once again, Angelique takes her place lying with her back to us in the car, and we drive about six minutes down the road to Madame Jeremy's villa. As soon as we arrive, a sleepy Angelique kisses her aunt, and then me, on both cheeks and whispers 'bon nuit', leaving us alone in the comfortable sitting room. 'There are the drinks,' Madame Jeremy says to me, gesturing at a table covered with expensive-looking bottles of cognac, whiskey, gin and many others I don't recognise. 'Help yourself, Noel. I will be back in two quick seconds.'

Five minutes later, she returns, having quickly changed from her rather businesslike cream silk trousersuit into something far more feminine, wispy and white. Although it flows loosely all around her, it also gives tantalising glimpses of her full figure. 'We must have music, don't you think? How about some reggae from Martinique?' In a moment, the room is full of soulful music and Madame Jeremy is taking the drink from my hand, placing it on the table, and putting her arms up so that she holds my shoulders close as she moves her hips West Indian style under her negligee. We dance staring into each other's eyes, then she presses closer and runs her hands down my back. I follow suit and as my hands descend, in one quick movement, I feel her slide the lacy garment off her body. Without missing a step, this amazing woman has disrobed and is naked in my arms. Her lips gently taste my neck, and then rise to my own lips. This kiss is so powerful that I suddenly lose the last of my self-consciousness; my anxiety about this woman has been eclipsed by the force of my desire.

She takes my hand in hers and says, 'Let's take a shower together, yes? To cool off from this hot, hot day.'

Watching her walk across the room and towards the stairs is a revelation. Her long shapely legs and perfect derrière, the side view of her full breasts, the way her back swoops down to her narrow waist, all draw me after her as if I was on a leash. Upstairs, I follow her into the boudoir and then the bright bathroom, pulling off my clothes as I go, leaving a trail behind me. She is waiting under the hot spray. Our mouths join in the rush of the water and I feel her hand on my nakedness, which flies upwards on the wings of her butterfly strokes. From within me, someone she had recognised but I had never suspected, a full-grown man, emerges out of the shell of my remaining boyhood.

Within minutes, I carry her to the large bed. The first time is urgent, overwhelming, but then it becomes a long, unhurried journey of exploration that lasts all night, long after the first sound of birds stirring in the trees outside her window. At times we simply lie in each other's arms, staring into each other's eyes, and say nothing. Once I even whisper, 'Thank you'. She smiles, but she does not reply. This night of love is the best gift. It solves so many riddles, heals so many pains. Thank you, Madame, from the bottom of my heart.

We stay in bed until late morning. Her niece has gone off early with friends. After a leisurely breakfast, Madame Jeremy suggests we drive back to the campsite, pick up the others, and go to lunch in St Tropez. When we arrive, we find Peter alone, very pleased to see us since Babis and Lena had left him sleeping to go the beach on their own. The three of us drive down to the coast and Madame Jeremy takes us to lunch at the 55 restaurant on the beach. The scene is wild, with celebrities like Brigitte Bardot and Sid James at nearby tables, with many of the most exotic and beautiful people in the world acting silly in their tiny bathing costumes all around us. It's a party that seems like it will never end. I wish that I could stay here forever. But when we meet Lena and Babis on the beach later, Lena says that she has to meet people in St-Paul de Vence in the next day or so, and Babis insists that we are all going along.

'You should see the rest of the coast, Noel,' Madame Jeremy tells me. 'But I will come to see you. Let me organise hotels for you. I know so many people on the Riviera. Tonight, however, you will come back to my place, no?'

'Yes,' I say. 'Definitely yes.'

That night we talk honestly about our lives, and about the unexpected forms that happiness and romance can take, and the coincidences that bring two very different people together. She has far more life experience than I have. It is the first time that I feel a deep bond like this. I want to tell her that I will miss her tremendously and that I want her to say, 'You must stay. You cannot go with your friends.' I want to tell her that she has made a man of me. But she accepts our fate with a wisdom beyond my own, and although I believe her words of sad regret, I can see that she is doing the right thing. I hope that she can read my emotions.

The next morning she calls a taxi to take me back to the campsite, because she says she cannot bear to prolong our goodbyes. She holds my face in her hands and kisses me and says, 'Believe me, the last thing I wish is for you to leave. But I will see you in Cannes very soon.'

I think, 'Not soon enough,' but get in the taxi and don't look back as we drive away from her villa.

On our journey to Cannes, I am not the only person in mourning. Lena has told Babis that she must go off on her own soon, perhaps even that afternoon. He drives in silence, staring straight ahead and ignoring Lena's playful banter and jokes. When we reach Cannes, we quickly find the hotel that Madame Jeremy has booked for us. It is owned by a charming couple: a Yorkshireman named Edward and a Frenchwoman named Collette. 'You must be Noel,' Edward says. 'We're putting you in J's favourite room, as she requested. You'll sleep well there, mate.'

'Thanks, Edward.'

Babis comes over and whispers, 'Lena likes this place so much she's decided to stay the night, so I'll take her up to St-Paul tomorrow and then we can go on to Nice.'

We spend the afternoon walking the famous crescent-shaped waterfront of Cannes, drinking in cafés, enjoying a boisterous dinner in a backstreet bistro. Back at the hotel, I fall into a deep sleep in the four-poster bed. It's not the sun that awakens me around dawn, but the warmth of my lady's naked body snuggling up close to me under the cotton sheets. She has driven straight from closing her restaurant. Her hands explore me eagerly and she cries, 'Ah, I see you are up already!'

'Very up, as you can see.' We stay in bed for hours, until our hunger for food overtakes our hunger for each other. Then we meet the others. After breakfast on the terrace, I say my final goodbyes to Madame J. She has insisted on booking a table for us at the Hotel Colombe d'Or in St-Paul de Vence. 'That is where many artists used to stay and eat, before they were famous and rich. Look at the pictures and sculptures. You will find Picasso, Matisse, many surprises there. And the food is simple but good,' she instructs us. 'It's a must that you go there. If I didn't have to get back, I would love to go with you.'

Really, for me, this is the culmination of my summer. My first great love affair. Although there are many days of the journey before we return to England – with brief stops in Nice, Monaco, Genoa, Portofino, Milan, Lake Como, across Switzerland to Germany, and finally the car ferry from near Amsterdam – this final parting with Madame Jeremy in Cannes is the bitter-sweet end of a glorious holiday. Before we board the ferry back to England, I write one last postcard. This is to my father, to thank him again for subsidising my trip 'to Russia'.

Now back in London, we find that all our passports have mysteriously disappeared – we have no idea how we came to lose them or who stole them. I have the option of applying for a British or Trinadadian passport and opt for the latter.

Returning to college and concentrating on studying is difficult after the highs of the summer. One evening my friend Sidney comes to my bedsit with his girlfriend for dinner. They bring along one of her friends, a very beautiful Trinidad girl of Indian-Syrian background named Sonja, who is a student radiologist. Sonja is, I can see, from a good background and rather shy. We are definitely attracted to one another, and a slow courtship begins. One night, after several months of dating, she agrees to spend the night with me.

Our relationship develops quickly. I arrange to move out of Maria and Constantine's house and into a flat shared with several other students, so that Sonja and I can spend every night together.

One day at college, out of the blue, the Dean summons me to his office.

'Sit down, Mr Charles. I understand there is a gambling den located here on our school grounds. Please find this den of vice, and ensure that it ceases to exist. Immediately.'

'Yes, sir,' I say. 'It's news to me, but I will investigate.'

'As Social Secretary, this is your responsibility.'

I am very bummed out, especially by the idea of having to return to the Underground to get to classes. I approach the two poker organisers and suggest that they move the game up to my apartment in Hampstead. They reluctantly agree, but are delighted when the game really begins to take off. Now it can continue all weekend, from eleven in the morning until six in the evening, both days. Before long, the game is welcoming local businessmen who arrive with more cash than any of us have ever seen before. Within a few weeks, I am pocketing £400 or more each weekend.

My lifestyle continues to improve, of course. I become a true London nighthawk, hanging out at the Flamingo on Wardour Street on Fridays, or the Roaring Twenties on Carnaby Street where you can get high on hash just by stepping in through the door. I think I am so cool that I let my studies slide until the point where I simply don't show up at school anymore. It is difficult for me to concentrate on Economics with my pockets stuffed full of £20 notes.

And then one day my girlfriend Sonja announces that she has missed her period.

'How did this happen?' I ask. 'We took precautions…' Though withdrawal was the only precaution we had been taking up to this point.

'I don't know,' Sonja says.

'What shall we do? We could get married,' I suggest, for I do truly love her.

'No, my parents would kill me. They want me to become a radiologist.'

Eventually she seeks counsel at the hospital where she works. The bemused social worker suggests foster parents for the child, and condoms for us. Seven months pass very quickly. We are both studying hard, and Sonja's pregnancy is a strain on our relationship, but we continue to love one another. A baby girl is born and we name her Lisa. Three days later a Mrs Horness comes to the hospital to collect her new foster child. (One day, years hence, I will find Lisa in Trinidad and bring her back to Barbados with me.)

Within months, despite our efforts to always use condoms, Sonja gets pregnant again. We learn this just as my mother arrives in London. She has come to England both to check up on me, and to look for a house to buy where I can live and, presumably, my parents can stay when they visit London. I am very tempted to confess everything to my mother. After all, I know how much she adores little girls. If I told her, perhaps, in her excitement at being grandmother to a little girl, she could solve all our problems.

I go so far as to say, 'Mother, what would you say if I told you I have a daughter?'

'Boy, stop talking nonsense. I don't want to hear anything like that from you.'

If she doesn't want to hear about the first-born, I think, surely it is pointless to mention the second one on the way. And then an emergency strikes the very next day. My mother receives a telegram saying that my father has had a serious accident and is in hospital.

'I have to go home at once and Noel, I want you to come back too. Your father's business will need you as long as he can't work.'

In the end, I spend almost four months away in Trinidad. While I am gone, a second little girl is born and we name her Penelope. But, by the time I return to London, Sonja has vanished. Years later, I learn that she has married and reclaimed Lisa from her foster parents. Happily, this leads to a reunion with Lisa in the 1970s and she comes to stay with me in Barbados for over a year before returning to Trinidad. As for Penelope's fate, that remains a lifelong mystery.

After my return to London, I find it very difficult to concentrate on my studies. While I am still making money from the poker game that takes place in my Hampstead flat, I begin to spend my nights wandering from one hotspot to another, particularly around the Cromwell Road. At the time, there are a number of clubs that combine drinking, dancing and gambling in the area. I have a lot of friends and we often meet up in these clubs. One evening I visit a club called the Cromwellian. It is well decorated, elegant and my friend and I enjoy a drink at the empty bar downstairs, then head upstairs to the pristine gambling tables. Again, I am very impressed by the taste and expense that has gone into the club, but surprised to find so few customers. We have the tables almost to ourselves, and the lack of other players definitely detracts from the excitement of the casino. At one point, I say to my friend, 'This is a really nice place but completely dead. I don't get it. The owner must be a real arse.'

Soon afterwards, as we are leaving, one of the managers comes up and stops me, 'Tony Michel would like to buy you a drink.'

'Who is Tony Michel?'

'He's the owner of this club. That's him over there. He's waiting for you.'

As I follow the manager, I realise that the croupier upstairs must have reported my remark. I feel my stomach contract. What kind of trouble have I got myself into now?

'Sit down and have a drink with me,' says Tony Michel, rising to shake my hand and introduce himself. He doesn't seem angry, but rather he's wearing the face of a worried club owner who has a room full of empty tables. 'So you like this place, but you don't like me? You want to explain?'

'Look, I don't even know you. I really like this place, and I just can't see why you aren't doing a roaring business here. I didn't mean to be insulting, but I was trying to figure out what is wrong. Maybe you're not promoting the place properly.'

'I'm open to any ideas you might have. That is if you have any ideas beyond rude wisecracks.'

I tell him that I have lots of ideas. 'I've helped other people with their clubs, and I know the scene in London very well. In fact, if I were going to open my own club, it would probably look a lot like this one.'

We talk for several hours. He offers to pay me a fee for any new customers that I bring to the club. I ask him to have several hundred membership and VIP cards printed up, and once these are delivered, I go to work. I make the rounds of all the clubs I normally frequent in London, and when I see my friends, or any likely punters, I talk up the Cromwellian. Interested people are given free membership or, depending on the level of their bankroll, VIP cards.

The effect is dramatic. Within a few weeks, the Cromwellian is starting to take off. After two months, it's one of the hottest clubs in Swinging London, packed every night with pop stars, the theatre crowd and the young glittering Chelsea set.

Tony and I have become friends. He's keen to have me in his club every night, where I mix with the crowd and assume ever greater managerial responsibility. He asks me what I think is fair compensation for all the work I've done. I've been thinking about this, and am ready with a proposal. 'I would like six per cent of all the gambling take.' I don't expect him to agree to this figure, it's just my opening bid. But, to my astonishment, Tony says, 'Let me sleep on that overnight, but my initial reaction is that it's fair.' And sure enough, the next day we shake hands on the deal.

The casino at the Cromwellian continues to thrive. In particular, we host a regular group of guys who run a car park concession out at Heathrow. They love to bet big, and they lose big. One of them always arrives with his pockets stuffed full of cash, and manages to lose everything by the end of the night. I always make a point of giving him a hundred quid after each of these sessions so that he can drown his sorrows and take a taxi home. I am making serious money now, more than I ever dreamed of making, and my social life is in high gear, but nothing this good seems to last forever.

Still, it's a shock when some tough East End thugs – apparently linked to the notorious Kray brothers – start trying to muscle in on our business. Tony Michel calls me aside one evening and, because I have had words with these thugs, advises me to go on a holiday. He says he will sort it out, but it's better if I disappear for a while.

By this point, my college friend Peter has moved to the island of Mallorca, so I decide to pay him a visit. In fact, having first come to the Spanish island to work as an ordinary businessman, Peter has somehow ended up running two of the earliest discotheques in Palma – the Babalu and the Toltec. It's great to see him, and even better when at a poker game in his office one night I hit a string of wonderful cards and clean out the entire table. So, for the rest of my stay, I have piles of cash – at a time when everything on the island is dirt cheap under Franco's oppressive economic regime. Needless to say, I have a marvellous holiday enjoying the best restaurants and clubs in Palma's Terreno nightlife district.

I linger for as long as possible on the island, and the longer I stay, the more I think this is where I belong permanently. This conclusion is only reinforced when I finally do return to London. Tony Michel has disappeared. Nobody knows where he's gone, or even if he's still alive. This remains true as I write these words, so I have to conclude that Tony was the victim of some very foul play. In any case, the bright lights of the Cromwell Road appear a lot less exciting to me when I return. I hit a few casinos, win some pots, hit some numbers on the roulette table, but my heart is just not in London anymore.

Mallorca

In 1964, I leave England and move to Spain – to the magnificent island of Mallorca. There I meet a number of people who will become good friends for life, but looking back now, many years later, I see clearly that the most important thing that happened to me on the island was meeting Inga-Lill. Not only would she become my wife but, without her, I would never have started my club Alexandra's. How I met Inga is a story worth telling.

Back on the island, I manage to continue my winning streak at the poker table, and am still receiving money from London. I also pick up some work as a consultant for Mike Jeffrey, the legendary English rock manager whose clients include Jimi Hendrix and Eric Burdon and the Animals. My job is to help him establish and manage his new nightclub, Sgt Pepper's.

I find a lovely apartment in the Edificio Sol in raucous Terreno, and soon begin to share it with a pretty English girl named Willow, the recently divorced wife of my friend Brini. Although Willow and I get along very well, share the same bed, and enjoy each other's company in almost every way, it's not really a serious love relationship, at least not for me. Indeed, I'm probably closer to my best friend Jose Maria Fortezza Castro, whom I first met while managing the Cromwellian club.

Jose is larger than life, very generous and fun loving, with hundreds of friends in Mallorca and from all over Europe. He was one of Spain's foremost waterskiers until, during a routine practice, he had an accident in which the boat ran over him and the propeller cut through his life-vest and mangled the muscles in his arms and back. His survival was a miracle. Yet as soon as I arrive on Mallorca, the first thing he wants to do is teach me how to ski at the Palma Nova Ski Club. When we are not out on the water, we hang around the club's seaside café with a wild crew that includes George Best, Steve Klein, Mike Jeffrey, Susan George, Riki Lash and Peter Newman.

One day at the club, Jose asks, 'Do you like Stan Getz's music?'

'Sure, why?'

'Pepe and I met these two Swedish girls yesterday. Very nice girls. They are big jazz fans and told us they wanted to go to Barcelona where Getz is giving a concert this weekend. So we're taking them. I am going to book some rooms at the Ritz, where the manager is an amigo. I just thought maybe you and Willow would like to come along?'

'Definitely. I would love to see Barcelona.'

We land at the Aeropuerto de Barcelona about six o'clock on Friday evening and take taxis into the city. Jose's friend has arranged for us to have three opulent suites. Willow and I go up to ours, while Jose and Pepe find that the Swedish girls are not keen to be separated. This means the two hot-blooded Mallorquins will have to share one of the suites. It's not what they planned, but they have high hopes of hooking up before the weekend is over.

We all meet in the lobby downstairs and set out to have some fun. I have already decided the two Swedish girls are good news: intelligent, sophisticated and very sexy. We spend a couple of hours exploring the Ramblas and the Gothic Quarter, staring up at Columbus on top of his waterfront plinth, and wandering through the colourful markets. After drinks in a café near the Placa Catalunya, we make our way to the famous Las Caracoles restaurant, which Jose assures us, serves the best food in Barcelona. After a fabulous seafood feast, we set out to paint the town red at a succession of bars and nightclubs in the Barrio Chino. The area is still a flourishing red light district. The two Swedish girls aren't bothered by the hookers or the crowds of drunken US Navy sailors who swagger up and down the narrow streets, although they do cling more closely to Jose and Pepe as we walk from club to club. Finally, after dawn, we all return to the hotel. Willow and I make love before we fall into deep, deep slumber. It's late afternoon when we finally get out of bed.

Tonight is the Getz show, but in a café near the hotel I suddenly begin to feel awful. Dizzy, with my skin clammy and then burning hot, and a sudden stabbing pain in the guts. I try to ignore it, and Willow doesn't seem to notice. However, by the time we reach the theatre, I am really ill. I tell Willow, 'I must have eaten something bad. I've got to go back to the hotel. You enjoy the show.'

Outside on the pavement, I am looking for a cab when one of the Swedish girls, Inga, comes up from behind and takes my arm. 'Noel, are you all right?'

'No. I must have eaten bad shellfish. Going back to the hotel now. I'll be OK. You have a good time.'

She insists on accompanying me, telling the taxi driver where to go, and then escorting me up to my suite. As soon as we are in the room, she calls the desk and, speaking in Spanish, asks them to send up a specific medicine. It arrives a few minutes later, and she pours the nasty looking, horrible tasting fluid into a glass and makes me drink. Lying back on the bed, I wish I could be sick. Suddenly, that wish is granted. I race for the bathroom. When I come out 15 minutes later, Inga is waiting to put me into bed. What a weird situation: her perfume is turning me on, at the same time making me want to vomit again. 'You should go back to the concert,' I tell her.

'I am staying with you.'

'Listen, Inga, thank you so much for looking after me, but I just want to be alone now. Please go back to the concert.'

Any other time, I would accept what she is offering, but the timing is completely off. I just want to be alone. She stares at me with huge blue eyes flashing concern, and a bit of hurt, but then she nods and gives me a chaste kiss on the cheek, turns and leaves. (Apparently, when she arrives back at the theatre, Willow gives her a ferocious tongue-lashing about chasing 'her man' and being a 'Swedish bitch', while Inga bites her tongue and thinks, 'You don't deserve him if you don't know how to take care of him.' Fortunately, I am fast asleep and far away from all of this.)

Later, Jose is on the telephone saying, 'You missed a far out show, Noel! Why you eat bad fish, anyway? Come on, get off your ass. We going for dinner and then dancing all night.'

'No way, Jose. I am finished for tonight, man.

Willow comes on the telephone, obviously drunk. 'Noel, why did you take that Swedish bitch up to our room?'

'Willow, believe me, I didn't take anyone anywhere. My stomach is in a million different pieces. You go and have fun with the others. If I feel any better, I will try to meet you later at a disco.'

It's many hours later and a naked Willow is crawling under the sheets, trying to get me excited, moaning, 'I missed you, missed you,' until I get the message across. She lies beside me playing with herself for a long time, but is too drunk to reach a climax, then falls asleep and begins to snore. I suppose it's at that moment that I think the beginning of the end of our relationship is here. It doesn't help to have images of Inga flashing through my mind as I pull the pillow over my head to drown out Willow's alcoholic rasps.

My revenge comes later that afternoon, when Willow wakes up with the worst hangover of her life and we have to rush to the airport. She throws up several times on the aeroplane back to Palma, and while we are waiting for our luggage she has to run for the lavatory. Inga takes this opportunity to approach me.

'Thanks again for looking after me,' I say.

'Jose has told me a lot about you,' she says, eyes staring straight into mine. She sticks out her hand to shake, and I kiss her on each cheek. What does she think I am? What has Jose been saying to her?

'It's been a pleasure meeting you,' I say.

'I hope we will meet again.' She kisses me once more on the cheek, turns and walks away without a backward glance. Meanwhile, I note that Jose and Pepe are looking bemused. Neither of them has scored with either of the Swedish girls, and now they have to be content with quick pecks on the cheek. They had taken their chances and so it goes: rolling the dice in love is not unlike rolling them across a casino table. Win or lose, at least you are alive. So, too, Inga has made her play, and I am somehow annoyed although not sure exactly why. I tell myself that Willow is a sweet girl and a good roommate. Why should I mess this up for a cold-hearted Swedish girl?

The answer is gradually revealed to me over the following months of autumn and winter, as Inga refuses to take 'no' for an answer. Wherever I go, it seems, she soon turns up, sometimes with other Swedish girlfriends, but always with her sights set straight on me. I am polite, and friendly, but careful never to flirt with her, or encourage her in any way.

Finally, one night at the after-hours bar called Jack el Negro, where I stop after a night spent hanging out with Steve Klein in his club Sloopy's, all my pals are gathered at the bar. In the middle of them, somehow having infiltrated my tightly knit Terreno clique, stands Inga. I order a drink and before I know it she is trying to tug me out onto the tiny dance floor. I resist her at first. Everybody in here knows I am with Willow. And I think that I'm too cool to fall for aggressive girls who think they can have their pick of any man just by snapping their fingers. And get rid of them with another snap. The trouble is that Inga just looks too fine, and is too intelligent, and genuinely funny, for me to resist for very long. So we dance, and we move very well together, and it all gets extremely intense, with people stopping to stare at us. My friends don't comment, but I know they are talking about us. Finally, I stop dancing and say goodnight and walk straight out of the bar as fast as I can. Otherwise, I know it will be impossible to resist going home with her.

Early the next morning, the phone rings and I hear Inga's voice. I can feel my heartbeat rising, even as I try to sound annoyed. 'What do you want? I was asleep.'

'Noel, I am sorry but I have to see you.'

'What's wrong?'

'Something is weird and you are the only one I trust to ask…'

'Can't you ask me on the phone?'

'It's so embarrassing. It's just, when I was brushing my teeth this morning, I saw that my tongue was all black. Is this right? Will it stay like this, or does it mean I am getting the plague or something?'

I had to laugh out loud. 'Were you drinking the red wine last night at Jack's?'

'Yes?'

'Well, he serves the cheapest Mallorquin rotgut and that's what it does to your tongue. Don't worry, it's not the plague – and you can brush it off.'

'Brush my tongue? I've never done that before.'

'Well how do I know what you've done with your tongue before?'

'Well, perhaps I could show you?'

I have to laugh again. And so, finally, I agree to meet her at her apartment later that morning. So begins one of the major, most tangled, deepest and must sensual relationships of my life.

Although Inga can speak at least seven languages fluently – all the Scandinavian ones, English, Spanish, French and German – and has been well educated at an American university, there is something innocent, almost naïve, about her that I find very attractive. After I break-up with Willow, who frankly is not too bothered and soon has a new boyfriend, Inga is quickly accepted into my group of friends. We fall deeper and deeper in love to the accompaniment of the music of Otis Redding, Sam and Dave, the Stones, the Beatles, Bob Dylan.

I have to make regular flights back to England, and Inga – who is working for the major Danish tourism company Spies, has to return frequently to Stockholm. As often as possible, we travel together to these places.

On my first visit to see Inga in Stockholm, she takes me to Döbelnsgatan to meet her divorced mother and her three sisters.

(Inga's father, a successful dentist, has just married a younger woman. It will be a considerable time before I meet him.) The ladies give me a very warm welcome, as if I am already a member of the family, with a huge hug from her mother. It's a warm July afternoon and Mamma is in a very talkative mood, asking many questions and then answering them herself before I can reply. In contrast, Inga's three sisters – Pia, Titti and Gull – are shy and stare at me with polite reserve.

Mamma insists, despite Inga's protests, on showing me baby pictures, including the obligatory ones of a naked infant Inga in her bath.

'What is it like in Trinidad?' asks her sister Titti.

I try to describe my island, but Mamma interrupts, 'You must be very hungry, Noel. I will cook a Swedish dinner for you. We must shop for food. Come on, you two, come with me, ja?'

We head for Östermalms Hallen, her favourite market, where she seems to know everyone, and banters and bargains with great gusto. I offer to pay for every purchase and, although she makes a fuss, she graciously accepts each time. Finally, loaded with groceries, we head back to Mamma's car. She drives like a daredevil and I wonder how she has avoided running over a dozen people by the time we get back to the house. She and Inga head straight into the kitchen, leaving me to be entertained – and interrogated – by the three younger sisters. I soon feel like I have been adopted into a clan of beautiful, warm-hearted Swedish women. Who could ask for anything better?

Later that evening, back at our hotel, I am still in a wonderful mood. 'I feel like dancing, Inga. Are there any places to dance in Stockholm?'

'Well, there's my friend Tom Macksey's club.'

'An old boyfriend of yours?'

'No, he's an American who rented a room from my parents when he was here on vacation from the Canary Islands. He decided to stay and open a club in the Wenner-Gren Centre.'

'Well, let's hit it. The night's young.'

We take a taxi but upon entering the so-called 'club', which is a drab ground floor space in the cafeteria adjoining a student common room, I feel my heart sink. After everything I have learned in the nightclub and casino business in London and Mallorca in recent years, this place is an affront. There's no atmosphere, theme or energy in the place. Yet it is packed with young people and obviously making a lot of money.

Tom, who had left the States to avoid the Vietnam War, is a decent guy and Inga introduces us. We chat about the nightclub business for a while, and I ask him what other places there are in Stockholm. 'You can check out Restaurant Cecil. It was famous in the 1930s as a five-star restaurant. I haven't been there, but I hear they have a disco upstairs on Friday and Saturday nights.'

Basically, I am not very comfortable in this student club and it's Saturday night, so I ask Inga, 'Shall we check it out?' She agrees and soon we are in another taxi. The driver knows exactly where we are heading. Cecil's is a famous place in Stockholm, and located in a good spot for a successful club: on a street lined with boutiques and jewellery shops in the middle of the city centre. I start getting a bad feeling when the doorman pockets the entrance charge and rudely nods us towards the frosted doors. We pass the crowded ground-floor restaurant and head up the stairs to the disco, with the familiar sounds of Aretha demanding 'Respect' becoming louder as we ascend. The décor in the place is tasteful and relaxing, and the bar upstairs is jammed, as is the dance floor. But when the song ends, the DJ begins to babble in Swedish. He talks for a long time before the next song begins. And then, when that finishes, he launches into another monologue. Every time the atmosphere in the club starts to soar with the beat, it is aborted by another speech. It's annoying and unnecessary.

I head over to investigate. The problem is immediately clear. There is only one turntable and the DJ has to talk to cover the record changes. I smile and introduce myself to him during the next song, and suggest a couple of tricks that will allow him to make the transition between songs much smoother and faster. He tells me to have a go. In a few minutes, we have the place jumping.

In the taxi back to the hotel after dancing at Cecil's, Inga and I can't keep our hands off one another. It's been a fantastic day and a very romantic evening. When the cab pulls up, we're so entwined with one another that it takes a couple of minutes before we even realise that we've reached the hotel. It starts again as soon as we are in the elevator: our hands are under each other's clothes, we're kissing deeply and grinding into one another.

'I want you now,' Inga says, and punches the emergency button. The lift comes to an abrupt stop.

'I want you too, but not here. Let's go to bed.' I reach over and press the floor button again, and the elevator resumes its climb. She won't quit, and pulls me right out of my trousers. Fortunately, it's so late that there's nobody waiting when we arrive at our floor to witness our state of undress. Back in our room, we make love many times that night.

In the morning, I ask, 'Do you remember Peter's club in Mallorca – the Babalu?'

'Yes.'

'I have to fly back tomorrow, but while you are here, will you look around for a space about the same size as the Babaloo?'

She stares into my eyes and reads them like a book. 'Darling, of course I will. But is this really what you want to do?'

'I can't tell you how much I want this. Seeing how all the Swedish people loved to enjoy themselves last night, and seeing how few places they have to go, and knowing what I know about clubs, yes, this is what I want. But...'

'But what... Noel?'

'But only if you want to do this together with me. Do you, Inga?'

'Yes, I want to do it with you.'

'Then find a space for our club.'

'I will, my darling. I will find a space for us. Now we have to get up... did you forget we are meeting my father for lunch today?'

Stig, her father had invited us to join him for lunch at the Operakallaren restaurant, perhaps Stockholm's most exclusive gourmet dining spot in those days. Inga had taken a very long time getting ready to face her father, so we arrived more than an hour late. When we are brought to his table, Stig is pissed in more ways than one. 'So you finally made it,' he blurted in English, then let out an angry torrent of Swedish at his daughter.

'Papa, this is Noel. Noel, this is Stig, my father.'

'Very pleased to meet you, sir.'

'As you can see, I am not so pleased that I have been waiting here for more than an hour. You might as well sit down.'

Stig insists on ordering for everyone. The elaborate meal includes reindeer in a red wine sauce and a fantastic dessert of wild lingonberries, blueberries and strawberries. We drink beer and schnapps to start, followed by a very good 1961 claret. I am impressed, and decide his anger had been justified. I just hope he will soften his obvious disdain for me. Over coffee and cognac, Stig – in perfect English – suddenly asks me, 'So Mr Noel Charles, what are you intentions?'

'It depends on what you mean?' I say.

'Please, Papa, don't…'

'You are sleeping with my daughter. What are your intentions towards her?'

'Don't listen to him, Noel, he has been drinking too much!' protests Inga.

I notice that diners at the tables on either side of us have stopped talking and are hanging on every word we were saying. 'Excuse me, I must go to the bathroom,' I say, and rise from the table. I hope that Stig will get the hint and follow me.

Sure enough, three minutes later, he comes rolling through the door. I decide to turn the tables on him. 'Listen, Stig, you have four children with your ex-wife. What were your intentions when you got married to her? Now you are remarried to a much younger woman, what are your intentions now? What can I say about intentions? We can all have the best intentions, but what is more important is that I love your daughter very much, want to be with her, and we will see how things develop between us. My intentions are that we will be happy together for a long time.'

Stig stares at me hard, straight in my eyes, and then says, 'I was afraid of this – that I would like you.' He can barely keep the smile off his face.

When we come out of the bathroom a few moments later, he has his arm round my shoulders and is pointing out the voluptuous nudes painted on the ceiling. 'You know the Opera had to commission a second artist to paint those vines to cover their... you know, privates... because the public was so shocked by this mural.'

'Hmmm. Doesn't sound like the Sweden I know,' I joke, and it is with an enormous laugh that we rejoin his worried-looking daughter at the table.

Ten days later, she rings me in London, where I am deeply involved in the negotiations for a new nightclub deal. 'Noel, are you sitting down?'

'Inga, I'm very busy right at this moment...'

'Listen, I've found the perfect place for our club!'

I am impressed. She's taken the challenge seriously, but I am distracted by the new London deal. 'Inga, the timing right this minute here isn't good.'

But she won't take no for an answer, babbling away about what a great location this is, about how she has been all over Stockholm looking for my dream site. She needs my approval, I realise, and so I tell her to go ahead and describe what she's found.

'It's part of the Strand Hotel. It actually used to be a nightclub, and so it has almost everything you would need. Noel, it's fantastic.'

'I'm sure it's nice, Inga, but nightclubs in hotels are usually nightmares.' I have never liked patronising hotel clubs, let alone operating one of my own. There are too many rules, too many straight-laced management types breathing down your neck, too many hotel regulations that infringe on what you can do in the place. I say all this to her, but she doesn't give up. Instead, she becomes almost hysterical. How can I reject something I haven't even seen? What about all the days she's spent looking everywhere for our spot – and now I won't even take it seriously?

'Inga, I'm working on a big deal here, but I hear what you're saying. OK. I will put this deal on hold for a couple of days and I will fly to Stockholm. Are you satisfied?'

'When will you fly here?' It's Friday afternoon.

'Monday at the latest.'

'You'd better keep your word, Noel, or I will never speak to you again.'

I get the message, but that doesn't stop me from having a massive weekend on the town: dinners and drinks; the Scotch of St James and Harry's Bar; gambling at Erik Steiner's Pair of Shoes casino on Hertford Street and, late at night, drinks and dancing downstairs at Johnny Gold's Tramp. And throughout the weekend, Inga keeps phoning up to rave about this place in the Strand Hotel and to say, 'You'd better be here Monday, Noel, or you know what!'

She meets me at Arlanda Airport and, despite my protests that I need a bath and a rest, insists on having the taxi drive us straight to the hotel. As the Strand is one of the leading hotels in Stockholm, I am a bit sceptical about their desire to open a nightclub. Obviously they have tried it in the past, and it hasn't worked out.

The space has its own entrance, set apart from the hotel lobby. Immediately inside there is an ornate staircase that leads to the first floor, and large windows overlooking Stockholm waterfront. The décor is Victorian and expensively done, with thick carpets and velvet armchairs, lots of mahogany, all the decadent but distinguished charm I might wish for in a top-class club. Immediately I start to get ideas. What about crystal chandeliers, and velvet curtains? In this area we could put a roped-off VIP lounge. Inga shows me the dance floor, which is large enough and in superb condition. She touches a button and a stage automatically slides out of the wall. The lighting system is very professional, built to create atmosphere but also to support a full cabaret show.

'Inga, you were right. This place could not be better. It will only take a relatively small amount of money to get this up and running.'

I call London and put off the nightclub deal. Instead, I stay in Stockholm for another week. I pace every inch of the club, over and over, and draw my ideas for improvements on a sketch pad. I feel all my experience in London and Mallorca coming into sharp focus here. I had helped create some of the best discos of the swinging sixties, as a consultant for other people, but here I am looking at the possibility of my own club. Stockholm, I am certain, is ripe for opportunity – and who better to take advantage of it?

My philosophy of life is, and always has been, to take advantage of those moments when luck throws up an opportunity like this.

Chance is an essential element in life. While some people are wary of change, and need to move cautiously, resisting the urge to be reckless or extravagant, to go with the flow is my first principle. The chance to take advantage of Stockholm's dearth of good nightlife, and the fact of this perfect space being available in the Strand, have created a once in a lifetime opportunity that I must grab now.

We spend days debating the name for the club. I look through reference and history books, even the Bible, hoping to find a word or phrase that will conjure up the feeling of sophistication and decadence that I have in mind. I make a list of other clubs in London and elsewhere – and I pause at the name Annabel's, which is Mark Birley's famous, exclusive club in Berkeley Square. That's when it hits me: Alexandra's. My club in Stockholm will be called Alexandra's. I love the sound of it, the way it rolls off my tongue, cosmopolitan but slightly wicked.

Inga loves the sound of this name, but is having some doubts about the venture. 'I've never been involved in anything like this, Noel. I'm getting scared. You're moving so fast.'

'You have to move fast in this business. Once an idea is out in the world, if you don't follow it up, for sure somebody else will. And don't be scared. You are very intelligent and you charm people instantly. I can teach you what you don't know. I have no doubt that you'll pick it up quickly.'

I truly hope so, because Inga is vital to me in this project. She's Swedish, for a start, knows the culture and the people, and has a wide circle of friends. Above all, she is a woman, and I want to design this club with women foremost in mind. Her feminine judgment is essential to me in selecting things like fabrics for upholstery (gentle on the legs please), in the fine little details like placement of mirrors and vanity tables in the ladies' washroom. While all the menus and promotional materials can be in English, and all the staff must speak it fluently, a great deal of expertise in Swedish will be required – and I simply cannot begin to master Swedish, no matter how hard Inga tries to tutor me. I want the club to have an international flavour. English and Swedish.

'When do you want to open?' she asks.

'Just as soon as possible.'

Of course, the first requirement is a watertight lease with the Strand Hotel. Then, and only then, can we begin the renovations, install the sound system, refine the lighting, launch the promotional campaign and recruit the staff. Inga arranges a meeting with the director of the hotel. To my amazement, and great joy, we do the deal in half an hour. The hotel will get all the food and drink earnings, and we will keep the entrance fees. The contract is ready to sign three days later. I immediately engage Monica Zetterlund, one of the country's top vocal stars, to play at our grand opening night. I want this to be something people in Stockholm will talk about for months, years to come. And I am obsessed with every detail.

My nightclub deal back in London is forgotten. My life on Mallorca has been abandoned – until much, much later. Stockholm is my future now.

Stockholm

The opening night of Alexandra's goes well. The crowd is enthusiastic but, in my heart, I know it's not as large as it could be. I stand with Inga and greet every guest. There are a few local celebrities, but not the tidal wave of glittering international stars that I might have wished for. While the press coverage the next day is broad, it's also, I think, somewhat lukewarm. Launching a great nightclub does not happen overnight. While I might be slightly disappointed with our opening night, I certainly keep this feeling to myself. From the outside, my confidence in Alexandra's is unshakeable. I know we need more time – and a big break, a moment of supreme good luck. We need our chance to shine. The best publicity, like the winning bet on a roulette table, must come at just the right time.

Several weeks pass and then one afternoon Mr Smerberg, the Director of the Strand Hotel, asks me to come to his office. 'Would you be interested in helping us honour a contract which the Strand has made with the Swedish Royal House?'

'I most certainly would be.' Is he kidding? Any private party would be welcome, but a ball for the aristocracy! This is music to my ears.

When she learns the full details, Inga is speechless. I would be too, if I had any background knowledge of Swedish society. The event will be a debutante 'coming out' ball for Titti Wachtmeister, the aristocratic daughter of the Swedish Ambassador to the United States, Count Wilhelm Wachtmeister. The copy of the guest list given to us reads like Sweden's *Who's Who*: starting with Crown Prince Carl Gustav, his sister Princess Christina, Babbi Wallenberg, Carl Adam Lewenhaupt, the distinguished names go on and on. Attached is a detailed statement of royal protocol and ceremonial guidelines, which are to be followed to the letter. I can already imagine the press photographers lined up outside to capture the guests as they arrive in their limos – and the headlines the next day.

Caught up in the challenge, determined to raise our ambience to a regal level, I contact a local museum with an idea to rent six noble busts of historical Swedish monarchs and nobility. As soon as he sees the guest list, the museum director offers to loan me the busts without charge. Lady Luck is truly smiling on us now.

On the big night, long before the first limousine arrives, the press have begun to congregate outside Alexandra's. They all know the inviolable royal etiquette that forbids any photographers or reporters being on the actual premises during a social occasion. I have had numerous meetings with courtiers from the Palace who have gone thorough every detail of the evening, from the guests' first arrival, through the seating and service of dinner, to ending the night and departure. Inga has bought a beautiful gown from Margo's for the occasion. I am wearing a new tuxedo.

The first arrivals are a pair of Swedish socialites named Count PA von Rosen – a restaurateur from Stockholm and Kenya – and his friend Ove Dahlberg, both already regulars at our new club.

PA is a charming tall, tanned gentleman, with a voice that women find irresistible. During the first weeks after opening, he has brought singer Lou Rawls to the club, our first ever celebrity guest, and undertaken to introduce me to Stockholm's elite. Now he offers to stand nearby as I greet the arriving guests and discreetly whisper names and information to me. 'This is Anders Lettstrom. He's a good friend of the Crown Prince' and so on, all of it very helpful indeed.

As it happens, everything conspires to make this royal evening a fantastic success.

The centrepiece of Alexandra's is what I call the Great Table, for me, my friends and VIP guests. By 4 a.m., most of the guests have departed and Inga and I are seated there. Exhausted but exhilarated, we unwind together with PA, Ove and a few other friends. I have never seen Inga looking so lovely and happy. She is glowing, and thrilled by the fact that everyone has been calling her 'Alexandra' all evening. Suddenly one of my doormen arrives with a worrying frown.

'Excuse me, sir, but I have some bad news. The bust at the entrance has gone missing.'

'Hell! Are you serious? Someone must be pulling a prank. This crowd wouldn't steal anything. It will turn up, surely.'

'But what if it doesn't?' Inga worries.

'Sir, I have already reported it to hotel security and they have called the police. They will be here any minute.

'OK, we will wait, but I wish you had called me first.'

The two policemen are calm but clearly interested in the club. Middle-aged and serious, they take notes and then ask to see the guest list. When they read the names, they begin to blush and become very nervous. All of Stockholm's aristocracy have just been in this room. In seconds, they pack up their notebooks and leave. A potential criminal tragedy has suddenly become a Keystone Kops comedy.

When we are all alone, after the last friend and all the staff have gone, Inga and I sit with a bottle of Krug and words fail us. Instead of words, we let our bodies reach out and touch one another. Our deep kisses lead us onwards until her black silk dress falls from her soft white shoulders. She is determined to please me, and I am determined to please her. We lose ourselves in the lovemaking as she leans across the Great Table and her moistness grasps my hardness in a trance of dreamlike passion.

This is the night that truly launches our club. The night my career really begins. The night Inga becomes Alexandra.

My first task the next morning is to get in touch with the museum director who had kindly lent us the busts and inform him about the theft. Unfortunately, as soon as I get him on the telephone, I can hear the consternation in his voice. The police have already informed him about the missing bust.

'Unfortunately, Mr Charles, the bust was commissioned by Gustav the Fourth. It is unique. I am sympathetic to your position, but I must insist that you immediately compensate us for our loss.'

'How much?'

'500,000 kronor.' (About £50,000. Much later, I will learn the true value is more like 5,000 kronor.)

Playing for time, I say, 'I will get back to you as soon as I have spoken to my insurance people.'

'I will be waiting to hear from you, Mr Charles.'

In fact, I have not insured the club yet. So my next call is to the Director of the Strand Hotel, to see if the hotel's policy covers my premises. Of course it does not. I am hardly surprised, although I had dared to hope. I have to keep from kicking myself. Why hadn't I insured the club yet? I was pouring all the cash that I had and that we made into continual 'improvements' to the nightclub itself. I would have to think of something, and to stall the museum director for a while yet.

I open the club at the usual hour. I have seen all the photographs in the newspapers of guests arriving at Alexandra's. The publicity is tremendous for us, and just beginning. In fact, one of the very first guests is a journalist on one of Stockholm's biggest daily papers. He sidles up to me and asks if the rumour about the missing bust is true. I invite him for a drink and tell him the whole story, including the huge cost of the statue. I don't, however, tell him that I have failed to insure the club's contents against theft. He takes notes and, after downing a few more drinks, makes his way off into the night.

His story breaks the next day on the front page. 'Rare Statue Goes Missing at Alexandra's' is the headline. There are more photographs of the royal celebrities outside the club. By late afternoon, the television and radio journalists have all been to interview me. 'Alexandra' and I are suddenly local Stockholm stars. By the end of the week, all of Sweden is wondering what happened to the missing bust.

In a matter of days, Alexandra's is the hottest spot in the city, and we are the king and queen of the Swedish nocturnal realm. Business is fantastic. I am even contacted by Gröna Lund, Stockholm's answer to Tivoli Gardens in Copenhagen, who offer me a catering deal within the park. Every summer a series of world-class entertainment stars perform in Gröna Lund, where they will be fed by my kitchen, and naturally learn about the club itself. After their gigs, they will head for our late-night welcome at the club. The list of celebrities who stream through my doors – past the waiting newspaper photographers – is amazing: Elton John, Mick Jagger, George Harrison, Keith Richards, Billy Preston, Tony Joe White and many others. As a result, we have a permanent crowd of enthusiastic young Swedish groupies camped out in front of the club hoping to get autographs, or even something more personal.

In the end, as I write this, that statue is still missing and its disappearance remains a mystery. We never had to pay the 500,000 kronor – nor even the 5,000 it was actually worth. I suspect that one of the exalted guests at that party may have absconded with the bust of one of his ancestors and placed it on display in the ancestral home, but that, as I say, is only my fantasy. The truth remains unknown.

The nightclub business attracts all kinds of people, not just celebrities and royals. It's not a church supper and, although I am always careful and selective about my clients, sometimes it is impossible to know exactly who you are hosting.

One night I am nursing a Chivas on the rocks at the Great Table after Inga and all the staff have gone home. I have agreed to lock up once the last party has paid its hefty bill. There are ten of them, men and women, but not really couples, so far as I can tell. Swedish.

Noel and Alex outside Alexandra's, Stockholm, on its opening night in June 1969. In a matter of weeks the club became the hottest spot in the city.

Noel and Alex greet guests at their wedding reception in Umea in Sweden, a town north of the Arctic Circle where Noel was the first black face most people had ever seen!

Noel opened a second Alexandra's in Barbados. It was a complete departure from the beach shack style of other clubs on the island.

Noel and Alex with Sidney Poitier and soul singer Vin Cardinal at home in Stockholm.

Jane Olinikoff and singer-songwriter Lee Hazlewood were close friends of Noel's.

Alex with her family. Her parents, Stig and Inga, and sisters, Pia, Titti and Gull, immediately made Noel feel part of their family.

Before long Alexandra's was the most fashionable nightspot in Stockholm and visiting celebrities, such as David Bowie (above left) and Jack Nicholson (above right), were sure to include it on their itineraries.

Royalty, like Sweden's Princess Christina and her husband Tosse Magnusson, bought their guests to Alexandra's and were celebrated regulars at the Great Table.

Alex with Jan and Ulla Nalivykov. Jan's paintings, which lined the walls of both Alexandra's, were a big hit with the customers.

Swedish stars including Britt Ekland and Rod Stewart (above left), tennis champion Bjorn Borg (above right) and Agnetha Faltskog of Abba (below left) made Alexandra's their favourite night-time venue.

Noel and Alex with their good friends Peter Morgan, the Minister for Tourism for Barbados, and his wife Margaret.

And it's easy to see who is in charge: not the biggest guy, but the unmistakeable boss. And he has insisted on ordering nothing but the best. The table is covered with empty bottles of premium whiskey, vodka, cognac and liqueurs. Plus their bill says that they have downed a dozen bottles of Dom Perignon. The bill is going to more than cover the day's payroll.

As they all stand up and say their goodbyes, the boss and two of his biggest henchmen remain behind. One of these gorillas must be close to seven feet tall and built like a Sherman tank. Suddenly he is approaching me. 'Hey, Mr Skiffer says he wants the bill now.'

I rise and smile. 'Yes, I have it right here.' I hand it to him. He takes it back to the boss, who beckons me over.

'Can I help you?'

'It's late,' says the man. 'My name is Leif Skiffer. You must want to get home, right? I will drive you there. And we will settle this in the car.'

How could I have been so stupid as to wait for this group alone, without my bouncers or any of my staff? 'If it's all the same to you, I prefer to collect the bill here. And then I will take my usual cab home.'

'No, I insist that we drive you home. It's the least I can do to thank you for your hospitality this evening.'

I don't see much point in upsetting this man or the two gorillas. 'Well, that's very kind. Just let me turn off the lights. Do you want to meet me outside?'

'No, we'll wait here with you.'

So there is no chance of making a phone call to alert Inga. I turn off the lights and let them accompany me downstairs and out into the street. The summer sky in Stockholm is brightly lit even just before five in the morning. Their car is a black Mercedes – a huge, sinister car. As soon as we are inside, the goon who is driving screeches away from the kerb, down the block and then makes a sharp right.

'Aren't you going to ask me where I live?'

'Don't worry. Relax,' says Skiffer. 'I want to show you something.'

'I'm really tired. I would like to get home.'

'You're coming with me and then we're going to have a little talk. So sit back and shut up,' he says. Which is what I do, or attempt to do, as the car heads for the northern suburbs, and then out into the countryside. We fly past dense forest and the occasional farm. I am losing all my bravado. Who are these guys and what are they planning to do with me? There is no point in even thinking about fighting. These are three very tough, large men and I am one skinny little pacifist. It's deadly quiet inside the Mercedes, although I can see the speedometer and know that we are streaking through the empty woods at more than 160 kph.

We turn onto a dirt road that leads for several miles into the forest before we stop in a clearing beside an enormous Alpine-like chalet. Inside the main room has rough beams and a huge stone fireplace beneath a high cathedral ceiling. There is an iron spiral staircase leading to a second storey loft, and one entire wall is glass looking out onto a lake. I can smell the cedar scent of a sauna. One of the goons starts to build a fire and, as it's the middle of summer, that really worries me!

Skiffer goes to fetch a large bottle of Courvoisier and two giant crystal snifters. 'You sit there,' he orders, nodding at a place on one of the sofas. Then he puts the bottle in his mouth, yanks out the top with his teeth, spits it on the floor and begins to pour about eight ounces of brandy into one of the glasses. 'First we have a drink.'

'It's been a long day. I've had enough to drink and I'm exhau…'

'Either you have a drink or you have a problem. What's your name?'

'My name is Noel Charles.'

'Well, Noel Charles, you have my club. How did you get my club?'

I accept the snifter and take a sip. It burns all the way down my throat. 'What do you mean?'

'I have been negotiating with the Strand for years now. And they have promised me this club. And now you, a foreigner, a fucking kid, come here and they give you my nightclub. How does this happen, Noel Charles?'

'Well, I am truly sorry for this,' I say, my mind racing to find a way to defuse this man's anger, 'but I'm not the guy to be angry with. I just work for a company and they pay my salary. I front the club for this English company, and they did the negotiations with the Strand. I was hired in London, but I've never met the directors of the company who own Alexandra's.'

Skiffer sits down on the low coffee table opposite me and cocks his head, thinking. I am careful to look directly into his eyes. The silence begins to stretch into minutes. I stare at him innocently. Skiffer grinds his teeth audibly, and then gulps more cognac.

'You know what I am thinking?'

'No, I don't.'

'I could make you disappear. Believe me. Your body would never be found.'

I have to swallow my own terror before I say, in an attempt at a calm voice, 'Why would you want to harm me? I'm just an employee.'

Suddenly, he leaps to his feet. I brace myself for the punch, kick or whatever he is about to launch at me. Instead, he rips open the front of his shirt and sticks out his chest, which is covered with thick blondish hair. Then takes a cigarette lighter from his pocket and ignites the hairy bush. It makes a hideous smell. He laughs and slaps it out. 'I like you, Noel Charles. My soldiers should be more like you. You have cool and calm, no panic. Come with me. I want to show you something.'

I rise and follow him, to the spiral staircase. He stomps up and I follow behind. We are in a loft bedroom with a huge king-sized bed. He beckons me on into a large dressing room, with many suits lined up in an open cupboard. 'Look in the top pocket of any jacket in there,' Skiffer says. 'Go ahead, reach in the pockets.'

I shrug and do as he says. In the first top pocket, I feel some paper and pull out a Swedish note worth 10,000 kronor. That's worth about £1,000! 'There's one in every suit. Take as many as you like. There's your payment for the bill tonight.'

'Just one should do it, and I'll be happy to give you the change. I think your bill was about 8,600 kronor…'

'No change! You take more than one. Keep as much as you like, Mr Employee.'

'Look, I don't want to take anything from you. Whatever I earn is mine. I work for it. Whatever you earn is yours. I don't want anything that I haven't earned.'

'Are you sure? What do you want? You must want something?'

'I want you to send one of your men to the club tomorrow and I will give him the exact change that we owe you for your bill,' I say. 'And now I would ask you to drive me home. I really am exhausted. It's been great to see your place here, your wonderful home, but...'

'OK, Noel Charles. We go back to Stockholm. But first you must drink your drink. It is bad manners not to finish your drink.'

Downstairs, I manage to down the cognac in steady sips and eventually, having changed into a new shirt, my host indicates that we can go out to the car. It takes almost an hour for his gorilla to fight his way through the morning rush-hour traffic to the centre of Stockholm. I tell them where I live, but first Skiffer insists on a detour to Kumsgarten. We pull up outside an art gallery. 'I own this place,' he says, and the two of us get out and enter the shop.

'Choose any one you like,' he says, gesturing at a wall full of rather beautiful landscape paintings. The girl sitting at the far wall behind the antique desk has risen, but is careful not to speak unless spoken to first.

Who is Leif Skiffer, I wonder? An art dealer? The boss of Stockholm's gangster class? I will never find out exactly.

'You know, I don't want to take anything from you, Mr Skiffer.'

'Listen, Noel, if you don't accept a gift from me, you are going to wish that you did.'

'OK, I'll take that one,' I say, indicating the nearest picture.

'Good choice,' he says, grinning. Then he goes and lifts it off the wall and hands it to me. 'It will look great on your dining room wall. Now let's go.'

Back in the car, Skiffer takes a card out of his wallet and writes something on the back. 'You take this, with my private number. If you have problems, you call this number. They will always get your message to me. But, I think, you will have no trouble in Stockholm now.'

'Thank you very much.' Who, I think again, is this guy?

They drop me outside my apartment building and I make my way upstairs, to find Inga in a state of high anxiety. 'Noel, where have you been? I was very worried... what's that? A painting! Have you been at another museum all night perhaps?'

I explain the 'kidnapping' to her and ask what she knows about the story behind Mr Skiffer. She knows nothing. Later Inga finds out that Skiffer is married to the daughter of a prominent Swedish government official, which may explain his swashbuckling arrogance, but other attempts to learn more about him over the next days elicit very little information. 'Better you know very little,' is one thing she is told. 'What you don't know about him cannot hurt you.' Skiffer is a mysterious and daunting individual who, it turns out, will become a loyal customer and even a good friend. In the months ahead, he always makes a booking in advance, always arrives with the number of guests he has promised, and always behaves like a perfect gentleman, as well as a most generous host. Moreover, he always pays in cash. Naturally, I make a point of according him the greatest respect when he is in the club, often inviting him to free rounds of drinks and chatting with him at his table.

Then one night he calls personally and says, 'Noel, I want a table for eight tonight. However, my friend, please do not come to join us at the table tonight.'

'Why, Leif? I don't want to snub my best customer.'

'Look, I am bringing the boxer Ingemar Johansen. You know he's just been knocked out by Floyd Patterson, so right now Ingemar does not want to look at any more black people. OK?'

When the Skiffer party arrives, I make a point of going straight to the table and inviting everyone to a free glass of Dom. Then I sit down next to Leif. He roars with laughter and says, 'Why did I know you were going to do this? Well, Noel Charles, meet Ingemar Johansen, Sweden's greatest boxer.'

'Nice to meet you,' I say, lighting a cigarette but careful not to raise my hands, even for a shake. The evening turns out to be a great success, and even Ingemar looks happy when he departs in the early hours of the morning.

The nightclub business is never boring, but unfortunately it is one industry that truly lives up to the old Chinese curse 'May you live in interesting times'. About four months after our rise to the summit of Stockholm's nightlife world, I am in a cab on my way to work. Inga has now, to all extents and purposes, become known as

Alexandra – and even I always call her 'Alex'. I am in a wonderful mood today, and even the fact that I know she is out spending a fortune on new clothes doesn't take away from my euphoria. We're packed in the club each night. It seems that every celebrity who comes to the city has Alexandra's on their 'must visit' list. My bank account is fatter than it has ever been before.

The previous night had, in fact, been our 'fourth month anniversary' celebration. Celebrity hairdresser Vidal Sassoon, a friend from the clubs in London, had arrived with a group of beautiful models. And my buddy, soul singer Vin Cardinal, had treated the club to an impromptu medley of the biggest Motown hits. By closing time, I had been sitting there with Vidal discussing the idea of opening a chain of Alexandra clubs across Europe. Fortunately, a voice inside me had whispered, 'Easy does it, buddy. One step at a time.'

Now as I approach the Strand Hotel, I see Alex standing by the entrance to the club loaded down with shopping bags from Stockholm's most luxurious boutiques. Why isn't she going inside? Why is she just standing there and staring at the doors? As soon as my loafers hit the pavement, and I approach her, I can see exactly what the problem is.

The double doors are secured with thick loops of chain and a huge padlock. The refrain from a Motown hit rattles across my brain: 'chains, chain, chains'… but we're not talking about romantic love here.

'Noel! Do you understand what this is?'

'Baby, I don't have a clue. You better get up to the director's office and find out? We're been paying our rent, that I know for sure.'

'I go now. You wait because I don't want you to lose your temper with him.'

'Well, either he gets this chain off immediately or I am going to go ballistic.'

I go for a walk around the block to try to sort out my feelings and understand what could be the possible explanation. It makes no sense that he would just close the club. After all, the hotel was making handsome profits through the provision of food and alcohol for such a successful nightclub. Then a thought forms in my mind… a feeling that Alex – fuck it, Inga – is not telling me something here. I think that I should have gone with her to see Director Smerberg. After all, I had allowed her to conduct all the final meetings about the contract, since all the legal language was Swedish, and I was in such a rush to get the place transformed into my vision of a great nightclub. Much, much later, I will look back and suspect that Inga's relationship with Smerberg may have been deeper than simply business – and that his closure of the club may have been based on his jealousy of me.

'Noel, I am sorry,' she says now, her face a deep dark cloud when she returns to meet me outside the entrance. 'It is my fault.'

'Explain what is your fault please…'

'The contract is only four months, not four years. He promised me at the time that if everything went well it would convert into four years. A few weeks ago he said that he was pleased with the way it has been running, and if we continued with this it should be possible to give us four-year contract. But just now he told me that he is sorry, his directors are not happy with the publicity that we have been getting and he won't take the chains down…'

'You never told me about the four months. You told me four years! That we had a four-year contract! Do you think I would have invested all this money and work into a four-month contract?'

'But Noel you were in such a hurry, and I was so sure it would be success. And look, it has been a great success.'

'And now we are chained out of our own club. We have to hire some lawyers. Let's call our friends and…'

Dozens of frantic phone calls to our regulars, some of the leading socialites and businessmen in Stockholm, all confirm the utter gravity of our predicament. I had signed a contract good only for four months. But it was watertight and I have no recourse whatsoever. And although I am tempted to blame everything on Inga/Alex, in my heart I know that this is my fault. I am the one with experience in contracts for nightclubs, not her. How could I have allowed her to work out these crucial details without any oversight, without translating the contract for me word for word? I am at fault, and try as I might, I cannot shift the blame onto the woman that I love.

Over the next few days, I contact all my regular customers and all of them are aghast at what has happened, and in mourning for their favourite after-dark refuge. We go out and meet our friends for drinks in other Stockholm clubs, like my friend Leif Vestlund's Lord Nelson, where I occasionally DJ. But it is never the same. There is much talk about my finding a new venue, and I am continually sick when I think of all the money I have tied up behind those chained doors, including all the sound equipment, the lighting, furniture and decorative features. Then one evening I get a call from a former customer who says, 'Noel, this may not interest you, but I may have a temporary solution for your problems.'

'Really? Tell me more.'

'I am a shareholder in a brand new hotel called the Blue Avenue.'

'Really?'

'Yes, and we would love to have you open a club there.'

The only problem is that the hotel is located six hundred kilometres north of Stockholm in the city of Umea. It isn't actually north of the Arctic Circle, but the people there, my friend assures me, are desperate to have a good time during the long, long nights. In fact, it's a university town, which is always good for club business. Well, I know that beggars can't be choosers. And I also know how quickly a fat bank account can become an overdraft. So we accept.

We arrive in Umea with high hopes, but the culture shock hits us like an eight-foot snowdrift and a sky where the sun never shines. In fact, it's the middle of winter and the roads are banked with enormous walls of white ice, while 'daylight' consists of a few hours when the southern horizon betrays a slight twinge of radiance. I can't walk outside in any of my shoes, and immediately have to purchase a pair of arctic-proof boots. But the biggest shock is what I see on the faces of everyone in the city. I am the first black person any of them have ever met. Amidst all the blinding whiteness of the landscape, the flawless white skin and the blonde hair, any chance I might have of 'blending into the crowd' is laughable. I don't seek the spotlight, but in Umea there is no escaping its glare whenever I leave the house.

We take a suite in the Blue Avenue Hotel and get to work. I have to start from scratch, without access to any of the sound or lighting systems, furniture, decorations or even records that are locked up back in Alexandra's. I don't have the money to operate on my usual scale of luxury. However, the customers who flock to our Red Spot disco aren't really bothered by the relative lack of glamour of our premises. We quickly see that their eagerness to let off steam and dance the night away will spread across the town of about a hundred thousand residents without requiring promotion.

It's a 'mom and pop' operation basically: Alex collects the cover charge at the door, which we get to keep, and I control the sounds in the DJ box. Our deal gives the hotel control of the bar receipts, but it's not a bad arrangement since I haven't had to sign a lease or pay any rent.

Umea is a university town. We have a steady stream of younger people hungry for nightlife, all enjoying themselves, drinking and dancing, grooving to the beat. It's also not uncommon for many of the people to ask if they can touch me. There's no racism involved, simply innocent curiosity. They want to see if my skin is as velvety as it looks to them.

This will never make us rich, but it does provide an adequate living while I am still seeking a new Stockholm venue to re-open Alexandra's. An unexpected bonus comes along when I realise that a great many of these people cannot dance. I announce afternoon dance classes and immediately dozens of women sign up for them.

As the long winter finally begins to thaw, Alex and I find that we are becoming popular members of the Umea community. We are invited to many homes for lunch or dinner, and later to picnics and barbecues, which often last until three o'clock in the morning in the summer. In the winter we are more likely to end up naked in the sauna, then running outside to roll in the snow. It's all very cordial and cosy, but I have to admit that I miss the action of a big city and the excitement of running a major club. I am, above all, a night creature, not an outdoorsy person. Naturally I am keen to follow up every possible lead about a possible new club venue in Stockholm, and frequently make the long drive south on scouting trips.

Alex stays behind to keep an eye on the club, and I find that she is growing increasingly irritable with me. She makes no effort to hide her growing jealousy about all the women who flock to my dance classes – indeed who flirt with me during the evenings at the Red Spot. And she is very suspicious about my trips into Stockholm.

I suspect she is just as restless in Umea as I am, and that we both believe that we need to get back to Stockholm as soon as possible if we are going to keep our relationship from becoming a constant series of angry arguments.

Fortunately, I get a telephone call one afternoon from my friend Leif Vestlund, owner of the Lord Nelson disco in Stockholm. 'Rolf Drangle is in serious financial trouble at Cecil's,' he tells me. 'The landlord there is Borje Brun. I suggest you give him a call today before the word gets out.'

I do as he suggests and, the very next day, find myself sitting across a table from Brun. He says that, for the right price, he could be persuaded to do business with me. However, he refuses to answer any questions about Rolf Drangle's lease.

'Why won't you tell me how long the lease is for – and give me some idea of when you would be willing to negotiate an agreement with me?' I ask.

'Well, I don't know if you have the money I am looking for.'

'How about giving me first option on the club?'

'That'll cost you too,' says Brun.

'How much?'

'I have a figure in mind.'

In the end, I go away frustrated by Brun's vagueness but determined to do this deal. One of the first things I need to do is line up my backers, and so I make a phone call to Tom Macksey. Then I decide to take the bit between my teeth and call Rolf Drangle directly, telling him that I have been to see Brun, and arranging to meet him that very day at Cecil's.

He's waiting at the bar when I arrive. I immediately notice the lack of customers.

'Hey, what happened here?' I ask. 'This has been one of the prime restaurants in Stockholm since the 1930s?'

'That was then, this is now. You want a tour of the place?'

I follow him through the main dining room and into the kitchen, which is very large and impressive – larger even than the dining room.

Then he shows me the elegant salon that can accommodate eighty people in exquisite style at private dinner parties. He shows me the disco upstairs, which I have already seen, and then we sit down to talk. I get directly to the point, 'I understand you're in trouble here. I've been to see Brun. And I think you and I could do a deal.'

It doesn't take long, thanks to Inga's old friend Tom Macksey's financial support, and within three days the deal is completed. Tom and I are partners, while Rolf retains 25 per cent of the original company.

I am elated. I am going to have a stake in Cecil's and be able to re-launch it as the new Alexandra's. Of course, there will be some refurbishment necessary, and suppliers to contact. Fortunately, the profits we've made at the Red Spot in Umea have allowed me to pay back the suppliers in Stockholm. Suppliers are the lifeblood of a nightclub, and without their goodwill the business is not going to work. I am away from Alex for less than a week, but when I arrive back north, she is in a state.

'You should be thrilled. We're going to re-open our club in Stockholm very soon. Why are you so angry at me?'

'Noel, how can I trust you, or what you say, when you are constantly flirting with all these women? How can I know what you have been doing down in Stockholm?'

'Alex, this jealousy thing is making you crazy. How do I know what you have been doing here in Umea while I've been away?' In fact, I have never given it a second thought. I am not a jealous person by nature, and I have assumed that Alex and I have a secure, committed relationship.

'You always stop to talk with these silly girls who just want to get you into bed!'

'Baby, these are not silly women they're our customers. We have to keep them happy. They want to talk; I talk. They don't change my feelings for you one little bit. Maybe you should talk to the customers more, you know?'

'That's your job. I am just supposed to collect the money.'

'Alex, you know that's not true. You speak their language. You are the best hostess in the world. Listen, do you want to get married?'

'What did you just say?'

'I asked if you want to marry me?'

She stares at me very hard, and then slowly crumples to the floor in a dead faint. I guess – correctly – this is her way of saying 'yes'.

Two days before our wedding, which is going to be held in Umea as a quiet but elegant affair with family and a few friends, Alex's mother and sisters arrive, followed by her father Stig – whom I like immensely, ever since our first meeting.

Now I am very pleased to welcome Stig, and all the rest of Alex's family, for our wedding. That first night we host them at the Red Spot for a raucous evening of drinking, dancing and endless laughter. There had been some anxiety about this family reunion, but Stig wisely has left his new wife back in Stockholm, and the group gets along famously.

The next night – on the eve of our wedding – some of my male friends in Umea insist on taking me out for a traditional stag party, which includes gambling, eating and a vast amount of alcohol. The next morning I have a vicious headache, which persists throughout a day of frantic last-minute preparations. Finally, however, I am standing in front of the altar in Umea's Blue Avenue Hotel, facing up the aisle to see my lovely bride. She looks absolutely radiant, and I have no hesitation when the moment comes in declaring my eternal love for her.

At the restaurant where we hold our reception dinner, Stig wastes no time in making jokes at my expense during his speech. I laugh along with everyone else, my mind focused on the beauty of my bride and on my sincere desire to make a family with her. I want to have children and to raise them with love and understanding. I know that she will be a wonderful mother.

As for a honeymoon, it would have to take place in Stockholm – a working honeymoon as we raced to prepare the old 'one-turntable' Cecil's for it's re-launch as the new and glorious Alexandra's with a spectacular sound system built by OK Krantz.

Shortly after the wedding, Alex and I move down to Stockholm and begin the intensive work of refurbishing the club. Happily, her three sisters throw themselves into this task as well, with great energy and dedication. I feel like I am truly a member of a Swedish family now. The girls have been educated in a system that encourages frank, direct questions about all social issues – sex, drugs, birth control, abortion. Sometimes they ask me questions that leave me shaking my head. My strict education in Trinidad was very puritanical compared to this. As we talk, while we are hanging new crystal chandeliers, draping velvet curtains and arranging new furniture, I feel like I am also revisiting my attitudes to parts of life that I found too 'embarrassing' to speak about in the past.

The work goes quickly and, to my surprise, we are ahead of schedule. We have already sent out the invitations for the select opening night, but even right up until the last minute I am at the club, polishing crystal and sweeping floors, until Alex exclaims, 'Noel, do you want them to arrive and see you dressed like a workman? You must go home right now and change your clothes!'

Our opening night in June 1969 is everything I can – and do – hope for. The guest list is even more impressive than the royal debutant party that had been our shining moment at the first Alexandra's. By special invitation, we host Crown Prince Carl Gustav, Princess Christina, Prince Orsini and all the leading members of Swedish high society. Needless to say, the press is camped outside. The newspapers will be full of glamorous photographs and headlines proclaiming Alexandra's 'renaissance'.

On our second night, the guest list is almost as exalted, but the club is twice as crowded. This crowd has not come by special invitation but of their own volition so eager are they to return to their favourite night-time playground. All of our regular customers seem to show up, and I don't stop shaking hands, kissing cheeks and slapping shoulders until the early hours.

One of the problems that had plagued Cecil's is its location. The street – Biblioteksgatan – is no longer the fashionable address it once was, and hosts a few mediocre shops and offices while two-way traffic dribbles through it during daylight hours. Within six months of Alexandra's re-opening, a dramatic transformation has taken place. New fashionable boutiques have opened, expensive jewellery shops and cafes, and the rental price of square footage on the block has actually doubled. Traffic has become so intense that the city has made the street one-way. Such, I like to think, is the influence of our Alexandra's.

Over the next few years, Alexandra's will reign alone at the summit of Stockholm's nightlife. While summers are slow, as Swedes take off to catch their share of the sun in the Mediterranean, each autumn season explodes with excitement. Our regulars can't wait to return to their favourite watering hole, and the list of celebrities we entertain grows longer and longer: from tennis stars like Bjorn Borg and Arthur Ashe, to rock stars like Manfred Mann and Frank Zappa, as well as most of Sweden's top performing artists. I am particularly pleased when we take a reservation for the American actor Sidney Poitier.

Back when I worked at the Cromwellian club and casino in London, I would occasionally be offered jobs as a film extra by one of our regular customers who was involved with the actors union Equity. One of these jobs turned out to be at Shepperton Studios on the set of a film called *The Long Ships*, which starred Poitier, Richard Widmark, Rosanna Schiaffino and Russ Tamblyn. I had gone straight out to the studio from my night shift at the club. Hours were spent fighting the yawns as I waited for each new camera position to be set. One day Poitier's stand-in was ill, so they asked me to replace him.

The stage was set for a storm scene. Huge paddles were whipping tanks of water into a frenzy. Fans blew thick mist off large blocks of dry ice, and huge hydraulics were tossing the 'deck' of the Viking ship. Yet in the middle of all this, I fell asleep.

Richard Widmark was furious. 'This is my fucking scene. Sleep on somebody else's time!'

I bolted awake and made my apologies. After the scene had been shot, somebody told me to take a cup of tea to Poitier. I found him talking with the voluptuous Rosanna off to the side of the sound stage. 'Would you like some tea?' I offered.

He ignored me.

'Can I give you some tea, Mr Poitier?'

He ignored me again.

My pride was hurt and I lost it. 'I don't need this shit,' I muttered.

I walked off, dropped the cup and saucer on the floor, and went straight home. Over the years, I had regretted that incident many times. My stubborn pride had got the better of me, and I had been deeply embarrassed after being ignored by a man who, in fact, was one of my idols. Who could have blamed him for wanting to be alone with Rosanna Schiaffino? Would I have behaved any differently in his situation? Of course not.

So when Sidney Poitier arrives at the club, I make a very special effort, including a sign on the Great Table that reads, 'Guess Who's Coming To Dinner'. As it turns out, we get along famously, especially after I remind him of the story of our first meeting and the cup of tea he scorned. Much champagne is downed and the party goes on until closing. It's only the first of many evenings Sidney will spend with us, both at the club and in our Stockholm apartment.

You can never predict when your life will change dramatically. Nor do you notice when that change starts, when you have started down a new path, often not until much later.

For me, it begins in the kitchen – not surprisingly, since I love kitchens, and cooking, and the smell of freshly ground spices and garlic – but this is not one of those good kitchen moments. I have just let myself through the back door of Alexandra's, at eight in the evening as usual, into our large bustling kitchen where I like to consult with my chef first thing upon arrival every evening. Suddenly a hand grabs my arm and slams me into the wall. 'Who the fuck are you?' says my attacker, as his hand comes up to grasp my throat. He has a rough American accent.

One of my staff shouts, 'This is his club, asshole.'

'It's true. Let him go,' says another American voice. I turn to see who is speaking. It's someone from the US embassy and an occasional guest at the club. 'Sorry, Noel. You OK? These Secret Service guys get wound a little too tight sometimes. Please accept our apologies.'

The hand lets go of my throat, I shake my head and say, 'I'm fine, but what the hell is this all about? I'm not used to being assaulted in my own kitchen. And we're in Sweden, not the United States, so who gives you the authority to be here anyway?'

'We're here to look after Senator Ted Kennedy. Didn't the embassy reserve a table?'

'What the hell has that got to do with this?'

'Standard operating procedure; we have to secure your premises.'

I stare hard at him. The arrogance is unbelievable. 'With all due respect, shove your standard operating procedures. I have royalty, national presidents, Gulf sheikhs who all come here but never have I allowed this kind of security invasion. This is my club and you are here without my permission. Get off the premises now.'

The guy looks sheepish and flustered. 'We have to secure your club as Mr Kennedy won't go anywhere without security.'

'Then he will have to find another place to party. I want these gunslingers out of my club now. They are a menace – to me, and to my customers.'

Scowling, the Secret Service men leave the premises about five minutes later, and the embassy attaché follows on their heels. Within thirty minutes, we get a call from the embassy cancelling the Kennedy reservation. I couldn't care less, although I notice that the huge burst of adrenalin I had in the kitchen has left me with a strange feeling in my chest. It's a twinge near my heart that comes and goes. Not a sharp pain, but worrying.

The twinge continues throughout the evening. In fact, it grows slightly worse. When I leave for home, I can tell that Alex, nestled close beside me in the cab, is in the mood for one of our long, sensual lovemaking sessions. And I, too, am in the mood. I'm not sure my body is though. Soon after we arrive home, I feel the first sharp pain and realise that my body is definitely telling me to call for help. My mind flashes back to the life I have been living. I exist on very little sleep: we're invited to every opening and gala in Stockholm these days, receive far more invitations to dinner parties than we can possibly attend, and there is always a new star in town who wants to be entertained until very late in the club.

At 5 a.m., I find myself flat on my back in the emergency room at Karolinska hospital with wires and tubes stuck into my flesh, the chest pain still coming and going, my fear worse than anything. A sedative helps to control that a bit, and I sleep, only to wake up into an endless ordeal of EKGs and blood tests, stuck on a ward of ailing bodies, hidden behind a flimsy green curtain. I hate the lack of privacy even more than the pain in my chest. It brings me thoughts of how it must have been for my mother when I was born in the hospital in Trinidad. And it brings inevitable thoughts of my own mortality. How can this be? I am too young to die. It doesn't help when they move me into intensive care.

Quieter, strapped to the EKG machine, I have nobody for company during the long night except the glare of the machine's monitor. Many of the nurses are young, beautiful women – and I feel terribly embarrassed in their presence. However, one older nurse, a Finn, resembles Mother Teresa (I think) and I confide my anxieties to her. 'You must be patient and rest. Dr Strom is a very good doctor,' she tells me.

'I thank you, Nurse Ribbing, for looking after me so well.'

'I am off for two days tomorrow. You must let the other nurses take care of you too. Don't be so shy. You run a big nightclub, you mustn't be shy.'

'When will you be back?' I ask in desperation.

'Don't you worry. And I won't tell these pretty nurses that you are shy of them.'

The next day I take her words to heart and attempt to overcome my shyness. In fact, I hand out a few free passes to Alexandra's, and these bring me lots of smiles and kindness from the nurses. (As a result, I also begin to get morning reports from the nurses who've taken the passes on what happened in the club the night before.) Dr Strom finally arrives to say that so far all the tests have been inconclusive. They are going to have me talk with a psychologist, Dr Kellberg, who he's brought along.

They ask me detailed questions about my lifestyle, and I am honest with them about the long hours I keep, and about my eating, drinking and smoking habits.

When I've finished, the two doctors stare at me, almost in disbelief, then go away for five minutes to confer. When they return, Dr Strom says, 'You are lucky to be alive, Noel.'

'You have definitely been pushing your luck,' Dr Kellberg says. 'Now you must certainly take six months convalescence.'

'Why, if you can't find anything wrong with me?'

'Nobody can carry on living at your pace and expect to survive. You are only 29 years old. Now here you have been hospitalised with a heart problem. If we don't have the exact diagnosis of the problem, we do have an exact picture of your life. The tests rule out cardiac arrest, but your heart has obviously been abused.'

They put me into the coronary care unit and prescribe a special diet to rebuild my system. I feel very relieved. If I can heal myself simply by resting, by eating well, by sleeping regular hours, how lucky! It seems I have a second chance here, and I do not want to be a fool and squander it.

The next day, during her regular visit, Alex – who has been doing a great job of running the club during my illness – shows up with my friend Archie. He had been a croupier in the Chemin de Fer game at La Discotheque on Wardour Street in London the night I had one of my biggest wins. I had been busted out of that game with only a sixpence to my name. On my way out of the club, I had put that into a slot machine and won a £6 jackpot. I went straight back to the table, where I ended up passing eight times. Then Archie and I had gone to another club where there was an all-night high stakes poker game and we had both won very big. We'd celebrated with a champagne breakfast at the Inn on the Park accompanied by two stunning girls. Ever since, Archie and I have been the best of mates.

I've had a night to think and now I tell them both about the doctors' recommendations the previous day. 'What am I supposed to do about the club – if I'm supposed to retire for six months to convalesce? I love my life. I don't really want to change any of it.'

'But your life is killing you, Noel,' Alex says. 'The doctors tell you this! I am still very worried about you.'

'Don't be worried. I think the worst thing happening to me now is being cooped up in here, with all these tests draining my blood. And all these sick people around me.'

There are tears in her eyes. 'Noel, I love you. You must do what the doctors say.'

They have brought me flowers and Archie has given me a book that is wrapped up in fine paper. The nurse comes and tells them that visiting hours are over for the day. 'Enjoy the book, Noel,' Archie says, with a big wink. I feel an enormous urge to get out of bed and follow them off into the Stockholm night, to feel the electric atmosphere back inside Alexandra's as the music draws everyone to the dance floor, as the crystal glasses rise in joyful toasts.

Left alone on this grim ward, I wonder how I am ever going to follow the doctors' orders. Where is the magical potion that is going to take my old personality and change it into that of a sedentary invalid? How does a man used to speeding along in the fast lane suddenly slam on the brakes – without skidding off the road into madness. Eventually, with the help of a pill from the nurse, I fall into a deep sleep.

I wake up feeling a burst of restlessness at 3 a.m. and, looking around, my eye falls on the gift brought by Archie. Unwrapped, it turns out to be a book about erotic art. On the first page is an inscription that reads: 'To my dear friend Noel, Don't be shy. Have a good one. Archie'. Looking through the pages, I begin to get aroused. Sex hasn't crossed my mind since I've been in the hospital, but now I begin to surrender to the urge. It doesn't take long to have an orgasm, and a powerful one at that. The book goes flying off the bed into the monitor, which sets off an alarm in the nurse's station. Within seconds, a pretty young nurse arrives and quickly understands the whole scene.

'Someone has been a naughty boy. Good, you must be feeling much better. Come on then, let us connect this machine again. And I will put this book here under your pillow for tomorrow, so you can get some sleep now, ja?'

The next day I am moved to another four-bed cardiac ward. One of the men coughs all the first night, continually waking me, but he is gone in the morning. The other man disappears two mornings later. When I ask a nurse about them, she explains that both men had died in their sleep. The panic that rifles through me at that moment is indescribable. I must get out of this place... as quickly as possible.

My clothes – the ones I arrived in weeks earlier – are hanging in a small cupboard in the room. I dress as fast as I can and head out into the corridor, down to the elevators and press the button for the ground floor. We stop at another floor and an attendant wheels in a gurney with a corpse covered in a sheet. That does it! No doubts about escape now, I make a dash through the lobby to the street. In fact, I feel dizzy and my legs are weak from all those days spent flat on my back. The street seems confusing, all these people shouting, cars honking and I feel myself pouring with sweat at the effort. I manage to get to the pavement and wave for a passing taxi. Once I get a cab to stop, the actual drive to my apartment feels like a rollercoaster ride that will never end. Upstairs, I rip off my clothes and collapse into the welcome softness of my own bed. I sleep for two days straight, while Alex keeps vigil over me, mops my perspiring brow and worries.

When I finally wake, she is sitting at the foot of the bed. 'What time is it?' I ask.

'Noel, do you realise that you have been asleep for two whole days? Who cares what time it is?'

'Well, didn't the doctor tell me to get lots of rest?'

'Do you realise what you have done, Noel?'

'I've come home because I can't stand to be around all those dying people.'

'No, you've broken the law.'

'Huh? In my sleep?'

'It's against the law to leave a Swedish hospital without a doctor's consent. Dr Strom has called and says you must return to the hospital immediately. He was very angry, but I have done my best to keep him from calling the police. I told him that if you have a criminal record, you won't be able to run your nightclub business.'

Reluctantly, after a bath and a shave, I get dressed in fresh clothes and together we return to the hospital. Dr Strom is waiting. He gives me a fierce lecture and makes me promise that I will stay until officially discharged. 'You're lucky I didn't report you. If your wife didn't love you so much, and if my wife didn't love Alexandra's, I would have reported you to the police. Actually, I have to admit that I love your nightclub too.'

Several days later, I am officially released from the hospital. I am back at Alexandra's that night. Try as I might to adopt the new 'healthy' approach to my life, I find it very difficult. Within a day or two, I am living just as I have always lived, sitting at the Great Table with a Chivas in one hand, a cigarette in the other, beautiful women on both sides of me, interesting people talking the night away.

The next day I arrive to hear that a 'trade delegation' from Barbados has booked for the evening. I am excited to meet this Caribbean crowd. In all my years in the clubs in London and Mallorca, I have never met a VIP from the West Indies. When the group arrives, I watch them from a distance. They are dressed elegantly and behave with impeccable manners. Alex chats with them, then comes over and tells me that the Prime Minister of Barbados would like to meet me.

We go back to their table and I am introduced to Prime Minister Barrow. In fact, I recall having met him once very briefly before – at Carnival in Trinidad. I had been in the Trinidad Hilton when his assistant, Carlton, had invited me to join their table.

'Yes,' says Errol Barrow. 'I remember you. It was the Trinidad Hilton, wasn't it? Do have a seat. Let me introduce you to Peter Morgan, our Minister of Tourism. And this is…'

After all the introductions, we begin a lively conversation that includes many compliments on the club and lots of laughter about the differences between Stockholm nights and Caribbean nights. Soon we are all on a first-name basis. Nobody is in a rush to leave, and so we are still having a blast when the lights suddenly go bright at 3 a.m.

'This is the first time a nightclub has ever closed on me,' says Errol. 'How astonishing that it should be Alexandra's, which I like so much. In any case, it's been a great night, Noel.'

'It's been a genuine pleasure having you and your friends here tonight Errol,' I say, adding, 'I hope you will come back soon.'

'Noel, a club like this is exactly what we need on Barbados,' he says. 'Would you consider lending us some of your expertise as a guest of my government?'

'It would be a pleasure. I am rather busy running this place, but it would be nice to get some sun.' Already I am thinking: this could be the perfect way to follow my doctor's orders and convalesce, on the beaches of Barbados.

'I'm going to have Peter call you tomorrow and arrange a lunch. I don't waste time when I get a good idea like this, Noel. I like to move quickly.'

'So do I. Let me give you my private telephone number. Have Peter ring me when he wakes up tomorrow.'

Two days later I meet with Peter Morgan, the only white man in the Barbados government, at the Operakallaren restaurant. Over a fine lunch of mussels and grilled fish, we discuss tourism on the island. We finalise the details of my invitation to Barbados. The Prime Minister and his delegation will depart Sweden on 1 November 1969, and I will follow a week later to investigate the possibility of establishing a sophisticated, high-end club on Barbados.

The day before my departure, I take a night off from the club at Alex's insistence. It's going to be a long flight and I will need to be rested. Although I fall asleep early, I wake up in the middle of the night. I've been having a vivid dream about Barbados. There is no sign of Alex. I look at the clock and see she isn't due home for another hour.

The buzzer rings from downstairs. I work the intercom. It's our friend Marion, and I let her up. She's a handsome woman, a real outdoors type and she is accompanied, as always by her husky dog Butch. She likes to spend her weekends hiking and skiing with her dog and friends up north. I had asked her to recommend a going-away present to give Alex. Now here she is with an adorable puppy in her arms. It's a jet-black cocker spaniel, just a few weeks old. We sit down to play with the puppy and, before long, Alex arrives. She is thrilled with the dog and can't thank me enough.

'Marion,' I whisper to her as I see her out later, 'You're an angel. This was the perfect present.'

Early the next morning, Alex accompanies me to the airport. She suddenly becomes very emotional. 'Noel, I don't want you to go to Barbados. I have a bad feeling about this trip. It's going to change things, I am sure.' She clings to me and I give her a long, lingering kiss.

'Don't you worry. It's an opportunity for me to rest, just what the doctor ordered. You should be happy I'm taking this healthy break.'

I have to wipe the tears from her cheeks as she refuses to break our embrace. 'I have to check-in now,' I say gently and finally she lets me go and steps back. I approach the immigration officer and we have a few moments of confusion about my entry visa. Eventually, we find it and I am allowed to go through the security check. I set off the alarm, and have to be searched and empty my pockets. I turn to go through it again and see Alex standing back at the edge of the crowd, in floods of tears. It sparks a very sad flashback to my mother standing on the quayside in Trinidad the day I boarded the *Ascania* to leave for England. I turn and pass through security with no problems on my second attempt.

At the airport bar, I bump into a Russian whom I know from the first Alexandra's. He used to be captain of the hydrofoil that made regular crossings between Leningrad and Stockholm. We'd had a deal in which we swapped the caviar and vodka he brought from the USSR for dinner and drinks at the club. Now he is telling me about his adventures the previous evening in the new Alexandra's. 'Why weren't you there, Noel?'

'Doctor's orders,' I tell him, and excuse myself to do some last minute shopping. I want to take some of my favourite gourmet Swedish foods down to the island. While the shop is sold out of gravadlax, I stock up on smoked reindeer, pickled herring and salmon roe. Then I hear my flight announced.

It's 9 November 1969. When I settle down into the large comfortable seat, a familiar face in a purser's uniform approaches me. In fact, it is another customer from Alexandra's and he is intent on giving me the best possible service, which translates into an enormous goblet full of Chivas Regal.

We're flying via Copenhagen and Zurich, with a plane change in the latter. In Copenhagen, I leave the plane to make a quick local telephone call to Stefan. He is my Danish restaurant manager, very experienced, who spends every other weekend with his family in Copenhagen. We're more than just owner and employee, but good friends as well. Now I make sure that he has no further questions, since he will be assuming all my responsibilities for ordering food and drink and supervising the back of house. Alex will continue to be the hostess and to oversee all aspects of customer service in the front of house. Stefan assures me that he has everything firmly under control, and I thank him.

When I re-board the plane, I feel relatively secure about leaving the club for what may be, I think, as long as a month. I am ready to start a new kind of life. And so I settle in for the long hours of flight, including the plane transfer in Zurich, a glass or two of champagne, a good dinner, more Chivas and then a long deep sleep.

I wake up with the pilot's voice in my ear. 'Ladies and gentleman, we are experiencing some turbulence as we pass over the Azores. Please return to your seats and fasten your safety belts.'

I bury my head back into the seat and fall asleep again quickly. It's the only way to deal with a frightening flight. Then I hear a soft Swedish voice whisper, 'Sir, will you be taking tea?'

I look up and see the stewardess, her blonde hair in a corona of bright light around a beautiful face. Outside the cabin, the sunset on the horizon is filing the sky with gold, purple, orange flames. 'Yes, please. Are we almost there?'

'We'll be landing in Barbados in about an hour.'

'It's all gone so fast. Asleep is the only way to cross an ocean, I guess.'

'I have been to your nightclub, Mr Charles.'

'Have you? That's wonderful. Did we meet?'

'Yes, and another time at Bisana's house. Do you recall?'

'Oh, with all those intellectuals from the university? Yes, I remember that.' But I don't remember her. All those pompous eggheads must have blocked out her extraordinary beauty, and I had been there with Alex, of course.

'I am from Sweden, but I live in London,' she says. 'My parents moved there when I was a little girl. My name is Astrid.'

'It's very nice to meet you, Astrid.' We shake hands.

'Please tell me – did you ever find the statue that was missing from your club?'

I laugh. 'Well, in fact we…' But the pilot's voice interrupts me.

'Ladies and gentlemen, we will be landing at Seawell Airport from the north, after approaching along the west coast of the island. Please return to your seats now, and fasten your safety belts.'

'You can tell me another time,' Astrid says. 'I'll be at the Hilton for the next five days. Perhaps we can have dinner sometime?'

'That would be more than a pleasure. I'll give you a call.'

'I look forward to hearing from you then. Now I must go.'

Once she has gone, I sit back and close my eyes. Starting a new life – a quiet, restful, virtuous life – is not going to be easy.

Barbados I

A warm Caribbean breeze caresses my face as I take my first steps on the island. The low colonial buildings of Seawell Airport look so quaint compared to the sleek modern jet aircraft that crowd the tarmac. Palm trees sway beside the terminal. It feels very good to be back in this part of the world, far from the icy streets of Stockholm, the leaden skies of London. Yet, even at this moment, I experience a twinge for what I've left behind. Will Alex be able to cope in my absence? Then the moment passes, and I enter the arrivals hall.

The dark-faced immigration officer wears an immaculate white uniform. 'Welcome to Barbados, sir.' He stamps my passport. 'Have a most pleasant stay.' I thank him. My heart lifts as I scan the crowd of faces beyond the Customs area.

There he is – the Prime Minister himself – chatting amiably with one of the baggage handlers. Talk about a VIP welcome! I step forward and shake the hand of the man who has changed my destiny. He flashes a warm smile and says, 'Hello, Noel. Good to see you.'

'It's very good to see you too, and to see you looking so well, Mr Prime Minister.'

He turns to the baggage handler and says, 'Mr Charles will identify his luggage. Take it out to my car please.'

'OK, Dipper,' says the man.

I make a quizzical expression, and the Prime Minister laughs. 'People here call me "Dipper", as you'll soon learn, Noel.'

Fifteen minutes later, we are chatting away in the Prime Minister's large white Mercedes as he drives us along the coast road beside the gorgeous turquoise sea. 'The little village we're coming into now is called Oistins,' he says. 'This is where the first Charter of Barbados was signed, in 1652, in a pub called Ye Mermaid's Inn. We received our self-rule in return for pledging our loyalty to Cromwell. Now you'll see the village has been thoroughly modernised, but the fishermen here still are some of the best on the island. Come at four every afternoon when they sell their daily catch.'

Soon we arrive at a complex of buildings called the Maresol Apartments. Within seconds of parking, we are greeted by a man who had been one of my boyhood heroes, the legendary Bajan cricketer Everton Weekes. He personally takes my bags to the residence, where I will be staying. The owner is waiting, along with his wife: it's none other than Peter Morgan, the Minister of Tourism. His lovely wife, Margaret, has prepared a spread of local delicacies: sea eggs, flying fish, fish cakes. She offers us drinks, and I have a Chivas, while the Prime Minister opts for gin and kola tonic.

After we eat and drink, Everton takes me to my room. We pass through a private garden with lush flowering hibiscus plants. The room itself is very comfortable, cosy and bright. My luggage has already been unpacked and stowed away. Everton asks if I would like to have a nap, but I feel – despite the very long flight – completely energised. In fact, I feel fantastic. Barbados feels, from the start, like my destiny, filling me with new strength. I have always followed my gut instincts, rather than detached strategic planning. So far, my gambler's intuition has never failed me. I tell the great cricketer that I only need ten minutes for a quick shower and shave, and then I would like to continue with the programme. Errol has already told me in the car, 'There are three people I want you to meet right away. Each one will be important to your project.' Why waste a single minute of my first day?

As we travel at speed in the Mercedes, heading west towards Bridgetown, Errol gives me a stream of fascinating information and insights. I feel like I am with the King of Barbados. Every few moments someone waves at the car or honks their horn. We cruise past the statue of Lord Nelson and the central police station, past a crowd of waving schoolchildren, along blocks of interesting local shops and bars. Eventually, we are out on the open road and then pull up in front of a house named Calais. We park and meander up a footpath to an open doorway. The sounds of the *Mikado* opera come through the door, along with the aroma of home cooking.

'Dipper, welcome!' booms a voice. 'Come and join us. Meet some good friends of mine.'

'Hello, Clyde. This is Noel Charles, who has just arrived from Sweden. Noel, this is Clyde, my soft-spoken but immensely talented lawyer.'

We are standing on the open, second-storey terrace of a house built on the cliff edge at Prospect St James with a spectacular view of the sea below us, and in the distance a necklace of white sand beaches heading to the north of the island. It's early evening, and the moon is already visible in the dusky sky. This is the first of many visits to this house. Our host, Clyde, is seated with two attractive ladies, drinking cocktails. It seems that he cannot speak except at full volume, as he shouts, 'Donald! See what these gentlemen want to eat. We have an excellent flying fish, stuffed with tiger prawns and papaya. The girls enjoyed it. Won't you have some?'

'Tempting, but we ate at Peter's an hour ago. Donald, I think Noel might like a Chivas with lots of ice. And I'll have my usual,' says the Prime Minister.

'Of course, Dipper.'

'Errol, it's very nice to meet Noel, but I need to talk to you in private for a bit,' Clyde says. 'Can I suggest that Noel takes these ladies down to the lower balcony. Don't hesitate to enjoy their company, Noel. Have some good Bajan fun. And you'll get a better view of our amazing underwater nightlife down there, as I have lit this cove with nocturnal spotlights.'

'I'd love to get a closer look.'

'Let me show you,' says one of the ladies. Both of them are attractive, young and dressed in revealing outfits. I am unsure what the deal is, but I don't want to be a bad guest.

As we stand directly above the illuminated cove, I can see schools of vividly coloured fish attracted by the lights. The stars are becoming visible above us, and the air has cooled. I sip my whisky and find myself whispering, 'I must be in Paradise.'

One of the ladies giggles and says, 'Yes, you must be. Look at that… the stingray over there! We call him "Hoover."' I let my eyes follow her pointed finger. The graceful creature is slowly fanning its way across the cove.

'Thank you for showing me,' I say. In response, she laughs again and kisses me quickly on the cheek.

A few minutes later, Clyde's voice booms, 'OK, we've completed our conference. Bring the distinguished gentleman back up here, ladies.' So I am led inside and up to the second floor. Apparently, there's no time for a second drink, as Errol thanks our host. Soon we are back in his car and heading northwards along the coast.

It's not far to his own house – called Kampala – at Paradise Beach. We park and a man throws open the door before we reach it. I immediately recognise Carlton, Errol's right-hand man, from our first meeting in the Trinidad Hilton. We have a chat and Carlton leads me to the kitchen, where he again offers me snacks and makes me another drink, as well as a gin and kola for his boss. But when we return to the living room, the Prime Minister is stretched out on a long sofa with his eyes shut and his breathing deep and regular.

'I thought we had another couple of stops tonight,' I say, 'but it looks like Mr Barrow has reached the end of his road.'

'Motley can wait until tomorrow,' says Errol, his eyes still shut. 'I am sorry, Noel, but you're right: I guess I have run out of petrol. Finish your drink and Carlton will run you back to Maresol.'

In the car, with calypso music playing softly over the radio, I chat with Carlton about Stockholm, and then about my island, Trinidad, and its Carnival. 'What did you think of Clyde?' Carlton asks suddenly.

'An impressive man, and a fantastic host too. Didn't really have much of a chance to talk to him.'

'He tries to shock people, but pay that no mind. You'll like him more when you get to know him.'

'I'm sure that I will.'

Once I am back in my room at Maresol, sleep comes easily. It seems only seconds before I am awake with the sun streaming through the yellow curtains. When was the last time I had the pleasure of seeing a sunrise? I jump out of bed. There is a knock on the door. It's a young maid with a tray full of tea, toast and fresh tropical fruit. 'Is it possible to swim in the sea here?' I ask.

'Yes, sir, at the beach, 15 yards away. But be careful of the coral and the currents. Don't go and drown yourself.'

'I learned how to swim on Trinidad when I was seven years old. I can take care of myself.'

'You be careful anyway, man.' With the tray all set up on the table, she pulls back the curtains and reveals the stunning azure waters of the Caribbean. In fact, there is a door leading straight outside. When she is gone, I find my trunks and slip them on. I am outside and halfway down the path when I hear Everton's voice calling. 'Noel, the girl tells me you wants to swim?'

'That's right. Where's the best place, Everton?'

'In de sea,' he says, and laughs. 'You be fine.'

I reach the edge of the water and stroll along, noting how the morning sun makes the water so transparent, how the light glints off the low swells and bounces off the silver palm leaves. I run straight into the sea and swim out as far as I can. In less than 24 hours, Barbados has captured my soul. Of course, I love Trinidad and Mallorca, but as I stroke my way out into the Caribbean, and then roll over to float on my back, I think that neither of those islands compares to this. I take off my trunks and swim naked for a while. Pure bliss; total freedom. The doctors had told me to rest and heal. Where better than on this enchanted island?

When I return to the beach, I lie down on my towel in the morning sun. Soon, a very tall Bajan walks by and pauses. He introduces himself as Patrick, a neighbour who lives in the nearby Glenroy Apartment complex. 'You must be on holiday,' he says.

'Yes and no,' I tell him. 'It's a working holiday.'

'Where have you come from?'

'Stockholm.'

'You missed the sun up there, I expect.'

'I can't tell you how much I missed it. This is paradise.'

'Paradise if you can stand it, yes.'

I laugh, but note a subtle warning in his remark. 'I think I can stand it.'

'I'm sure you can.'

We chat for several more minutes, then he makes his departure. 'See you tomorrow,' he says.

'Until tomorrow, Patrick.'

I have to force myself to rise and walk back to the Maresol. In my room, I shower and then change into fresh clothes. I wander out and meet Margaret, and ask her if I can use a telephone to call my wife in Sweden. She graciously takes me to a phone and then leaves me in privacy. I try Alex at home, and there is no reply. Next I try the club, but she's not there either, so I leave a message. Then I dial the number that Errol had given me the previous evening. Carlton answers, then quickly puts me on to the Prime Minister. 'Noel, I was about to ring you. We have a lunch scheduled here with your architect. Ben is Nigerian, a wonderful chap, who does most of our government work. Shall I pick you up?'

'Don't trouble yourself, Errol. I can take a cab.'

My taxi driver is a charming streetwise Bajan named Stephan. We get to chatting about the island, and he is full of interesting – and honest – insights. By the time we reach Kampala, I have asked him if he will be my personal guide and driver for the duration of my stay. He seems pleased to accept. 'I wait for you now, yes?' he asks. 'Later, I take you some places no tourist ever see. The true Barbados, yes?'

'Yes, please. Looking forward to it.'

Errol is looking refreshed and completely businesslike this morning. We sit down in his parlour and launch immediately into a serious discussion. Where should the club be located? Should it be built from scratch or converted from an existing building? What kind of budget will I require? What about hiring and training staff?

In the midst of our conversation, Ben arrives. I had been somewhat wary since Errol had told me about him, based on my own history of dealing with architects, and Nigerians. However, from the first moment we meet, I am fully at ease with Ben. He reminds me of my old friend Zihute, the tribal prince from Ghana who befriended me at the poly back in London.

'So what do you do exactly for the Bajan government?' I ask.

'I provide advice on national projects. What do you do, my friend?'

'I work with food, beverage and entertainment.'

'Here in the Caribbean?'

'I was born on Trinidad, but my work has been done in Europe: London, Spain and Sweden.'

'Let me tell you, Ben, this man runs the best nightclub in all the world – in Stockholm,' Errol says. 'I can't begin to tell you how much we enjoyed ourselves in his establishment during our recent visit. That's why I have invited Noel here. Our island needs a nightclub that is truly world-class. And Noel is the man to help us achieve that.'

Carlton summons us to the dining room, where we continue to discuss the project from many different perspectives over a delicious lunch. At its conclusion, Errol says he has to leave for another meeting, but invites us to continue our meeting in his house. However, Ben says there is a possible site that he would like to show me. I agree. My new driver Stephan is waiting, but I tell him that I will be driving with Ben and that he should check by the Maresol later that evening.

The building Ben shows me is located in Bridgetown at a place called the Pierhead – a wharf located on the Careenage Canal in a district of warehouses and small moored fishing boats. The building itself is close to one of the two bridges spanning the canal, very close to the sea. Immediately, it looks like an ideal space to me – and reminds me of a place outside Milan called Lago Maggiore where boats anchored at a jetty and ferried people from the lake's islands to the mainland in order to party. I am clearly excited, and Ben and I chat away for another hour or two before he drops me back at the Maresol.

That evening I place another call to Alex. She answers, sounding cheerful; clearly exulting in her new role as the sole supremo of Alexandra's while I am halfway across the world. However, her cheerfulness fades noticeably as I gush with excitement about the beauty of the island, the fun I am having and the great prospects for a new club here.

'Noel, you are supposed to be resting. Are you up to your old bad habits, and working so hard on just the second day you arrive there? Oh please Noel!'

'Come on, baby, my health couldn't be better. I am feeling great.'

'It sounds like you are over-indulging.'

'Nothing of the sort. I'm hanging out with the Prime Minister and other government types and concentrating on serious business. I haven't been near a bar or a club since I arrived.'

'Yeah, sure. Well, we've found a place in Norway,' she says, changing the subject. 'That's where we should open our next club.'

I am annoyed. I can't remember having such a stilted conversation with Alex before. She seems to be completely dead set against even considering a club on Barbados.

'The important action is here on Barbados, not in Norway,' I say. 'Listen, I have to run now. I'll call you soon.'

'Don't hang up yet,' she says, suddenly uncertain.

'I miss you, Alexandra.'

'Noel, what is wrong? Are you annoyed with me?'

'I want you to come down here. Very soon.'

'Of course, darling. I will come there.'

I hang up and, despite my best instincts, dial Astrid, the airhostess, at the Hilton.

'Noel, I was wondering if you were going to call me. Yes, I would love to have dinner with you. Tomorrow I'm leaving for New York. Great, I'll see you here at eight.'

After hanging up, I take a hot shower and muse on where to take her. The previous day, in the car, Errol had pointed out a sign for a restaurant called Bagatelle. 'One of the best on the island,' he'd said. So that will be our destination. I cannot stop puzzling over Alex's strange attitude on the telephone. The fact is, even as I am about to take another woman out for dinner, I know that I love my wife very much indeed. What I heard in her voice just now disturbs me, but there is little I can do about it tonight.

Bagatelle is located in the hills of St Thomas, a parish overlooking the chic west coast of the island. It is owned and hosted by a sturdy English gentleman named Nick Hudson. As we drive up to the coral stone plantation house, once the home of Lord Willoughby, the Governor of Barbados in 1650, I am acutely aware of how attractive Astrid looks in her short black strapless dress.

Her tanned shoulders and long blonde hair, gleaming with highlights from the sun, would make any man who accompanied her the envy of his fellows. In the cab, she has kept up an amusing patter about her excursions on the island and her efforts to fend off randy beach boys. I haven't said much. Realising this, she suddenly asks me, 'Have you spoken to Inga – I mean Alexandra – since you arrived?'

'Yes, this afternoon in fact.'

'Will she be joining you here?'

'I hope so. We've never been apart for very long before. It's a bit difficult.'

'You must miss her.'

'Yes, very much.' I realise that this is not exactly seductive conversation on my part, but I cannot be dishonest about something – someone – who means so much to me.

'Do you think you really know her, Noel? I mean, really understand her?'

I think this is a bit odd, a bit insinuating, but put it down to women's inherent competitiveness. 'Yes, as well as anyone can ever know another person, I think I know her.'

'That must be a wonderful feeling,' says Astrid. 'I'm not sure I have ever felt like that about someone else.'

We enter the restaurant and are confronted by Nick Hudson himself, dressed, rather bizarrely, in a full-length skirted dish-dash. 'Welcome, come in please. Golly, you're a beautiful young lady. You are a lucky man, Mister… ?'

'Noel Charles. I'm a guest on the island of the Prime Minister.'

'Oh yes! Of course, I've heard all about you and your legendary club in Stockholm. So glad you came tonight. Errol is not here, but do please say hello to him for me when next you see him. I'm afraid we are rather full at this minute, so please allow me to buy you a drink while we prepare a table for you. Won't you follow me into the bar? Or would you like to dine with the rest of us at the Great Table, named after your Great Table at Alexandra's!'

'Why not the Great Table? We're not expecting Errol to join us this evening.'

'Come then and let me introduce you to your fellow guests…'

Hudson makes the introductions so fast and casually that I almost cannot keep track. There's the famous London photographer, David Bailey, with the striking young international model of the moment, Penelope Tree. A Canadian accountant named David Allison and his wife, and Hudson's own girlfriend, Sherry Hunte. With us, that makes eight in total. Nick suggests that the Beef Wellington is his house specialty, but the personalised menu offers many other tempting dishes. I am seated between Astrid and Penelope, and it's difficult not to feel extremely flattered in these circumstances. Soon our glasses are filled and the meal stretches out over several hours, a truly world-class meal too. I am very impressed with Nick Hudson's charm and professionalism. Indeed, he goes far beyond the professional host's role when, coffee having been served and brandies being sipped, he invites us all up to his private apartment where he would like to play some classical guitar for us. But it's getting late, and I know Errol will have a busy day scheduled for me, so I make our apologies and tell him that next time I would be honoured to hear his recital. Astrid smiles graciously, although I can tell she is somewhat surprised.

However, when we reach the Hilton, we are confronted by a hotel security man who does not know me and demands to know my room number. Astrid gives hers, but the man says, 'Not yours. Only guests are allowed on the property after midnight. I want to know his room number.'

I shrug and turn to see Stephan waiting in his taxi. She calls goodnight at my back, and I wave with my hand. I am furious at the hotel security, but recognise that, as an official government guest, the last thing I want to do is make a scene.

Over the next few days, I find myself caught up in a dream state of total relaxation and pleasure. Even the business meetings are a pleasure, for there is nothing in the world I enjoy so much as creating a vision for a new club and then making that vision a reality.

Of course, it's not all business meetings or looking at sites. Each night is a new adventure, a bar hopping whirlwind – with my Swedish doctor's orders to convalesce largely forgotten. Sometimes on my own, other times with Errol, Clyde or Ben. I quickly become a regular at Bajan hotspots like the Pepper Pot, the Island Inn and a little disco called Mary's Moustache. After all, if I am going to conquer the night scene on Barbados, I have to know the territory better than anyone else.

I make frequent telephone calls to Alex in Stockholm, but find these often end in tricky moments of mutual puzzlement. Something is shifting between us, I sense, but I cannot really put my finger on it. Of course I trust her, and she professes to trust me. And the business itself seems to be flourishing, as ever, under her sole management. Still, I want her to come down to Barbados, but she always manages to avoid making a definite commitment to this.

Since I am so close, I decide that I ought to visit my mother on Trinidad. It's less than an hour by air, and, in truth, I long to see my wonderful island birthplace again. It will be a mini-holiday, and no doubt a bit of a healthy break from my Bajan revels. The island really has captured my soul and makes me feel almost like a teenager again.

I should have known better. Whatever romantic dream of family I have briefly conjured up is rudely shattered when I arrive at my old home on Trinidad. My mother is obviously surprised and perturbed by my appearance. She asks not a single question about my life in Stockholm, my new wife, or my plans for Barbados. I suppose I had wanted to be greeted as the prodigal son returned, with a bit of affection and gratitude. In truth, it takes me less than ten minutes to wish I had never come. My mother is scornful and visibly annoyed at my sudden appearance.

At least I have one friend who is very glad to see me. Oswald 'Gus' Augustine is someone I first met during Carnival back when I returned to Trinidad after my father's accident in the early 1960s. He is now the owner of the locally famous – indeed infamous – Excelsior Bar and Lounge. Located on Abercromby Street in the centre of Port of Spain, this is a raffish establishment (and knocking shop) known for its delicious food – conch stew, spicy shrimp and pork dishes – that, after one of Gus's excellent *smokeables*, can put fire in a man's belly before he decides to go upstairs to one of the bedrooms (available on an hourly basis) and tend to his other appetites.

'Noel! Man, ah was jus tinkin bout you,' exclaims Gus when he sees me across the bar. He's quickly on my side and engulfing me in a huge bear hug. 'What you drinkin man? You hungry now? You want something else, mon, you know what I mean?'

'Let's start with a cold beer, Gus. It's hot out there. How are you doing?'

'Much bettah to see the like of you, man. How is your mother? Is she OK since your father passed away?'

'She's OK, and that was my excuse for coming down to see you, Gus. I've been on Barbados the past few weeks. Thinking of starting something up there.'

'Why not right here, man? Why you want to go to Barbados, when you a Trinidad boy from birth? Now heah your beer, how about a smoke too? Fine Colombian, just to break the ice…'

So the afternoon passes into evening, and a mellow reunion becomes a new adventure, far from recuperative, a long way from doctor's orders. Gus suggests we get in his car and go for a cruise around some of the city's other nightspots. Of course, it is a weeknight, and most of Port of Spain is a ghost town, the streets empty save for the occasional forlorn hooker or drunk. We hit a couple of empty bars and then end up at Choy Aming's club at the top of the Salvatore building. There I find a pretty 'hostess' whom I have known for years: Foxy. She is pleased to see me, and turns on her most seductive charm, but I seem to be immune. In fact, I am still rankled by the cold reception I received from my mother. I tell

Gus and Foxy that I had better leave, since I am planning to fly back to Barbados first thing in the morning.

'Man, you don't need to leave tomorrow, do you? I was thinking to take you to the Panyards tomorrow. Them will cheer you up proper, Noel,' says Gus. 'I reckon you need to hear some of that Panyard music.'

I think about his words. Gus is right. I need to connect with my island, even if I cannot connect with my mother. The calypso sound of the Panyard music sleeps in my soul. Why shouldn't I awaken it?

'Gus, that's a great idea. I'll put off my flight for a day. Meet you at your place, at noon?'

'I be there, Noel.'

When I wake early the next morning, in my old room, my eyes sweep across the familiar surfaces of my childhood. So many memories – good and bad – cry out from the past, but I don't want to go there. This room is so much smaller than I had ever remembered. I quickly rise and go out into the kitchen, put a kettle of water on to boil, then go outside into the garden. I gather flowers, noticing the smell of cotton sheets drying on the line, the shrieks of nearby children playing, the last dew drops on the bougainvillea petals. I think, 'How strange that this little house, on this small island, could be the source of all my greatest joys and my deepest pain.'

I go to my room, dress and then telephone for a taxi. Half an hour later, I enter Gus's saloon and find him puffing on his chillum.

'Hey, Noel, look at the long face on you, man. Heah, take a few pulls on this. It will bring your smile back, an let me fix you some breakfast. I bet you ain't had nuthin to eat yet.'

I smile and reach for the chillum. 'You know how to make a man feel welcome, Gus. Sure, I could eat something.'

An hour later, Gus asks me whether I want to go hear the Invaders in Woodbrook. 'They got an iron man down there make your knees bend around backward. We go find him, sure.'

As soon as we near Woodbrook, I can hear the high ping of singing steelpans, Trinidad's gift to the world. There is nothing like its pure magic. I could be snowbound north of the Arctic Circle in a dark cabin and one note from a steelpan would zap me right back to the Caribbean at the speed of light. The iron – usually crafted from old car brake drums and played with short steel sticks – holds together the other 'pans', the soprano, cello, tenor and bass. The iron is the engine, and any band that has two irons could claim to have an 'engine room'. Likewise, any band without an iron would be something of a joke, unless playing classical music.

Carnival is coming in a few weeks, hence all over the island the pans are tuning up and practicing their hearts out. We suddenly come to a park where a band of dozens is gathered. Several hundred more people are watching and listening. They make a mighty river of sound, and the crowd will be floating on this river all day and into the night. I feel a burst of island pride as we get nearer.

In the centre of the action, on a small elevated platform, is the conductor. And nearby is the 'iron man' – although in this case the 'man' is a woman. Gus blurts, 'Look at dat iron man, Noel. She got that ting a ling singing for us. Whooo weee. She won't never let go.'

Even women who play the iron are called 'iron men'. This music belongs to the people, born out of their ancestors' struggle to survive the colonial oppression. The conductor – the Maestro – raises his hand. 'OK now, let's take it from the top again. But let's change it from 'ting ting, ting a ling' to *ting a ling ling, ting ta ling*. Everybody got that? One, two and three…'

Away they swing, perhaps a hundred musicians in all, weaving a harmonic wall of sound in perfect synchronisation, so powerful, so sweet. I close my eyes and float away on this beautiful music. My happiness is beyond description.

'You hear dat Eli Mannet pan?' says someone nearby in the crowd.

'Oh yeah, he's sweet for the soul, but we got a hidden weapon up the road. You hear dem Starlife, mon? Dey is de kings of steel.' It's all part of the fever, the run-up to Carnival, when two weeks of total social decadence will envelope the island in panyard music, extravagant costumes and wild dancing.

Gus and I spend hours mixing with the panning crowd in my old neighbourhood. Finally, he drives me back to my mother's darkened house. I will take an early flight out in the morning. When he embraces me to say goodbye, Gus says, 'You looking better, Noel. You got your soul refreshed, mon, and that mother thing off your back. Now why don't you come back heah for Carnival, mon? I will introduce you to the Pundit – the spiritual leader – next time you come.'

'I'll see what I can do to make it happen, Gus. Thank you again. You were just what the doctor ordered.' And so I return to the little house where I grew up but never seem to be welcome.

My first day back on Barbados offers an unpleasant incident. After rising early and taking my usual swim, I meet up with Patrick on the beach, along with two of his friends. We laze in the sunshine for longer than usual, as I tell them about the panyard scene I had witnessed in Trinidad the previous day. Feeling very chipper, and without an agenda (Errol had called and said there was a barbecue at Culloden Farm the following evening that he wants me to attend), I invite the others to lunch with me at the Southern Palms Hotel a couple of hundred yards up the beach.

The restaurant is empty so we find our own way to a table. Then the waitress arrives with a nasty expression on her face. 'I must ask you all to leave,' she announces.

'Are you closed?'

'No, but no beach bums are allowed in here.'

'Is that so? We're not going anywhere. Please get the manager.'

We wait for quite a long time before a white man in a suit and tie saunters into the dining room and up to our table. 'I'm afraid you will all have to leave…'

'Hello, my name is Noel Charles. What's yours? And can you please explain why you are refusing to serve us?'

'The waitress told you why,' he says, crossing his arms.

'Are you a native of Barbados?' I ask.

'No, I'm a British citizen. What does that have to do with anything?' His voice has assumed the most snobbish middle-class English accent imaginable.

'It interests me… greatly,' I say, fighting my anger.

By this time, other guests – all white – have entered the dining room and are watching us closely. A black person usually does not express open defiance to a white manager on Barbados, and I can see the Bajan waitresses pretending not to observe, but actually hanging on every word.

'It's hotel policy not to serve non-registered guests who wander in here off the beach,' says the manager.

'Hotel policy can go to hell. You are going to serve us,' I say.

'And who is going to make me?'

'I am a guest of the government – staying up the road with the Minister of Tourism. Would you like me to call and ask him to intervene, or will you serve us lunch?'

At that, the English manager grits his teeth to stop himself from saying something. He looks from me to Patrick, to the others. Suddenly, a Bajan waitress accidentally drops a tray of plates behind us. The manager's head turns sharply in her direction. He is obviously grateful for the distraction. Waving his hand dismissively, he mutters, 'Oh go on and have your bloody lunch…'

He stalks over to reprimand the frightened girl who has dropped the tray. I follow him with my eyes, determined to make him regret it should he overreact. If he fires her, I will see to it that his tenure on the island is a short one, if it's the last thing I do. Barbados is such a blessed island; how can such racists be allowed to poison our atmosphere?

My life on the island proceeds at a tropical pace. To a certain degree, I am at the mercy of people like Errol and Ben when it comes to advancing my dreams. It's not unpleasant. On the contrary, it's far too enjoyable. There's the barbecue the following night at Culloden Farm, with the Prime Minister and his wife Carolynn, the Minister of Tourism and his wife Margaret, Carlton and Ben, a few others. Everyone is affable, enthusiastic, relaxed and full of laughter. I don an apron and carve the meat, and later am happy when egged on to recount my exploits in the gambling clubs of London. Errol drinks lots of gin and kola; expressing his impatience to see a new Alexandra's open on his island. I can only agree with him. Secretly, I wonder why he is not doing more to advance the project as quickly as I would like.

The next day sees the island flooded with tourists from the *Queen Elizabeth II*, which has docked early that morning. I duck into Barclays Bank in Bridgetown to change some money, but my 10,000 Swedish kronor note causes some consternation. Fortunately, Errol has already introduced me to the manager, Hal Kirton, who is happy to exchange my money for $4,000 Bajan. I shop for new swimming trunks and waterskiing gloves, since Everton has booked me a slot for three o'clock that afternoon at the Willie Hassel Water Sports concession at the Paradise Beach Hotel.

When I arrive at the Paradise, it's easy to find Willie Hassel – a bronzed muscular man with sun-bleached hair and a friendly smile. 'How well can you ski?' he asks.

'I have slalomed, and had a couple of lessons from the waterski champion of Spain. But that was ages ago. I need a refresher.'

'You've come to the right place. You'd like a lesson?'

'Yes, if I can have one with you please.'

'It'll cost you a little extra, but of course.' I pay him on the spot, and he notices the large amount of cash I have in my Moroccan shoulder bag.

'Better check your bag at reception. Ask for Mark Ward. He'll show you where to change too.' The Paradise Beach Hotel is a sprawling white Colonial building set amidst lush tropical gardens on a long sprawling beach of golden sand. The reception area faces the beach and I easily find Mark, a young man who turns out to be the son of the owner. He locks my bag into the hotel safe, and asks, 'Would you mind if I join you? I usually go for a ski at this time of day. I can spot for you.' I tell him that will be great.

Willie offers me a rum punch to 'loosen up' before we go out in the boat, which he will be driving, with Mark in the back. I go for a warm-up swim, and then we set out in the boat. Mark and Willie are an excellent team, and soon I have dropped one of my skis and am cutting back and forth across the wake, having a fantastic time, thanks to their constructive tips. When it is all over, Willie says, 'That wasn't bad at all, for your first day back on skis. Same time tomorrow?'

'Definitely,' I say.

Once I am back in my room at the Maresol, I decide to call for reservations at the Bagatelle restaurant for the following evening. Nick Hudson himself answers the phone. 'Dear boy, I am so glad you called. I've been trying to get your number all morning. I want to invite you for cocktails tonight.'

'I was thinking of an early night. I just went waterskiing and I can already feel my muscles burning.'

'No, dear boy, you can't refuse. This is a command performance. Penelope and David are dying to see you again. And so is Ingrid! It's her birthday.'

'Ingrid?'

'Ingrid Bergman, silly man.'

Of course I know her, having spent a wonderful evening with her in Stockholm the night Lars Schmidt introduced us. We had clicked on sight, laughed the night away. 'In that case, of course I will be there, Nick.'

'See you around eight then, Noel.'

Just as I am heading for the shower, there's a knock on my door and a summons to the phone. This time it is a call from my Swedish journalist friend, Gunnel Hessel, who writes features for *Svensk Damtidning*, Stockholm's top magazine. A great supporter of the club, she had written many flattering stories about us. Now she is ringing to say, 'Alex has told me all about your plans for Barbados. So exciting, Noel! I am going to come down and write a story about what you are doing, OK? It will be great advance publicity. And I need a holiday.'

'Absolutely!'

'Can you find me a room?'

'Sure. You can stay here at the Maresol – the owner is the Barbados Minister for Tourism. You'll like Peter. When are you going to arrive?'

'I'll look into tickets now that I've spoken with you. But very soon.'

We say goodbye and hang up. My favourite anecdote about Gunnel is the night she encountered Woody Allen in Alexandra's. He was sitting with all of us at the Great Table, watching the pretty girls go by (as one does in Stockholm), when Gunnel attempted a sneaky interview by asking, him, 'Do you dance?'

'Yes.'

She rose and walked out onto the dance floor. Woody didn't budge. She came back and said, 'Hey, I thought we were going to dance?'

'You asked me if I danced. I do, but not now. Maybe later.'

So much for the interview. Gunnel took it in her stride and sat back down. She never did get that scoop, but she liked to tell the story on herself. Having her in Barbados will be another distraction, and also good for future publicity, as she pointed out.

When I arrive at the Bagatelle, the party is already in full swing. Penelope Tree is the first to spot me, and throws her arms around me in glee. 'Come here, Noel. We've been waiting for you.' But Nick Hudson intervenes and drags me off to the kitchen. 'You're dining with Ingrid and she wants you to sit next to her. Now get out there and keep the great lady happy, because I have to whip up a birthday cake. God help us all.'

Ingrid's face shines with recognition when I approach the Great Table, and I kiss her on both cheeks. We settle down to a delightful evening, with great food and lots of champagne, reminiscing about Stockholm, talking about my plans for a new club, and her plans for her 'secret' hideaway on Maycock's Bay on the north end of the island. Ingrid lives very much by her own rules, and has been coming to Barbados for years, but always in a very low-key manner. She hates the flash of paparazzi cameras and stupid gossip items, but she always seems to have her sense of humour in great form.

Tonight it is tested when Nick brings her birthday cake to the table. There is only one candle, and the cake looks delicious, but when he insists that she cut it, she can't make a dent. It's rock hard under the icing. The whole table cracks up, but nobody laughs harder than Ingrid, with tears of happiness streaming down her face.

'Maybe if I brought you an axe. The same one I am going to use on my pastry chef's neck,' suggests Nick. 'Actually, my own neck! I think I had better find a new recipe. I'm so sorry Ingrid. Let's have more champagne – on the house.'

When it's time to go home, Ingrid invites me to visit her home at Maycock Bay sometime. 'I want us to meet again before I have to leave for LA. And I hope you have your club open by the time I come back next winter.'

'I hope so too. You must come to the opening night!'

'If I can, I will.'

If I can ever find a site and get all the million things accomplished that I need to do, I think, then it will be a brilliant opening night with Ingrid Bergman as my guest of honour.

It's 5 a.m. when I arrive back at Maresol, and the telephone is ringing in the hallway as I pass. My instinct tells me it must be Alex calling from Stockholm, and I am correct. I fight back my guilt – for ignoring doctor's orders – and tell her all about the scene at Ingrid's birthday dinner. For once, she doesn't scold me, but there is something else in her voice: 'Who else was there? Which other women?'

'Nobody else,' I say. Could word about my date with Astrid have reached her?

'When are you coming home, Noel?'

'As soon as I have found a definite site and begun the first stage of planning and finance. I thought you were coming here?'

'I just can't. The club is far too busy. We have this Midnight Sun festival coming up. And film premieres and corporate parties, and a couple of travel nights. Here, I'll read you the reservations book.'

I listen in silence, and appreciate her dedication to the job. Clearly, she is making the club her top priority, and I feel far away from it all. But she is my wife and surely my partner Tom can hold the fort while she comes down for a visit. We have a woman named Gunilla Park who would be fine as the lead hostess. What is the point in paying all these people if my wife can't join me for a couple of weeks holiday? Then she says, 'Gunnel Hessel was in last night. She said that she had spoken with you and that she was coming down there.'

'That's right.'

'I'm sure you will take good care of her, Noel. It's important that she remains our friend.'

'Of course I will. You know I am always a good host.' I resent her attitude, but bite my tongue and change the conversation to small items of chit-chat. What's the staff gossip? How is the kitchen coping? Is it very cold? By the time we hang up, my resentment has disappeared and all I want to do is put my head down on a pillow.

I am awakened at noon by Everton. I feel very sore from yesterday's ski lesson, and my first move is to try and cancel today's.

But Willie insists that I keep my appointment. It's a very hot day. By the time I have driven to the Paradise Beach, gone out on the skis for 45 minutes, and taken a shower, I am feeling rejuvenated. I decide to see what the Prime Minister is doing, and invite young Mark to accompany me. We pull into the drive at Kampala to find the white Mercedes parked, a sure sign that Errol is home. However, Carlton informs us that he is having a siesta. A maid brings us a couple of cold beers and shortly we are joined by a sleepy-eyed Prime Minister.

'Noel, welcome. And nice to see you Mark. How are your parents?'

'They're well, thanks.'

'How are things progressing, Noel?'

'Well, I am waiting to hear from Ben. Haven't heard from him since the barbecue. And I am a bit concerned, because I have an important Swedish journalist about to arrive to write a story on our new venture. I'm not sure what I'll tell her, at this rate.'

'Hmmm, I had better give Ben a call. And you should too. By the way, have you called your wife? She's worried about you, Noel?'

I raise my eyebrows in surprise. 'Excuse me?'

'She's called me twice in the past couple of days. Very concerned about your health.'

'I spoke to her early this morning, in fact.' I am stunned that Alex has been calling the Prime Minister behind my back – and not mentioning it to me. Was she checking up on me?

'I should mind my own business, I know,' says Errol, 'but I sense that she is missing you terribly. Hate to hear Alex so miserable, she's a fine lady.'

'That she is. I hope you told her that I was fine?'

'Oh yes. I did my best to reassure her. Well, we'd better both chase Ben to see what progress he has made.'

My mind is reeling. Always a private person, I simply can't comprehend why Alex would want to call the Prime Minister without telling me. On a recent call, she had nagged me relentlessly: 'When will it be built? Will it ever be built? Is this project real?' I had assured her that it was going to happen, but the precise dates were as yet far from predictable. There were too many bridges still to be crossed.

'Thank you, Errol, for putting up with Alex's anxieties about me. I am sorry for the trouble. We'd better be off now. I am sure you have a full schedule for the rest of the day."

'No trouble at all, Noel. Look after yourself, you hear? Don't want to make your lady any more anxious than she already is by your absence.'

Mark and I say our goodbyes and I head for the Maresol. I can't help feeling betrayed by Alex. Still, I resist the urge to telephone her in Stockholm. Instead, I decide to have a quiet evening and an early bedtime. For once, I keep my promise to myself.

In the morning, Ben rings first thing. The Prime Minister has kicked him back into gear, and he asks me to meet him for lunch at the Crane Beach Hotel. Built on a cliff, our table is on the edge of a terrace a hundred feet above the pounding surf on the southeast coast of the island. Over a lunch of fresh fish and lobster, Ben shows me the plans he has drawn up for the Pierhead club. They look impressive: three storeys of open space, spiral staircases connecting levels at each end, a glass wall facing the water, with an open kitchen and even elevators for the handicapped. His first estimate is three million Barbados dollars. By the end of a delicious lunch, and genuine progress on my latest project, I feel exhilarated. Now if we can just turn these plans into solid reality…

Gunnel arrives a few days later. Weary from the long flight, she also seems oddly tongue-tied in my presence. This is unlike her. Gunnel is one of the most outspoken people I know in Stockholm, always direct and honest. Now I find that, although she embraces me warmly at the airport, she can't seem to meet my eyes in a direct stare.

Peter and Margaret have invited her for a welcoming drink. She soon confesses to being exhausted, and Margaret takes her off to her room. When I say, 'Get a good night's sleep, old friend. I'll wake you in the morning for a swim,' she nods, and I see tears in the corner of her eyes. Usually a tower of strength, she is clearly upset about something. Perhaps she isn't well. Could that be why she is here on the island? I decide to spend the rest of the night at the Maresol just in case she needs something or wants to talk. But there is no sign of her, so I turn in for an early night of my own.

In the morning, I wake Gunnel at eight thirty with a tray piled high with delicious tropical fruit and a sea egg omelette. 'When you're ready, I'll be having my coffee in the garden. Put on your swimsuit and we'll go down to the beach.'

Once she appears, we spend a pleasant couple of hours swimming and lazing on the sand. My friend Patrick arrives with his girlfriend Lily, and I introduce them all. Gunnel and Lily – who is German, rumoured to be a shareholder at Volkswagen and building her own house near the golf course at Sandy Lane – hit it off. They arrange to meet up the next morning so that Lily can give her a tour of the island.

The fortnight visit flies past. Unfortunately, apart from taking Gunnel down to look at the Pierhead site, there isn't much concrete information I can give her about the club. However, she is very keen to know as much as she can about Barbados, and tells the Prime Minister and Peter that she will do everything in her power to promote the island in her magazine as a winter destination for wealthy Swedes. (At the time there were only a handful of Swedish visitors each winter.) Basically, I devote myself to being her guide for the duration of her stay. However, I cannot help but notice that she remains awkward in my presence. Once, when I thank her again for everything she has done for Alex and me back in Stockholm, she says, 'It was for the club. Stockholm needed your club very much.'

So the whirlwind of food, fun and laughter stretches out through lunches at Luigi's, dinners at various restaurants, late nights at the Pepper Pot and the Island Inn. On her final night, Peter and Margaret host a bon voyage party in her honour with most of the island's VIPs in attendance. She thoroughly enjoys herself until the early hours of the morning. I walk her back to her room.

'Noel, I have a taxi coming very early in the morning. Don't bother to wake up. We can say our goodbyes now.'

I kiss her on both cheeks. 'It's been a fantastic time. So glad you came down, Gunnel.'

'Thank you for making it fantastic, Noel. When will you be coming home?'

'I'm not sure. It all depends on how soon I can get this project really underway. Things take a lot longer down here than they do in Sweden.'

'But what about Alex? Do you miss her?'

'Very, very much.'

She pauses for a long moment. 'In the spirit of our friendship, I must say that you should come home now, Noel.'

'I value your friendship immensely, Gunnel, but I don't see how I can come back yet. I've already invested a great deal of time and money here. I am determined to see this through.'

'So you're happy here?'

'In some ways, yes, but, of course, I miss my wife, and my home. Do you think I am staying because I'm happy here?'

'Only you can answer that, Noel. If you feel that you must stay, do what you believe is right…'

'That is what I am doing…'

'But if you want to save your marriage, you should do what is right for that and go home now. I cannot say anything more. Goodnight.'

Standing there outside the closed door of her room, I absorb her words, but I won't allow them to register. Creating the new club has become all-important in my mind. Still, when I return to my room, I find that sleep just won't come to me. I think about Gunnel's words, over and over, and finally conclude that Alex and I are the victims of circumstances we can't really control. The only answer seems to be to speed things up on Barbados, and hurry home to Stockholm the first moment I can get away.

Little do I realise that it will be five long months in all before I will be able to leave Barbados. Five months of frustrating twists and turns: planning meetings with Ben; strategic conferences with the Prime Minister, various lawyers, Clyde; endless detours and problems, before it becomes clear that the Pierhead site is never going to become a reality. Why, I am just never clear on that. Is it something in the tropical Barbados way of life that forbids working towards a realisable goal in a reasonable, logical way? The fact that it is government-owned land bothers me. What are the hidden political and business motives lurking beneath the surface, motives which I can only glimpse fleetingly? What is the Prime Minister's real goal? And Ben's? Over the months, our relationships remain good, but beneath the surface there is growing tension – at least on my part.

Finally, the day comes when I say to myself, 'This is my dream. If I want to make it a reality, it can't be with the government owning the property. I must act, as I always have, completely independent. Being a connected "insider" has got me nowhere but deeper inside a murky labyrinth of complications, red tape and personality problems.'

Over the months, I have come to admire the set-up at Nick Hudson's Bagatelle Great House. One afternoon I make an unannounced call on Nick and ask if he knows of any other similar grand Colonial houses on the island that might be for sale?

'No, not offhand. But I know who will,' he says. 'Let me call Margaret Leacock. She's the top estate agent on the island, with connections to all the old families. Have you met her?'

'Yes, I went to a cocktail party at her house at Sion Hill a few weeks ago. She seemed very nice and intelligent.'

'Her husband is the best neurosurgeon on the island. They operate at the highest levels of society. I'll call her and let you know what she says.'

'Thank you, Nick. I really appreciate it.'

Sure enough, two days later, he rings with good news. 'Margaret knows of a property that sounds just the ticket. It's an old plantation house, the nearest one to Bridgetown. I wouldn't mind seeing it myself. So get over here by 11 o'clock this morning and she'll come by and take us for a viewing. It's all arranged.'

'Brilliant, Nick. See you at 11.'

Erin Hall Great House is located on three acres at Collymore Rock, halfway up the hill from Culloden Road, and only a stone's throw from the Prime Minister's main home at Culloden Farm. I doubt if even he knows that it is available for sale at this time, such are the formidable intelligence-gathering powers of Mrs Leacock. Also in the neighbourhood are the Anglican Bishop's residence and the People's Cathedral.

We drive up to the house's high coral walls along a curving road that leads us into an impressive entrance, and onto a circular driveway. In the centre stands a giant bearded fig tree, while the drive itself is lined with mahogany trees. The house is a huge mock-gothic castle, complete with turrets, with a wide carved mahogany door at the top of broad coral steps. A long L-shaped veranda wraps around the front of the house, off which several high doorways lead into the elegant downstairs rooms. All the rooms on the ground floor have 12-foot high ceilings with elegant plasterwork and fittings.

Mrs Leacock graciously shows us around. There are two huge drawing rooms, spanning the entire front of the house, and behind these a vast dining room leads to the ample kitchen. In the main foyer, an imposing staircase leads up to four enormous bedrooms, two on either side of the landing, then a doorway out to a balcony and the mini-tower to the west. All the windows in the house are leaded, with interior and exterior shutters, able to withstand the worst hurricane winds. In the back are a large courtyard, a stable block and cottages for the gardeners and stable hands, along with herb and vegetable gardens inside high hedges, and even a folly-like windmill. To the west is an orchard with plantain, banana and citrus trees, inhabited by a small tribe of playful green monkeys.

The estate has the unique character of a great colonial plantation on Barbados. It matches – more than matches – my vision for a new Alexandra's. Nearby is an old cattle and poultry complex which has now been converted for use by the Barbados Dance Theatre, with its own parking area.

'It's marvellous,' I whisper to Nick.

'Is this what you had in mind?' he asks.

'This is exactly it.'

They're asking less than $130,000 US. Make them an offer. It's been on the market for ages, apparently, but only in the most discreet way. Make an offer and I'll bet they accept it. The family that owns this never comes to the island anymore. This is a white elephant and they just want to unload it.'

I speak with Margaret Leacock, and make my offer. She says she will communicate with the owners that same afternoon. Since it's Friday, I suspect there's a long nerve-wracking wait ahead of me over the weekend. Not only that, but a further delay before I can return to Stockholm. If the offer is accepted, for a start, I will have to raise the finance to make the buy.

Back at the Maresol, I try to reach Alex in Stockholm. She's neither at home nor at the club. It isn't until Saturday afternoon that I reach her and, from the sound of her voice, I guess that I've woken her up. It's early evening in Sweden. 'Who is this?' she asks.

'It's your husband. Remember me?'

'Oh… yes. Hold on a minute,' she says, frazzled. 'Hi darling, so when are you coming?'

'Listen, I've found a fantastic site. A true Great House.'

'To live in?'

'No, for the club. It's a genuine plantation Great House. I've made an offer and am waiting to hear from the owners.'

'So I guess I can't expect you to come home for a while, huh?'

'Not as soon as I wanted, but I just made the offer yesterday. I've got to secure the finance, and start planning the refurbishment. This place is incredible, Alex. It's an elegant estate, like a castle, with beautiful detailing everywhere. Very classy.'

'What about me? Your wife?'

'I am doing this for you… for us!'

'Oh yes!'

'Where have you been the past day and a half? I've been trying to reach you…'

She ignores this and says, 'So you have no idea when you are coming back here?'

'I will call you Monday when I know more.'

'Sure, you do that!' She slams down the phone.

I can't help but think of Gunnel's warning, 'You must go home now.' Is it already too late? Why such a childish outburst… and what kind of life is she living? I know that I must get back to Stockholm as soon as I can. I hope the owners give a quick response to my offer.

Fortunately, on Sunday evening, Margaret Leacock rings me and says that the owners have accepted. They would like to move quickly. I promise to move as quickly as I can. Then I telephone David Allison, who has a working relationship with the manager at Barclays Bank, Hal Kirton, and by the time I go to bed, I have an appointment for 10 a.m.

My high hopes are not exactly rewarded when, at 9.55 the next morning I approach the receptionist in Barclays and identify myself, saying I have an appointment with the manager. 'What exactly is this about?' she asks rudely.

'I think that's for me to discuss with Mr Kirton, don't you?'

'Sit down over there,' she orders, nodding at some sofas.

'I prefer to stand. It's ten o'clock. What's the problem?'

'I need to know the nature of your business with Mr Kirton, sir.'

'I want to borrow half a million dollars. Perhaps you'd like to authorise that?'

She flushes, and clears her throat. Behind her, Hal Kirton emerges from his office. 'Hi there, Noel, I was wondering where you were.'

Seated in his office, I describe the property I want to buy and my plans for the club. I have brought my complete portfolio from Alexandra's in Sweden. It contains press cuttings, letters from distinguished guests and government officials, copies of my licenses, lots of photos of superstars sitting with me at the Great Table, and a short business plan for the Barbados Alexandra's project. 'I want to use a loan from Barclays to purchase and develop this property – one of the prime original plantation houses left on the island – while everything else will be financed through my Swedish business.'

Hal cuts me off. 'Look, Noel, I've got an early lunch scheduled on the east coast, and I have to prepare some papers. Why don't you let me think about this for a while, then I'll get back to you with my thoughts.'

Perhaps it's my own pent-up impatience after five months of trying to launch this project and being given the runaround by everyone on the island, combined with the pressure I feel to get back to Stockholm and salvage my marriage, but I react abruptly. 'Don't bother, Hal, I get the drift. Sorry to have wasted your time. I'm sure I can find another bank that will take me seriously on this.'

'Well, if that's the way you feel…'

'It certainly is. Goodbye, Hal.'

I storm out of his office and out of the bank. My head is rushing with anger and determination as I walk down Broad Street in the middle of Bridgetown, under a glorious blue sky, surrounded by a cacophony of traffic, tourists and tradesmen. Up ahead, I spot the sign for the Chase Manhattan Bank. Without breaking stride, I find myself walking straight inside and up to the customer service counter, where I ask to see the manager.

'Please have a seat and I will tell Mr de Costa that you would like to see him,' she says sweetly. 'I won't be a second.'

In two minutes, the young manager – David de Costa – is standing in front of me, extending his hand with a warm smile. 'Please come into my office. Tell me how I can help you, Mister…?'

'My name is Noel Charles. Perhaps I can best introduce myself by letting you have a look at this,' I say, handing him the portfolio. 'I should tell you, up front, that I have found a great property which I want to develop into the premiere nightclub on this island, a sister to the club I own in Stockholm.'

I watch as the manager leafs carefully through the portfolio, his eyes popping as he comes to the photos of Sidney Poitier, Mick Jagger, the Swedish Royal Family, Arthur Ashe, Ingrid Bergman, on and on. 'Those were all taken at my Great Table in the club, where I personally host VIP guests.'

He nods. 'Will you have a Great Table at your club here?'

'Of course, and you I hope you will be a frequent guest, should you finance my purchase of Erin Hall.'

He laughs, but nods. 'Erin Hall, is it? I know the place. It's a living landmark. Great place for a top club. I didn't realise it was for sale.'

'They've accepted my offer, yes.'

He leafs through more pages, pausing to study the business plan for a few minutes. 'So we would take Erin Hall as partial collateral for the loan?'

'Yes, of course.'

'This all looks very feasible, Mr Charles. I am pleased you have come to see me. I suppose I can meet all the superstars I want, plus earn some reasonable interest on our investment?'

'Yes, indeed.'

'Well, I think you can conclude that we are going to grant you this loan, pending normal contractual negotiations and due diligence.

May I ask who it was that sent you to see me? I would like to thank them.'

'Mr de Costa, nobody sent me here. I followed my own gut feelings. And they have always proved to be my best advisors when it comes to doing business. I'm happy to see that they have proved correct yet again.'

'Yes, well I am happy that you feel that way. It is going to be a true pleasure doing business with you, Mr Charles.'

'Please call me Noel.'

'And call me David.' We shake hands on the deal.

'David, I have to make a trip back to Sweden very shortly, so I am going to have my accountant contact you about the loan agreement details. He will also be handling the purchase arrangements for Erin Hall. Is that OK with you?' I tell him the name of my accountant, who is well established on the island.

'Perfectly fine, so long as you are here to sign the contracts in person when the time comes.'

Once I have finished at Chase Manhattan, I have an urgent desire to get on an aeroplane and fly straight to Stockholm. I take a taxi back to Maresol. Then I realise that I have one more telephone call to make; one that I don't relish but which is unavoidable.

'Hello, Errol.'

'Noel, how are you?'

'Just fine, and I'll tell you why.' I explain to him that I have found a site for my club, have had my offer accepted, and this morning have arranged for all necessary finance with a bank on the island. I tell him the property is Erin Hall. I thank him for all of his generous help and hospitality, but explain that I just could not wait any longer.

There is a long silence, then the Prime Minister says, 'Let me understand you correctly. You are going it alone on this?'

'Yes, Errol, that's right.' In my mind, I suddenly hear my father's words from years before: 'Beware of politicians.'

'Well, Noel, I am rather surprised. But I think I understand. And I wish you good luck.'

'Thank you, I appreciate that, Errol. I am sure that I'll need it.' What I don't say is that, at this point, I trust my own luck far more than I do his official support. I tell him I am heading to Stockholm on the next available flight, but will return in a few weeks. He says to call him as soon as I am back on the island. This beautiful island.

Barbados II

It is 16 February 1972. Three years have passed since I first arrived on Barbados.

Tonight is the gala opening of Alexandra's Barbados. Despite the past few weeks of frantic painting, decorating, recruitment and chaos, I am ecstatic with happiness. Dressing in the bedroom of my rented house on the west coast of the island, with my wife Alex beside me, I think, 'Perhaps now we can start afresh, forget all our arguments and suspicions, even begin making babies.'

How did we get here?

When I arrived back in Stockholm after five months on Barbados, I had relatively little to show for my efforts. True, I had found an attractive property, one badly in need of restoration whose owners had accepted my offer to buy. But I had no signed contract. I also had a tentative agreement with Chase Manhattan bank to provide financing but, again, no signed agreement. I had made good new friends on the island, including David Allison, my accountant, and Nick Hudson, the owner of Bagatelle, both keen to help me. I also had, I believed, the continuing goodwill of the government, including Prime Minister Errol Barrow and Tourism Minister Peter Morgan. That was about it. In fact, my vision for a new Alexandra's was still two and a half years from becoming a reality.

In Stockholm, my nightclub business was still very healthy, thanks to Alex and Tom, and my dedicated staff. Of course, I knew that Alex needed my reassurance now more than ever, after my prolonged absence. Yes, there were some thunderclouds hovering over our marriage, clouds that neither of us could easily acknowledge, but I was sure that we could weather these storms.

I also had a number of urgent business commitments. Although many more visits to Barbados would be necessary, I saw that I could not continue to ignore my life in Europe. My soul might yearn to be in Barbados, but my mind and body had much to accomplish in Stockholm and elsewhere. And I was very aware that my business plan stated that the club in Barbados would be underwritten by the business in Stockholm.

The first thing I had to deal with was an ill-fated venture called the Festival of the Midnight Sun. This was a hugely ambitious three-day rock concert to be held in the Swedish town of Mantorp between 19 and 21 of June. Months before, I had agreed to help out my friends Julien Moulton and Jose Maria Fortezza Castro from Mallorca who were setting up the event. A vast array of top bands had been signed to play, including Bo Diddley, Manfred Mann, The Move, Arthur Brown, Juicy Lucy and Canned Heat. In my absence, planes had been chartered, personnel hired, caterers contracted, advertising and promotion launched across Europe. The event was being touted as Europe's answer to Woodstock – and indeed even the man who had organised the public health services at the latter, Dr William Abruzzi, had been hired. (In the end, his friendship would be the best thing to come out of this whole debacle, so far as I was concerned.)

Unfortunately, some ill-judged PR activity in Sweden proved disastrous. Advertisements in the Swedish press offered a free flight to Mallorca for lucky (and pretty) Swedish girls who would agree to hang-out in a new Palma disco which my friends Julien and Jose Maria were also launching. The disco opening was timed to coincide with the visit to the island of the US Navy's Sixth Fleet, and the thinking was that all those thirsty American sailors would flock to a bar full of beautiful Swedish girls, while at the same time it would be great PR for the upcoming festival back north. One Swedish newspaper dispatched a journalist to document what happened to the girls once they arrived in Palma. It was, as expected, a pretty wild scene.

The newspaper ran a leering account with salacious photographs for their scoop about the 'Festival of the Midnight Sin' which took place in Palma. As a result, Swedish parents clamped down on their children and refused to allow them to attend such a scandalous event. They had been preparing to sell 500,000 tickets – but only managed to shift 17,000. Fortunately, I had very little money invested, but after the debacle, after tons of wasted food was donated to charity and all the bands were paid off, my friend Julien lost his house as Jose Maria left him with the entire burden of debt.

My nightly routine at Alexandra's was always hectic, but never so much as during those first couple of months back from Barbados. To be sure, I didn't have to be cajoled into throwing myself enthusiastically into the nightly revelry and I thoroughly enjoyed all the management duties which I had missed while I was away. Our regular guests included the young Crown Prince, Carl Gustav and his sister Princess Christina, as well as almost every celebrity who came to the city. Each night, hundreds of people lined up outside the club just hoping to get a glimpse of the stars who might be there. Fortunately, working hard and partying hard: the balance of my life was built on this contradiction. Now I felt thoroughly rested and able to function at the top of my form.

But there were some unexpected challenges. For instance, there was the night on which we had to cope with a house full of celebrating high school students, an arrangement that should never have been made, but which I inherited upon my return. It ended up in a drunken near-riot with one of the students angrily assaulting Alex. When the police were summoned, they turned their ire – not on the drunken student who had shoved my wife through a glass door – but upon me. They wanted to take me to the station, but I refused, pointing out that Alex was injured and insisting on taking her to the hospital myself. In the end, I was charged but received a suspended sentence after our lawyer produced eyewitness statements from various adults present, including the good Dr Abruzzi who had been my dinner guest that evening.

Shortly afterwards, I was arrested again, completely without cause. This was after I had accompanied a group of friends and clients to a late-night club in the Old Town on a freezing cold evening. Somebody had stolen my coat in the club. Afterwards, when we couldn't find a taxi, we had gone into the Hotel Reisen to call one. My friends Lena and Peter had quarrelled on the street, and Peter had stormed off. For some reason, the desk clerk refused to call us a taxi. He said this service was only for guests. I tried to book a room, but he decided to call the police instead. When they arrived, I was arrested and locked up. In jail, various policemen walking by kept looking at me and whispering, 'Nigger.' Finally, Alex arrived to bail me out, but she was furious.

'Who was this woman you were trying to book a room with?'

'We were trying to book a taxi. I was with Lena! What are you talking about?'

'How could you do this to Peter?'

'I didn't do anything to Peter. Alex, for God's sake!'

'The police say you tried to book a room and when the hotel said they were full you became violent and abusive.'

'That's utter rubbish. You've never seen me be violent with anyone. How can you believe that? And there was absolutely nothing going on with Lena. I was trying to get a taxi so I could take her home, since Peter had walked off in a drunken tantrum.'

Again, the charges were quickly dropped and, apart from my new wariness of the Swedish authorities and my disappointment in Alex's lack of trust, no lasting harm was done. However, it certainly made me yearn for the peace and beauty of Barbados.

It was 1970 and everyone in Europe seemed to want to hold a rock festival that summer. Because of my success at Alexandra's, I was persuaded into 'consulting' on a number of these. The next one to cross my path was organised by our friend and client Thomas Johansson, chief executive of the Swedish EMI company, who had asked me to help out behind the scenes at a festival held on a small island off the coast of Finland. Alex and I flew over the day before the opening, and drove a rented car down the coast to the local school, where various rock bands were convening before being taken by shuttle bus across the bridge to the island. After being assured by Thomas that everything was cool at the site, we boarded the shuttle *with some of the musicians and set off. Unfortunately, there was a mob of drunken, stoned fans waiting at the bridge. Apparently there was a lot of bad LSD around, sold by a gang of tough American draft dodgers and Vietnam deserters. The crazed mob decided to attack the bus and, inside, we were shaken up violently. No police arrived on the scene for hours, and the entire festival was ruined by numerous drug freak-out cases. A fleet of ambulances was busy all night taking away the 'acid casualties'.*

That, however, was not the end of our European 'summer of love' festival tour. We had also promised to attend Italy's very first rock festival in Sicily – Palermo Pop – and had agreed to accompany a couple of stunning go-go dancers on the trip down. Moreover, once that ended, Alex and I planned to fly to Tunisia, where the Bourguiba government had invited us for an 'official visit' to thank us for the highly successful Night in the Desert Tunisian tourism promotion we had hosted at the club the previous winter, and would be hosting again this year.

The most fortunate thing that happened to us in Palermo was hooking up with a distinguished-looking, white haired Sicilian gentleman named Renso Barbera, who took it upon himself to be our guide and fixer throughout our stay. Although his English was limited, he always kept a pencil and pad to draw his thoughts when words failed. Under his protection, we saw all the local sights, were taken on excursions to picturesque nearby fishing villages, and were continually wined and dined by wonderfully affectionate Sicilians. We had a marvellous visit.

The festival itself went smoothly too, until the final day. My duties called for me to look after the English-speaking performers backstage. These included Duke Ellington's Big Band, Aretha Franklin, Georgie Fame and Arthur Brown of 'I am the God of Hell Fire' fame. One of my responsibilities was to convince Arthur that he could not, as he often did, take off all his clothes at the finale of his act. Not in Sicily, he couldn't. He took my word for it and promised to behave.

His act – wearing a helmet that shot live flames into the air – went over very well, electrifying the crowd. We all breathed a sigh of relief as he came off stage, and then was called back for an encore.

Suddenly, all hell broke loose when he started ripping off his clothes and throwing them into the crowd. Within seconds, the Sicilian police were on stage and led the star away in handcuffs, with a shirt in front of his groin.

The crowd was out of control now. I quickly pushed the next act – a chart-topping Italian rock group – out on stage. Halfway into their first song, the lead singer fell down. The crowd was throwing everything they could get their hands on at the stage. I asked Alex what was happening. 'Somebody said he's been shot,' she said. Things were getting out of hand. I went over and asked the great Aretha, who was scheduled to close the festival, if she could go on right then, and she gave her assent. In the end, this tactic worked as the crowd quieted down to hear the Queen of Soul perform. Happily, the next day we learned that Arthur Brown had been released without charges, and that the Italian singer had merely fainted, not been shot.

Alex and I spent a further fortnight on the island, touring its beautiful coast and breathtaking interior valleys from one end of the island to the other, under the beneficent guidance of Renso. We met his entire family for a memorable Sunday feast, and were moved by his tearful reaction when we told him that we really had to move on to Tunisia. He made us promise to come back very soon.

We had one final problem. We had not re-confirmed our flight reservations to Tunisia and, when I finally called the airline I was told that the next available seats were not for another month. We told Renso and he went off to make a telephone call. He came back to report there was a flight leaving that afternoon, fully booked, of course. 'Not to worry,' said Renso, 'I will drive you to the airport.' Lo and behold, when we arrived early, it turned out that a computer-glitch at the airline had wiped out all the recorded reservations. Passengers were to be issued tickets on a 'first come, first served' basis and our seats were duly confirmed. I looked at Renso; he shrugged and smiled a little sheepishly. In Sicily, anything is possible if you know the right people.

Our contact in Tunis was Hedi Ghabi, the cultural attaché at the Tunisian Embassy in Stockholm, a regular at Alexandra's and a good friend. His influence was obvious even before our aeroplane had reached *the gate, since the purser asked for 'Noel Charles to please identify himself.' Thus we were the first to exit the plane, and at the bottom of the stairway stood Hedi with another distinguished-looking gentleman, alongside a huge Mercedes limousine. This man was introduced to us as Didi Bourguiba – in fact, he was the President of Tunisia's brother.*

Thus began our red carpet treatment in Tunisia, which included stays in private villas and the best hotels, and the constant personal attention of the president's brother. It seems our Desert Nights promotional parties in Stockholm had received lavish coverage in the Tunisian press, and everyone we met was determined to thank us for helping to raise the country's international tourism profile. Not only were Alex and I swamped with invitations to all sorts of official and private dinners and receptions, but Didi Bourguiba made sure that we ended up in the best clubs and discos every night. During our excursions, Didi would regale us with fascinating lectures on the history of the country and its wonderful collections of important prehistoric, Carthaginian, Roman, and Islamic treasures.

Our visit to the country coincided with a tour by the Alvin Ailey Dance Company, a great favourite of mine. I had been an avid fan of modern dance ever since childhood, when I lived only two streets from the Beryl McBernie Dance Theatre in Woodbrook. We enjoyed a marvellous night at the Ailey performance in the Roman theatre amidst the ruins of old Carthage, and afterwards went to the US Ambassador's reception, where I was mistaken for a member of the company. Later, when Didi took us off to another disco, the DJ repeated the mistake by welcoming us as members of the Ailey company. There was nothing we could do: Alex and I proceeded to put on our own 'performance' as we danced our hearts out to James Brown's 'Hot Pants'.

One sobering incident during our visit was my reunion with Bjorn, a former DJ from my Stockholm club. He had come down to Tunisia a year earlier to start his own club. I had heard that it was very successful. When we looked him up, however, he was in a terrible state, having just learned that his local partner had taken off with all the money in the bank and all the furnishings, leaving Bjorn to cope with the disaster alone. It certainly made me think again about the dangers of 'partnerships' in my business.

One welcome result of our extended visits to Sicily and Tunisia was the renewed closeness between Alex and me. I was getting dressed one morning when she asked me from the bed, 'Do you think it will be like this between us forever and ever, darling?'

I went and kissed her deeply. 'Yes, forever and ever.' I felt such deep contentment that it conjured up the memory of my parents. They had a marriage that lasted 'forever and ever' until my father's death. Surely, that was possible for me too. Later that day, however, Hedi asked me in passing, 'Would you ever consider opening an Alexandra's here in Tunis, Noel?'

'I would love to, my friend, but I have already made a commitment to the Prime Minister of Barbados.'

Throughout those summer months and autumn of 1970, I spoke frequently on the telephone with David Allison back in Barbados. As he had predicted, it took almost five months before all the negotiations were finished. I flew back to sign the papers. This time I was met at the airport by Everton, who insisted that I stay at his home until I could find a suitable place to rent.

After signing the contracts, I immediately hired an architect named Miles Anderson to oversee the renovations and turn my vision into a reality. I had met him during my previous visit and was impressed by both his imaginative talent and his efficiency. While Ben had been a good friend, with lots of ideas, very little had been accomplished during the months I had tried to work with him on the Pierhead project. Now there was a great deal to accomplish before Erin Hall would be transformed into Alexandra's Barbados.

I called around to tell people I was back on the island. When I reached Clyde, the lawyer I had met on my very first night on the island, he was most welcoming. 'Come for dinner,' he said.

'I would love to. When?'

'Let me work that out. In the meantime, where are you staying?'

'Well, I am looking for a place to rent on the west coast, but staying with Everton for the moment.'

'So come and stay with me. It will be easier for you to look for your own place from here. I am sure we can find you something.'

'I might just consider that.'

'I have another friend on the island. Susie is her name and she's a young English teacher. Have you met Susie?'

'Don't think so.'

'I am sure you'll like each other.'

So I moved into Clyde's house and found that our two free-wheeling lifestyles combined easily, although a bit oddly, for a couple of weeks. We would communicate through the maid, leaving messages with her. I was out until late every night, and Clyde was out most of the day. When we did meet up, Clyde was generous with helpful legal advice.

Over the ensuing weeks, I managed to combine working with my architect, looking for a home of my own and a visit to Trinidad for Carnival. Of course, my absence was putting a strain on my marriage and frequent phone calls to Alex back in Stockholm usually ended with both of us wondering what the hell was really going on.

I began hiring people. One of the first was my friend Patrick, whom I had met at the beach near the Maresol when I had first arrived. As I had come to understand, Patrick was really a 'kept' man, living off his wealthy German girlfriend Lily, but now he was keen to gain some self-esteem through his own efforts. When he had approached me for a job, just after the papers were signed, I realised that I had never seen him do a lick of work. 'What do you do?' I'd asked. He explained that he was eager to do just about anything to earn some of his own money. If that meant working on the construction site at Erin Hall, fine. I told him that, so long as Miles the architect had no problems, he was hired.

One of the most important jobs that I had to fill was General Manager. I could have easily looked 'off island' to recruit someone with the necessary high-level experience. However, I knew that this would not go down well with the locals. One man I had my eye on was Leroy Critchlow, who worked as the Social Rep at the Sandy Lane Hotel. He had lots of flair and charm, although not a lot of managerial experience. As luck had it, Leroy approached me first.

'Why would you want to leave Sandy Lane?' I asked him.

'Because of the Golden Rule.'

'What's that?'

'It's the rule on Barbados, haven't you noticed? There are no black hotel managers on this island. And that's my ambition.'

'What about Ashleigh Sandiford at the Accra Beach Hotel?'

'OK, that's one. Name another?'

'Everton Weekes at Maresol.'

'That's an apartment complex, not a hotel. Listen, although I'm Bajan by family background, I grew up in Harlem. Opportunities there were pretty scarce. I know opportunity when I see it, Noel, and your club is one big opportunity that I would like to make my own.'

'Well, Leroy, I don't usually poach staff, but if you really want it, you can have the job. There are a few conditions though. You have to come to Stockholm for six months intensive training in all operations, so you know my systems and can learn exactly how I want the place to be run. Second, we never have racial or political discussions in the club, not with any customers or other staff. Finally, no chasing women while on duty. Nothing wrong with chasing women, it's human nature, but not on my time. OK?'

'OK, Noel, it's a deal. And I am very grateful.'

Of course, once he arrived in Stockholm, while an adept student who quickly mastered the various phases of management, Leroy found Swedish women impossible to resist. I chose to overlook his avid womanising. He reminded me of my friend, the civil rights leader Stokely Carmichael, who had come to Sweden to avoid the FBI and raise funds for the US movement. He soon became a regular at Alexandra's but acted like a kid in a candy store around all the gorgeous blonde Swedish girls.

Another person I decided to hire was my Stockholm in-house artist, Jan Nalivykov. Slim, good-looking, with an intense, almost tortured visage, Jan was married to Ulla, a stunning black-haired Swede. Somehow, the struggling artist had charmed me into making him a VIP member of the club during our first months. He had proceeded to run-up enormous bills, which he couldn't pay. In return, he would give us his paintings. These were unique, striking – both painful and peaceful – and very popular with our customers. I thought our Barbados club would be consistent with the one in Stockholm if it contained lots of Jan's work. I offered him the same deal: all the paintings in the club would be for sale and we would keep 50 per cent commission of those he sold. He happily accepted, and subsequently moved down to the island with Ulla.

Over the next year, we worked hard to completely restore Erin Hall. We discovered that the second floor suffered from devastating termite damage and this had to be rectified. A new roof had to be built. We had to install air conditioning, two large modern kitchens, three public bars and one service bar. We also furnished the place with lavish crystal candelabras and chandeliers and velvet curtains, which I ordered through our Stockholm club. There was a state-of-the art Krantz sound system installed, again via our Swedish business.

Since so much of our necessary equipment and furnishings would be coming from Sweden, it was fortunate that we now had excellent relations with SAS, the Swedish airline. These had been forged through a series of promotional parties, including those for Barbados and Tunisia. So I did not anticipate too much trouble in shipping out all the fragile crystal, fabrics and sound equipment. We also had good relations with British Airways, who were bringing down the Biba prints, wallpaper, lamps and gilt-edged mirrors I'd ordered from London, while BWIA was going to ship the lighting system from New York.

I finally found my own home on the island. It was called Dana Reef, a few houses up from Clyde on the outskirts of St James, right on the beach. An attractive detached house surrounded by trees, it was built into the cliff facing the western horizon of the Caribbean. I also bought a smaller house nearby called Quaco Bob. In the end I decided to move into this house – which today is the Cliff Restaurant – and put my guests up at Dana Reef.

I was moving back and forth between Stockholm and Barbados, keeping one eye on the construction at Erin Hall, the other on Alexandra's hectic Stockholm business. The latter became threatened when Tom, my business partner, began to act erratically.

Alex and I had been invited to visit Beirut by a man named Karim Abuj, who was starting his own nightclub there. He asked us to help him recruit some Swedish staff, and in return for our help, he wanted to show us a good time in Lebanon. Knowing that such invitations *were common, we accepted. On the eve of our departure, I telephoned Tom at home. His wife answered and I could tell immediately that she was upset. When she put Tom on the phone, I hardly recognised his voice.*

A long incoherent conversation followed: 'Want to know where money comes from?' Tom asked at one point.

'Absolutely, where?'

'From banks, asshole.'

'Tom, are you OK?'

'Sure, why do you ask? Sorry, asshole, you know, asshole. You changed my life. If only I could be you, maybe for a day. Please can I be you for a day?'

'Sure, if you want, Tom.'

'OK, I'm Noel for a day. But could I be you for as long as I like?'

'Who would I be then, Tom?'

'You could be me. You'd have to love money and fitness and family though...'

'Tom, do you want me to cancel my trip to Beirut?'

'No, don't do that. But remember to look in the pocket?'

'The pocket?'

'The pocket in front of you on the plane. I am very sorry. I've bothered you for too long, but now you are well informed,' he said.

In the end, despite my misgivings, we took the flight to Beirut the next day. Karim met us and drove us to the St George Hotel. Later we went to his club, where the svelte, blonde Swedish waitresses made a good contrast to the sultry, voluptuous Middle Eastern belly dancers who performed for his wealthy international customers.

Our week in Lebanon was fascinating, including visits to the Bekka Valley and Baalbek, where we spent an evening with singer Demis Roussos. We also toured the gold market and hit the casino. Unfortunately, on our last day I became ill with a fever and waves of uncontrollable nausea. As soon as I was back in Stockholm, I went to the doctor, who could not diagnose the problem, but insisted that Alex and I go into hospital and quarantine while all the other passengers were traced. After four days, I was feeling much better, but then we turned on the television.

There, on the screen, were pictures of our hotel in Beirut, the St George, in smoking ruins after it had been destroyed by a terrorist bomb. We had been very fortunate to have departed when we did, or we almost certainly would have been killed in the blast. A little later, Tom's wife called. He had suffered a total nervous breakdown after a series of bizarre incidents in the club, including one where he knelt in front of customers and begged for their forgiveness. He was now in a psychiatric clinic. I was very sorry for him, since he had proven to be a decent business partner, and hoped he would recover. In the meantime, I arranged for an old friend from my golf club in Mallorca to come to Stockholm and take over his duties, as I had to rush back to Barbados.

By the autumn of 1972, I was under serious financial pressure to get the new club in Barbados opened. We desperately needed a cash flow on the island, for our budget was being stretched very thin. Unfortunately, my architect Miles was behind schedule, although he was working himself and the construction crew day and night, hardly ever sleeping. Still, I insisted on a February opening. Everything was taking shape, the decoration was proceeding, the equipment was being installed and the luxury fixtures were arriving from London and Stockholm. Even the fine detail was planned. Our staff would wear aprons designed by Maria, owner of one of the island's leading boutiques, and these were being hand-sewn. Our English chef had already resigned from the Hilton. A guest list for opening night had been compiled with the help of the Prime Minister and others. All of Barbados was beginning to buzz about our opening.

One day at Erin Hall, I watched as Miles lost his temper with one of the local Bajan workers. I told him to take it easy.

'How can I take it easy? We won't be ready!'

'Yes, we will. Change the shifts, pay them more, and work right around the clock.'

'You're the boss. That might work.'

It was working. I can still recall the thrill when the Krantz engineers turned on the sound system for the first time. Workers came running to listen to the sound of T Rex blasting 'Get it On' through the fantastic speakers. It was an elaborate system which required maximum sound on the dance floor, but much more subtle sound in the other areas in order to allow conversation to flow easily.

Alex flew down a week before the opening night, just in time for a dinner party at Maria's. Errol Barrow was invited and he assured me that the load of Swedish crystal which had been sitting impounded in a customs warehouse at the airport for a week, under the scorching sun, would be released in the morning. Some of the crystal had already shattered in the heat, but I had managed to order replacements, which were due to arrive in time. In fact, for several days before the opening, one of the rooms upstairs at the Erin Hall was turned into an impromptu chandelier factory. It was painstaking work, made tolerable by the incredible display of dazzling prisms of light dancing around the room in the afternoon sunlight.

Nick Hudson and I had become partners based on a single handshake. Despite my wariness of partnerships, I had several reasons for believing that our arrangement – each of us would assume 50 per cent ownership of both Bagatelle and the new Alexandra's Barbados – would be a success. For a start, I was happy to get a share in what I considered one of the best-run and most attractive restaurants on the island. Secondly, I had accepted the fact that I would need to be in Stockholm half of the time to manage my nightclub there – after all it was the main source of my income at that point. I was convinced that Nick Hudson would be the best possible person to manage the Barbados operation when I was away.

All of us worked ourselves to the point of collapse during that final week before the opening. At one point, I rushed off to do a promotional interview for local radio. When the DJ, Olga Lope Seal, began to ask me questions on air, I suddenly froze; my exhausted mind went a complete blank. It was the ultimate horror show for any radio announcer: dead air. I was just too tired to speak. Finally, Olga thanked me and I beat a hasty retreat back to the club. And where the hell was the furniture?

In the end, it wouldn't show up until an hour before we were due to open. Which meant we'd have to greet early first-night guests in the car park, and hold them there with lots of free champagne until I could get everything arranged.

'Darling, the taxi is here. We must go this minute,' I say.

'I know, darling. I am almost ready now. How do I look?'

'You've never looked more beautiful,' I say. And it is the truth.

As we arrive, I see more than a hundred guests sipping champagne at a hastily arranged bar in the car park. For some reason, it reminds me of a scene out of a Herman Wouk novel that I once read called *Don't Stop the Carnival*. I wave at everyone and dash inside the club, strip off my jacket, and start shoving furniture into place like a madman. About thirty minutes later, I tell someone to let the guests come inside, don my jacket and fix a welcoming smile on my face.

'So glad you could come,' I say about seven hundred times this evening. 'This is my wife Alexandra.' Once the last guest is seated, I slip over to the service bar for a well-deserved Chivas. From what I can see, everyone is very impressed by the tasteful transformation of Erin Hall. I trust they will be equally pleased with what I am serving them tonight: beluga caviar from Russia, *gravadlax* from Sweden, fine wines from France, and Monte Cristo cigars from Cuba. Only the best, and cost be damned when what matters is making people happy.

The guest list includes the top-crust of Bajan society and government, along with their partners: Prime Minister Errol Barrow, Minister of Tourism Peter Morgan, Minister of Labour Philip Greaves, Leader of the Opposition Tom Adams, the Hon. Elliott Mottley MP, Minister of Communications Frederick Smith, Minister of Education Erskine Sandiford, the architect Ian Morrison, William Tywitt Drake of the Bereleigh Estate in Hampshire, legendary cricketer Everton Weekes, along with his teammates Clyde Walcott, Seymour Nurse and Charlie Griffith, C.O.W. Williams, George and Maria Eastmond, Lily Rully, Ashleigh Sandiford, Claude and Joanna Salvatore of Trinidad, Bruce Bart, Mark Ward and members of the famous musical group the Merrrymen.

Unfortunately, several hours later, I find the glittering atmosphere is rapidly being tarnished. People are smoking on the dance floor and stubbing out their butts underfoot, even dropping them on the new carpets. Plates full of leftover food have been abandoned in piles all over the club. Random inebriated people are wandering around with drinks sloshing out of their glasses. I have to remind myself that this is not Sweden, or Europe for that matter. For a number of my guests, who are lacking in European sophistication, this is the most elegant place they have ever visited. Bajan informality is wonderful, but I haven't designed Alexandra's to be a typical Bajan beach bar. The fact that a lot of guests have not bothered to wear evening dress should not surprise me. I have to pinch myself and recall that these are my guests, and that they are very welcome.

All in all, however, the evening is a great success. It's seven o'clock in the morning when I finally stand at the bar with a few of my staff – Bruce, Claude and Joanna – having just said farewell to the last guest.

'That was some party, eh man?' says Claude.

'And did you see that German woman with the see-through dress?' asks Joanna.

'That was Lily, Patrick's girlfriend.'

'Who is Patrick?'

'A friend of mine who worked on the construction here,' I say.

'Mon, that DJ bad for days. Where you find him, Noel?' asks Claude.

'That's Lee, one of my DJs from Stockholm. Anyone seen Alex?'

'She left an hour ago, catch a lift with the Prime Minister.'

'Good. I've got to get some sleep before I keel over.'

Over the next few months, all the synergy that I hope will exist between my club in Stockholm and the new one on Barbados begins to take effect. And all the time I have spent over the past couple of years in establishing credibility with airlines like SAS and BA proves its worth. Almost immediately, scores of familiar faces appear in our doorway: pop and film stars, wealthy aristocrats and corporate executives, even diplomats. Many of them are Stockholm regulars who have made the journey to Barbados just to check out the scene. And the word of mouth back in Sweden is good. As for airline staff and flight crews, I have always offered them special deals and free entry to my club, and they have now been telling passengers all about the new Alexandra's on Barbados. Within a month, business in Barbados is booming.

At the same time, I believe my marriage is blossoming again. Alex and I are having a second honeymoon when she is on the island, and working by my side every evening. We spend most days on the beaches, especially at Sandy Lane where she can chat to friends while I waterski. Just as in Stockholm, she makes Alexandra's a place where customers feel so comfortable they want to spend almost every night there. The Great Table is the ultimate VIP spot on the island.

Not to say that everything is a hundred per cent perfect – it never is in the nightclub business. My biggest problem is with the General Manager. Leroy has simply not worked out. In fact, just locating him is often a major problem. Finally, one evening I come across him in the office after a 25-minute search. He puts down the phone. 'Hey, I've been here,' he says. 'Talking to Lena in Stockholm. She's pregnant, Noel.'

I pause, trying not to show my exasperation. 'So what are you going to do about it?'

'Noel, I don't think I can handle this job. It's too much.'

'What do you mean – exactly?'

'I can't deal with these local Bajans. I will stay until you can replace me.'

'Then what will you do?'

'I have been offered a job as Night Manager at the Sheraton in Stockholm. I want to take it.'

There's no point in making an ugly scene. I have invested a lot of money and time in training Leroy, but now I set about trying to find someone else on the island who can be my General Manager.

One day talking with Everton Weekes, he says, 'Won't be much good for me to recommend anyone else – besides myself.'

'Are you certain you want to manage this club?'

'Piece of cake. I know all the Bajans, and I have been managing the Maresol for years.'

'Doesn't Peter need you?'

'I didn't tell you, Noel, but I quit that job a couple of months ago.'

'Welcome aboard then, Everton.' I suspect the legendary cricketer, and now good friend, can solve my management problem instantly, and I am proved correct. As well as his fame as one of the West Indies' greatest athletes, Everton has a confident, charming manner that guests find very appealing. There is no question about his honesty, and he is very reliable. I don't hesitate to leave him in charge whenever I am not in the club.

It's taken three years to open Alexandra's Barbados; now, over the next three years, the club will become famous throughout the Caribbean and indeed the world. Celebrities who become regular visitors will include Mick Jagger and the other Stones, singers Tom Jones and Engelbert Humperdinck, recording industry moguls Ahmet Ertegun, Clive Davis and Seymour Stein, Eric Idle and John Cleese of Monty Python fame. Scores of other visiting celebs make a point of visiting us whenever they visit the island.

Of course, the local Bajan Establishment comes to regard us as its own private country club. Errol Barrow invariably uses the club to entertain foreign delegations and to network with everyone who is anyone on the island. Local artists like Emile Straker, Lord Radio, Willie Carr and the other Merrymen form a calypso clique that always provides authentic atmosphere. And there is the wealthy expatriate set, men like Chris Darlington and George Drummond (godson of King George V and heir to Drummonds Bank) with whom I form deep, lasting friendships over a game of backgammon or a late night drink.

Some of the wealthiest people in Great Britain and Canada have a soft spot for Barbados too. Now the club has a regular Canadian contingent including the Buchannans, Griersons and the Bertonis. Of course, my Swedish regulars remain loyal to Alexandra's mystique. These include Virginio Marian and his supermodel wife Agnette Darin, along with Jannik Sunderstrom, the Sassoon disciple in cowboy boots, and her partner Johannes Bross, the actor, and her daughter Joanna, my godchild.

One of the most memorable encounters with celebrities on Barbados takes place over several visits by comedian and actor Richard Pryor. I am sitting at the Great Table with my old friend

Lee Hazlewood one evening when my doorman Patrick brings a familiar-looking figure towards us, along with the man's attractive female companion.

'Who's the nigger who owns this place?' demands Richard before I can say a word.

'This is Noel Charles, the owner,' Patrick says.

'You the owner? Nice to meet you. What do you want to drink?'

'I've got a drink, thank you.'

'No, no… buy all these motherfuckers a drink.'

I am, of course, already a fan of this man who many consider the greatest stand-up comedian of the twentieth century, have seen his films and heard about his wild reputation. Of course, this is the early 1970s and he is still peaking, with many of his best films yet to come, and long before his self-immolation while smoking crack – which he fortunately survived – and then the tragic revelation that he was suffering from multiple sclerosis which would ultimately end his great career. In many ways, it is a miracle he survived as long as he did, given that he is perhaps the most self-destructive man I have ever met.

Of course, I am not pleased to hear words like 'nigger' and 'motherfucker' in my club. But Richard Pryor, I see immediately, is a law unto himself.

When I introduce him to Lee, Richard says, 'I know your name. You're the singer, aren't you?'

'You got that right,' says Lee.

Pryor turns to me and says, 'Motherfucker, you got all these stars around you. One of these days, I hope I'll be a star.' Everybody at the table laughs, and Pryor turns to me. 'You play poker? Where's the cards. Get us a deck of cards.'

'We don't have any cards,' I say.

He jumps up and says, 'I'll get us a motherfucking deck of cards.' He goes to the door and hands Patrick a hundred dollar bill. 'Go get a fucking deck of playing cards and keep the change.' When he returns, he sits down next to his voluptuous girlfriend. 'How do you like my nurse? You're looking at her with adoring eyes, I can see. But when we get some cards, I'm going to whup your ass at poker.'

Everybody laughs again, including me, and the jokes keep coming in a non-stop stream of consciousness that I can't possibly duplicate, or else I would be a brilliant comedian too. At one point, he says, 'I want to tell you something. I don't want to play with this fucking Mickey Mouse money you got here. There's only one currency for me, and that's the US dollar. Them fucking Lincoln greenbacks, I only want to play with them.'

I nod and rise, go back to the office, unlock the safe, and return with a stack of US currency. The cards have arrived in my absence, and Pryor says, 'We're playing seven card stud. Nothing wild.' He shuffles, we cut for deal, I win and so I deal. The first hand comes and I have a small pair hidden in the hole. He bets a $100, I call, and deal. He gets a garbage card; I get nothing. I bet another $100 and he asks, 'How much money you got?'

'About $1,300.'

'Well, put it in, I'm raising you all in.' He takes out his huge wad of $100 bills and counts out 13 of them. 'There.'

I call and draw nothing but a deuce. I think that surely I've lost. I deal out the rest of the cards, and he shows his hand. Nothing! Absolutely nothing!

It continues like this, with me winning every hand, him betting like a maniac, while keeping up a hilarious commentary full of 'motherfuckers' that has everyone in stitches. At one point Lee whispers to me, 'I wish we had a tape recorder here. This is funnier than I've ever heard him before.' After he runs through the entire wad in his pocket, he asks his girlfriend for the back-up cash, which she produces from her purse. It's an even bigger wad. Meanwhile, the club closes, but we continue to play. Now that the place is closed, he openly begins to snort cocaine out of a little vial. It's not even powder. Chunks of it are dropping out of his nose as he jokes and bets and loses.

When he's lost all of his money, he says, 'I guess there's no way a nigger could get a loan around here?'

'Well I'm not a bank,' I say, 'but I guess I could swing an interest free loan if you are sure that's what you want.'

'You would lend me money, you motherfucker? You know me now, and you would *lend me money*! This nigger is crazy. He would lend me money. Did you hear this? Give me $5,000 then.'

I count out $5,000 from the huge pile of what was his money and we continue to play, until one hand when he has staked his last remaining bills. He asks, 'Can I raise this by $2,000?'

'If you want,' I say.

'You know I'm good for it.'

I just call the $5,000. And, of course, I win. He wants to continue, but it's almost daylight, and this whole thing is worse than stealing candy from a kid. I plead tiredness, and he agrees that the game is finished. 'My office will take care of what I owe you,' he says. And a few days later, after he has left the island, a cheque arrives in the mail from his office for the exact amount.

Over the next months, Richard calls me several times. 'Hey Noel, I'm in Louisiana, filming you know? If you want to reach me, I'll give you my number. But don't ask for me, ask for John Doe.' I don't know what that means, and I don't call him.

However, several months later, Richard walks into the club again, with a different woman, equally beautiful. The same routine begins all over again. Hundred dollar bills are thrown around the place, and just about every member of staff is lavishly tipped for some silly excuse or other. He sits down at the Great Table, insists on buying everyone's drinks, and announces, 'Noel, motherfucker, I brought my own cards this time.' Sure enough, he pulls out two new decks and slaps them on the table. 'Now we're going to play some serious poker.'

It is a re-run of the last game. Within an hour or two, all his cash is gone. He turns to his girlfriend and says, 'Hand me the other roll.'

'No,' she says.

'Give me my money.'

'NO. Read my lips, Richard.'

'I am reading your fine lips, baby, but it's my fucking money so give me my fucking money, you hear me?'

'Give you the fucking money? Why should I give you the fucking money so you can lose it to this guy? Why don't I just give HIM the fucking money, and then we can go home and fuck.'

There is silence all around the table. He looks at her a long time, then says, 'Bitch, give me my fucking ring.'

'I'm not giving you this ring.'

She waves her hand in his face, flashing a huge diamond engagement ring. 'It's my ring now. Here, take your fucking money.' She throws the wad of bills onto the table.

'Good,' he says. 'Now give me my fucking ring.'

'You are not getting this ring. It's my fucking ring. You hear what I am telling you?'

Richard goes crazy. He grabs the wad of bills and starts ripping them in half, then into smaller pieces and throwing them at her like confetti. Then, in an icy voice he says, 'You won't give me my ring, bitch?' He lunges across the table, reaching for her throat.

I grab him and others help me pull him back. He's thrashing and shouting, 'Let me at her. Let me at her. She's got my rock. I paid $20,000 for that fucking rock. Now she won't give it to me.'

'I've got your rock,' she says. 'And I've got your baby too, asshole.'

I turn to my English banker friend George Drummond and ask, 'Will you take her home please, George?'

'Delighted to escort the lady home, Noel,' he says. In a few moments, they have gone. After an hour of drinking, and listening to Pryor bemoan his fate, and complain about the woman who 'thinks she is such a big star' – though I have no idea who she is – he asks me for a ride home. I agree. Fortunately, when we arrive at his rented villa, his woman has locked all the doors and windows. So I offer to take him back to my place.

'I'll only come to your house if we can play poker.'

'Whatever you want,' I say. 'What about all the money you tore up in the club?'

'Fuck it. Let the cleaners sweep it up. You know my credit is good.'

Back at my house, we start playing and Richard is talking a blue streak, complaining about the woman, making me laugh, despite my own concern at how this scene has played out in public in my club. Shortly afterwards, George Drummond shows up and, in private, tells me that he's booked Pryor's girlfriend a seat on a flight in the morning, but to keep Pryor away from her until then. 'She's not very happy with him at the moment, to say the least. I will make sure she gets on that aeroplane tomorrow.'

I thank George, and return to babysit my guest. He sleeps most of the next day, we have an uneventful evening at the club, and he departs the following morning. I am very pleased we've managed to defuse a murderous situation, with not even a gossip item in the newspapers about the incident. Of course, unless I want the publicity, I have always been very discreet about keeping what goes on inside Alexandra's from the press. However, Richard Pryor could test anyone's discretion to the limit.

Of course, most of my customers are far less demanding, and my life at Alexandra's Barbados continues to feel charmed. Alex visits much more frequently, and I believe we are truly an established couple with a wonderful future. I also fly to Stockholm from time to time, to oversee the club there. It is still the jewel in the crown of that city's nightlife.

One result of my trips abroad is my conclusion, after about a year, that my partnership with Nick Hudson is not working as I had foreseen. Even when I am away, Nick never takes a managerial role at my club. Attorney David Allison insists that we have an agreement, and that I have to buy Nick out. I ask my accountant to arrange a meeting with Chase Manhattan to raise the finance for the buyout.

One morning soon afterwards I am called by a representative of *Who's Who in the Caribbean* who tells me that he would like to interview me in preparation for my entry into the book. I am pleased by this recognition, and so apparently is Alex, who happens to be on the island at the time. So, too, are my staff, who throw a celebratory party for me that evening after they hear the news. In truth, I feel vindicated, for my acceptance on Barbados has not been unconditional. Because I come from Trinidad – a 'Trini' – I have never really been accepted into Bajan society. There have been numerous small incidents that have made that clear to me over the years. I have even come to the conclusion that my early difficulty in securing the Pierhead project was down to my being an 'outsider'.

Unlike Trinidad, which is a truly multicultural island, Barbados was colonised solely by the British and their African slaves. While Trinidad is a rich island with great natural resources and a highly industrious economy, Barbados was a comparative backwater, primarily agrarian and producing little but sugar cane, until the advent of modern tourism. The black people on the island have been suppressed for centuries. When I arrived, the average salary for a maid was $20 a week. I insisted on paying $60 a week. While many disapproved, I thought that the change in fair wages had to start somewhere, and it might as well start with me. I was determined to pay all my employees reasonable rates. Despite all this I still regarded myself as an outsider to both the white and black communities on the island. Yet here I was being selected for *Who's Who*.

For their party, my staff bake me a cake in the shape of an owl. Am I really so wise? Well, I am about to find out the truth.

Following our private *Who's Who* celebration, the club begins to fill up with our regular customers. Alex isn't feeling well but she gamely stays around despite her bad headache. Finally, she accepts Errol's offer to drive her back to our house. Shortly afterwards, someone introduces me to Charlene Lackman, the Revlon heiress.

'My friends call me Charlie,' she says. She is a lovely young woman, with an interesting tale to tell. Apparently she had been on holiday in St Tropez recently, and was flying back to school when she got into a conversation with a Pan Am stewardess. 'I asked her where she got her fantastic tan. She raved about Barbados, especially your club here. You should really put her on the payroll.'

'Do you recall her name?'

'I think her name was Kristen. She was Swedish or Californian, or something.'

'I think I know her. She was here not too long ago.' I feel gratified that my policy of befriending airline staff has been proven effective yet again. Charlie Lackman is one of the top stars of the international glitterati set, and will surely spread the word among her friends. 'Come sit at the Great Table. And let me buy you and your friends a drink.'

This is my job, but it's also lots of fun. I am feeling great tonight and sure that it's going to be a late one, when Patrick comes to say that my accountant is on the phone. I take the call and David tells me, 'You're got a meeting at Chase in the morning. I think they will finance your buyout, but you'd better be sharp. We're meeting at 10 a.m., so promise me you will go home early and have a good sleep.'

'Will do, David. Thanks for calling. See you in the morning.'

I return to the table and make my apologies to Charlie Lackman and the others. Young Mark Ward, my waterski buddy who often stays at my house, is at the bar and is waiting for me, and after I tell Everton that he's in charge for the rest of the night, we drive back to my place.

As we pull into my drive, I see Errol's car is still here. I explain that he had driven Alex home earlier because she wasn't feeling well.

'I hope nothing's wrong,' says Mark.

'Nothing strange. Errol sometimes falls asleep here when he's too tired to drive back to his place.' I park and we go to the back door. It is locked. 'Now this is strange. We never lock this door. I don't even have a key. Let's try the living room window. That's always open.'

When I look through the window, I feel all the air rush out of my lungs. The day's elation explodes like a giant balloon stuck with a sharp pin. I rub my eyes, blink, unable to accept this. The Prime Minister is sitting in my favourite chair, his head back, eyes closed. In front of him, my wife kneels, her blonde hair spilling over his thighs, head bobbing, blocking the actual view of what she is doing.

Mark clears his throat, just behind me. It's not enough for me to witness this alone, but I have to be here with a young man who admires me, who will understand instantly what a humiliation this is for me. I turn and look at him, tears in the corners of my eyes.

'I'm sorry, man. Come on, we better get out of here before they see us.'

'This is my house. I live here. What do I care if they see us?'

'Keep your voice down. No, man, he's the top guy on the island. Whatever you are going to do, you'd better think first. You can't just charge in there. You're got to be careful, Noel, even though I know it hurts. Come on!'

We creep back around the side of the house. When Mark suggests that I put the car in neutral, and that we push it down the hill, as quietly as possible, I acquiesce. This kid is wise far beyond his years. He keeps looking at me with concern as we push the car and then start the engine out of earshot. We head to Enid's Bar on Baxter's Road.

Inside the little drinking den, I say, 'Chivas, and bring the bottle.' It's my bottle anyway, since Enid never usually serves anything but rum.

'Noel, I'm going to shut up, but there's one thing I want to say first. I will never tell anyone about this. My lips are permanently sealed. You can bank on that.'

'Thank you, Mark. I owe you for that and for thinking clearly back there. You know I don't have any legal rights on this island. I am here at the Prime Minister's pleasure, although I have applied for a passport. How could she do this? How could I have been so fucking blind?'

We drink for the next two hours, mostly in silence. The thoughts running through my head are explosive, but I know that I have to defuse them. I have far too much to lose on this island, with my business and all the money invested and borrowed. I decide that I will have to pretend that nothing has happened. This is the end of my marriage, and I can feel the hurt uncoiling deep inside me. I can also hear all the warnings from others over the past years, the 'Come home now, if you want to save your marriage' from Gunnel, softer hints from friends like Lee Hazlewood.

Finally, in a drunken but painfully clear-headed state, I say goodnight to Mark and drive back to my house. I find the two lovebirds still awake, chatting amiably in the living room as if nothing had happened between them. As if it had all been a hallucination. I tell myself that, for the time being, I have to pretend it *was* a hallucination. So I do a fairly convincing imitation of a man without a drop of jealousy or hurt in his body.

'Got an early appointment at the bank, so I won't have a drink, thanks. You two keep chatting, but I'm going to put my head down. Why was the back door locked by the way?' I regret asking the minute I hear the words leave my lips.

'I don't know, darling. I didn't know that it was locked. Errol has been explaining his plans to extend the summer tourist season on the island. Very interesting,' lies Alex.

'Dear boy, I was just about to leave myself. I'll let myself out. Don't trouble yourselves, I know the way,' says the Prime Minister.

I head straight for the bedroom, strip and get under the sheet. In a few minutes, Alex joins me, snuggling up close. I roll over and ignore her, but she presses her breasts against my back and strokes my nakedness. 'I thought you had a headache?'

'It's gone. I want you to make love to me. See, you want me too.'

Enraged, at her, at myself, I suddenly turn to her. Vengeance mixes with sexual desire. No, this is not love. It's animal sex, and it disgusts me even as I lose myself to its savage force. It doesn't last long, and I let my body go slack, roll off and turn my back. She hugs me as I pass out cold.

The meeting at the bank the next day goes well. They will finance my buyout of Nick Hudson's shares. And even as I sit there going over the details in the bank manager's office, I find myself thinking about the previous night's sex. It is turning me on. Never before have I felt such conflicting emotions at one time. The line between love and hate, desire and rejection, pride and shame – the line has been broken. I cannot decide whether I should drive home and confront Alex, throw her out of my life forever, or bury myself in her arms again.

Months indeed years will pass caught in this web of internal conflict. Keeping this secret and acting out my anger, it leads me into an obsession that becomes both depressing and ecstatic. My agony is self-inflicted, since I won't allow myself any honest resolution. As a result, my self-confidence takes a nosedive. I become paranoid. I have to second-guess every decision I make in the club.

Fortunately, Alex spends most of her time in Stockholm. When we are together, the rough sex binds us together in a way that neither of us ever talks about. At the same time, I begin to follow her, to spy on her and Errol as they meet for clandestine trysts, with me listening to their gasps and moans from behind a bush or underneath a beach house in the middle of the night. On top of everything, I have become a voyeur. The self-disgust that I feel makes me wonder if I am losing my mind. I come to depend on this compulsion, despite the nightmares that now keep me awake most nights.

I haven't felt anything like this shame since the episode with my friend Bash when we were kids on Trinidad and became locked into a sexual triangle with his maid Franka. Of course, when Alex is away, I now feel absolutely free to chase other women. So I have a number of affairs and one-night stands during this period, but instead of renewing my self-confidence, they just reinforce my feelings of paranoia and guilt – and anger. I am sure that Alex is taking lovers when she is away from me. Never for a second do I think she is restricting her adultery to Errol. Looking back, I think of others that I suspect she had affairs with like her friend Tom Macksey and the hotel manager in Stockholm who locked us out of our first Alexandra's.

So I am hardly surprised when, on an unannounced visit to Stockholm after a week of being unable to reach Alex by phone, I find a strange man in my bed at our home. Alex is nowhere to be found. I prod the sleeping figure and say, 'Who the fuck are you?'

'I'm Lasse,' says the tall, well-muscled blond Swede.

'You had better remove your ass from my bed, Lasse.'

'I think you should call Alex.'

'No, I don't think so. We can just sit here and wait for her.'

When she does enter the flat less than an hour later, to discover us both in the living room, the shock on her face gives me great pleasure. 'So darling, why didn't you just tell me our marriage is over?'

'What are you doing here, Noel?'

'I know, I should have checked into a hotel. And I will, but I wanted to see you one last time before I did.'

'Noel, it's not what you think.'

'Yes, why don't you go now?' says Lasse. 'She loves me, not you.'

My anger finally erupts. 'Get dressed, asshole, and get the fuck out of my house. Get out right now!'

The man looks beseechingly to Alex, but she just nods. Then Lasse stands up. He's taller than me, but suddenly he is on his knees and holding my knee. 'Please don't make me leave. Alex and I are in love…'

I turn to her. 'Are you watching this. Are you actually in love with this fucking wimp?'

'Please go, Lasse,' she says.

The moment the man leaves, sobbing loudly, she is on me. Something about being caught, and my anger, has excited her out of her mind. And, to my secret shame, I am excited too. The sex that happens next, all my efforts to 'punish' her, only fan the flames of our compulsion. I have never felt so trapped in my life, and it is my own fault. This is the darkest chapter in my life.

Located on the west coast of Barbados, Sunset Lodge is a massive four-bedroom ranch-style house with a two-car garage and maid's quarters. I rent it as soon as I return to the island. The garden is like a small park, and there is a large stable block. I love the flamboyant trees that blaze like fire in the afternoon sun, the flowing shrubbery and bougainvillea trees. Beside the kitchen, a lovely path leads past a scrawny little almond tree. For some reason, of all the features at the house, this tree captures my heart. I vow to nurture it until it grows fruitful and strong.

There comes a night when Errol, whom I have kept in the dark for almost three years about what I know, says to me in the club, 'Have you heard from George Moe? He's got your citizenship papers now.'

All I say is, 'Hey, that's great. I'll look him up in the morning. And why don't you come for supper tomorrow, Errol.'

I have dreamt about this day for so long. I have my declaration of independence worked out completely in my mind. I go straight to George Moe's office and collect my Bajan citizenship papers the next morning. That evening, I set the table, chill the wine, put the lobsters to steam in the pot. As soon as the Prime Minister, Alex and her mother come in from the garden, dinner will be served. Divorce will be for dessert. Just desserts.

'Was that a pinch of nutmeg I tasted in the sauce?' Errol asks at the table after we've finished the main course.

'Leave it to you to discover my secrets, Errol. Speaking of which, I know a secret too. I know that you have been my wife's lover for almost three years. I want to talk to you about this. Either we can talk here, in front of the ladies, or we can go outside. Your choice.'

His face has lost its customary arrogance but, without any bluster in his voice, he says, 'Let's go outside to the garden.' The women are dead silent as we rise. Alex and her mother sit and stare at us, their skin several shades whiter than usual, their mouths hanging agape.

'Errol, I first saw you with my wife in my own living room, three years ago. I've had to live with that memory. I have asked Alex, repeatedly, for a divorce. She refuses. I don't want a scandal. Not when it involves a man in your position.'

'A scandal like that might actually enhance my reputation,' he says.

'It won't enhance mine. And this is not about you, it's about me. By the way, don't kid yourself. You are not her only lover. There are other differences too, which cannot be resolved, between Alex and me. I want a divorce.'

'You know, Noel, I've always thought of you as the most sophisticated man I've ever met,' he says.

'There is a limit to my so-called "sophistication", Errol.'

He thinks it over and then says, 'Call her out here.'

I open the door and ask her to come. When she arrives, Errol glares at her and says, 'Why won't you give this man his divorce?'

'Well, Errol, what's in it for me?'

'She can have everything I own in Sweden, providing she leaves this island immediately. And stays away for at least two years.'

'Why two years?' he asks.

'If you must know it's because we've been caught up in this sick game, and I need time to get over it, and to find myself again. I don't want to see her for two years.'

'Let me speak to her alone,' Errol says. I nod and walk out into the garden. When I return, the ladies are packing up Alex's clothes in the bedroom. 'She agrees to your divorce terms.'

I nod, but say nothing. When the door finally closes behind them, I take a tour of my house. Not the building I am renting, but 'my house' as in my life, where truly I live inside my skin. I am not jubilant, but I do feel as if a ton of iron has been lifted off my shoulders. I feel a deep surge of sadness, and a sharp pain of failure, but I know those feelings will pass in time.

This night, for the first time in years, I sleep without nightmares. I will never allow my house to become so soiled again, no matter what dirty winds blow outside. And, although I have yet to realise it, some very dirty winds are coming in my direction.

Part Two

Sunset Lodge

Now I was free, but it was a different kind of freedom.

When, as a boy, I sailed away from the Trinidad wharf on my way to London, freedom felt like an ecstatic opportunity, a wide-open horizon, where all my dreams could be turned into reality. That freedom had empowered me.

Now, years later, I was again free – but in a negative way. I was rid of a marriage, rid of infidelity and betrayal, and hopefully rid of lies and obsessions. But my freedom felt more like an escape from prison than a journey towards the Promised Land. It was the beginning of a new and difficult part of my life. You don't escape from life. In my house you live it as best you can. I needed to put my house in order.

With my new status as one of Barbados' most eligible bachelors came lots of attractive temptation, but I was determined not to go crazy. In fact, I was still feeling lots of emotional pain, and was a bit wary of all women. I decided that for the foreseeable future the door to my heart would be a revolving one. In my position, running the resort's most glamorous nightclub, I could probably have bedded a new woman almost every night. Instead, I restricted myself to friendly dating, with women that I liked and respected.

My first concern was making the club run more smoothly. Alex had undoubtedly been very helpful to me in business, but she was gone and so, too, was my business in Stockholm. I needed someone who could step up and manage the place when I was away, and someone who was tough enough to handle a number of security issues. We had occasional problems with rowdy people, both at the door and inside, always the case with a nightclub. I am not a violent person, but my business – especially my clients – needed to feel safe and secure and I have always done what was needed. There was also the eternal problem of staff discipline, and particularly staff theft. I needed a strong, tough partner.

I had known Ozzie Cox since we were boys on Trinidad. To say he had 'rough edges' would be like saying a beach is sandy, but I always had respect for him. As young teens, we'd all looked up to Ozzie, who was a bit older, and we had relished his stories about forging documents to get work on ships and his vagabond adventures around the world. I met him again one night at the Flamingo Club in London during my first year as a student. That night he had warned me about a group of older hustlers who were sizing me up for a score, and he had taken my money and held it until we were safely outside, where he'd returned it. The next time I ran into him was years later at Heathrow, where I was changing planes on my way from Barbados to Stockholm. I told him about Alexandra's in Sweden and invited him to come over for a visit, which he promptly did. We put him to work on the door, and let him stay in the small apartment attached to the club. There had been a couple of incidents, but I always took Ozzie's explanations at face value. I hadn't seen him since Stockholm, but now I gave him a call and, within a couple of days, he arrived on the island.

I told him the situation and offered him 20 per cent of my share in the club if he would be a working partner. He readily accepted what were very generous terms, and settled into my guest premises at Sunset Lodge. Yes, he was a bit crude, with his merchant seaman's background, but he knew the nightclub business, was tough enough to deal with any problems at the door, and none of the staff would dream of stealing in his presence. I felt confident that the sophisticated atmosphere of our club would soon rub off on him.

Among the women I was dating at the time was one called Rosemary, who worked as a buyer at a department store in Bridgetown. It wasn't a serious relationship, but she was, I felt, a good woman with whom I could relax and talk openly, frankly, about our mutual problems and fears. She had helped me select new fabric for my staff uniforms. Soon, she had quit her job to go into the clothing business with a friend and partner. It was early days and she could barely afford to feed her children, so I took to stopping by her house with bags of groceries. In retrospect, I think she must have mistaken my intentions, believing them to be more serious than they were. I thought of her as a good friend whom I could trust, which is why I would turn to her for help later when I needed someone to look after my mother's estate. But I am getting ahead of myself here...

I am working in the DJ box one night when I see Nick Hudson being seated with a group of friends, some of whom I do not recognise, including a striking young blonde woman. Tall, lanky, upper class English, I think. I don't give her a second thought, as I am really into my sounds tonight, in a groove with the music, a kind of trance that I enjoy sometimes. I have a great audio system and the music washes away all my troubles, as it builds an irresistible atmosphere for my guests, raising their spirits on a soulful wall of sound.

'Noel, my friend, I would like to introduce you to someone,' says Nick Hudson, breaking my reverie as he stands outside the DJ box. 'This is Carina, my houseguest. Apparently you have mutual friends...'

I shake hands with the tall blonde. 'Welcome, Carina. Lovely to meet you.'

'Hello, Noel. Wendy Sonnenberg sends her love. I was just staying with her in New York.'

'Really. That's very kind of you to relay her message. I hope Wendy is well.'

'Why don't you come and join us for a drink?'

'Right now I am tied up here. Perhaps later. I can't leave my post just yet,' I lie. My regular DJ is upstairs and I could easily summon him, but I am enjoying myself. Why stop just to have a chat with yet another English bird down in the islands for a good time.

'Oh, OK. See you later then.'

Half an hour later, she is back. 'Don't you pay someone to play the music in here? Why can't you have a dance with me?'

'You want to dance?' I look at her again and become, for the first time, aware of how beautiful she is, especially her sparkling large eyes.

'Wendy told me you were a marvellous dancer. I want to see for myself.'

Flattered, and still a bit annoyed, I say, 'Hey, I'm expressing myself here. But give me a couple of minutes, and we'll have a dance.' I lift the internal phone and call the upstairs bar and tell my DJ to come and replace me. When the record ends, I put on a slow Barry White number and leave the booth. I take her in my arms.

By the end of the track, we are together.

Just like that. We both know it. I am overwhelmed, and I can see that everyone in the club is staring at us. They can see it too. I note Nick Hudson's seriously annoyed eyes on us, and the smiles of others at his table. I am confused, given that I have really been closed to such emotion for months now. How can I possibly be falling for a complete stranger? And I can see the feeling is mutual, for Carina looks confused and flushed as well, but she is not going anywhere. When the next track – 'Le Freak' by Chic – begins, we get straight into it together. My heart is pounding and I can feel that hers is too.

Shortly afterwards, Nick comes out to the dance floor and says, 'It's getting late and it's your first night. I think we'd better go home, Carina.'

She shakes her head, 'That's fine, Nick, you go ahead. Noel can give me a lift home, can't you?'

'Yes, of course.'

Nick walks off, obviously annoyed. It's not difficult to imagine the plans with which he had begun this evening. But we don't think of Nick, just dance together, and then talk with that fierce urgency of new lovers (although we're not yet lovers) until it's four o'clock in the morning. I leave Ozzie to lock up the club and drive her back to Nick's. Without talking, we both get out of my car and walk up to his private entrance. It's locked. Either by accident or in a fit of pique, he's locked her out.

'I can open a window for you, or you can come back and stay with me.'

'Oh Noel, I want to be with you. But this is the first night, you know. And Nick is my host, even if he's not being very gracious tonight. So if you could open one of these windows, it is probably the proper thing to do.'

I quickly find a window that is ajar and help her climb inside. We kiss passionately, for a long time, through the window, and it's all I can do not to follow her inside, but I know she is right.

'Promise to call me when you wake up?'

'I promise.' And I keep my promise later that morning. It's about noon when I drive round to pick her up. We go straight back to Sunset Lodge and directly to bed. Much later that evening, I drive her back to Nick's where she picks up her luggage. Carina moves into my house for the next two weeks.

Really, truly, we cannot get enough of one another. We make love every night until the soft Bajan dawn and a fresh breeze enter my bedroom. We have long conversations about our lives, our regrets and our dreams; amazed and overjoyed that we have found one another – physically, intellectually and emotionally. I haven't felt this way – in the first flush of love – for years. Just the touch of her hand or the scent of her hair can send my heart pounding. It's as if all that pain and regret I had been feeling had never existed.

Carina tells me about her modelling career, about strutting down catwalks with other top models. She talks about her friends in London and New York, and about her schooldays. But when she begins to talk about her childhood, I feel an alarm go off in my head, a distant alarm, but one that is persistent and will grow more intense the longer I know her. Lady Carina Fitzalan-Howard is more than just an upper-middle class English girl, much more. Her father is the Duke of Norfolk — the premier duke in the entire English aristocracy – and Earl Marshal of England. She grew up in Arundel Castle, daughter of the man who escorts the Queen into the most important ceremonial occasions. Moreover, he is the senior peer of the Roman Catholic Church in the United Kingdom. Finally, he is a Major General in the Grenadier Guards, who was awarded a Military Cross for bravery under fire in the Second World War. How, I wonder, will he react to his daughter's love affair with a black Trinidadian nightclub owner?

We spend our afternoons at the Sandy Lane beach, our evenings in the club. I show her my favourite places on the island, and we dine in some of my favourite restaurants and cafés. At the end of the two weeks, her return flight to New York is hanging over our heads like a black cloud. Finally, at the airport, she turns to me, and my gloomy face, and addresses the issue. 'Noel, I have to go back, and I don't know what to say. I didn't come down here expecting to fall in love. I have been so happy these past weeks. Now I just feel like there is a lot of thinking that I have to do. I will call you soon, I promise.'

In fact, she calls a few hours later, after the taxi from the airport has dropped her off in Manhattan. 'That was the worst flight I've ever had in my life. Not just because of the awful turbulence. Suddenly, just now, I realised that I hate New York. It is entirely your fault, Noel!'

I laugh and apologise.

'I am going to pack everything up tomorrow and move back to England. I will call you from there, as soon as I get myself sorted out.'

'I will be waiting for your call, Carina.'

My feelings of uncertainty and my yearnings are blocked temporarily a couple of days later when my sister Dorothy calls with bad news. Our mother has suffered a stroke. Dorothy is on her way to Trinidad, and I promise to get the next flight out and meet her there. What I find in the hospital is a woman who has aged greatly since the last time we met. My mother looks so frail in that big old bed, and she is paralysed down her left side. I know that she has suffered great loneliness ever since my father died. They were married for more than 30 years. She asks me about my brother Courtenay, and asks me to bring him to her. The fact is, I have not spoken with my brother in some years and don't know how to reach him, but vow to find out. Still, I feel a tinge of sibling rivalry. Instead of being glad to see me, all she can do is yearn for my brother. Of course, she has always been more comfortable with Dorothy. Nevertheless, I sit at her bedside all afternoon, trying to block the old bitterness and resentments from my mind, trying to amuse her with stories about my life in Barbados. She just looks annoyed and waves me away, asking for Dorothy to sit with her.

'I will find Courtenay for you. Some of his friends here are sure to know where he is.' Outside her bedroom, I hand Dorothy a blank cheque to cover the costs of her care. I am feeling very low and I go out and drive my rented car straight to the airport, straight back to Barbados.

Sitting at a table in the club with my friend Rosemary later that night, I spill out my emotions and an account of that day's depressing visit to my mother's bedside.

'You can't leave her alone in Trinidad now,' Rosemary says. 'You must bring her over here to Barbados and put her in a nursing home. Your sister can bring her, on her way back to New York.'

'My mother will never agree to that.'

'Well, the next time you go to Trinidad to see her, you bring me along. I will convince her that coming here is the best thing. You leave it to me.'

Which is what I do the next time I fly over. And, predictably, my mother forms an immediate bond with Rosemary. I can see that Rosemary is encouraged by this for more reasons than simply my mother's well being. My mother is not ready to leave Trinidad however, much as she might like Rosemary. In fact, I know Rosemary has strong hopes that she and I will get together in a serious relationship. Unfortunately, this is the last thing I want.

Over the past weeks, I have been talking to Carina in London almost every day. We're still getting to know one another really, and we talk for hours about our daily lives, our friends, what we feel about the fling that we've shared together. Suddenly, one afternoon she calls me in a fizz of excitement and intensity: 'Noel, I want to ask you just one question. You keep asking me when I am coming back to the island. Do you realise that, if I come back, I'm coming to stay, not just for a holiday. Are you ready for that?'

'That is exactly what I want you to do, Carina. Come and live here with me.'

'Are you sure? You have a great life as a single playboy or whatever you want to call it down there. Do you really want me to come there permanently?'

'Carina, I'm not a playboy and I don't have a great life here. All I want is for you to come here, for you to be with me... forever. That is how I feel.'

Two weeks later, she arrives with a great big smile and several large suitcases. This begins one of the happiest, and most unexpected, periods in my life. She moves into Sunset Lodge and, from the beginning, we start a routine that keeps us together most of every day and fills us both with happiness. I know that she will not be happy if she doesn't have something to do, some kind of work, and I find responsibilities for her around the club. Following several hours work at the club in the mornings, we spend our afternoons playing on the beach, waterskiing, taking excursions with friends. In the evenings, we may have dinner at another restaurant, but my main responsibility is to keep a close eye on Alexandra's. While I usually stay on the premises until after closing, Carina sometimes heads for home before me, in order to be awake and alert for her morning tasks at the club.

Up to this point, I have been renting Sunset Lodge, but now, with the new feeling of security I have from Carina's presence, I decide to buy the house. The owner accepts my offer, and I quickly arrange a mortgage through Chase Manhattan. So now I am the complete Bajan: both a citizen and a homeowner. I suspect, however, that neither my passport nor my land truly convinces the locals that I am anything but a Trinidadian interloper on their island.

I have been flying back and forth between Barbados and Trinidad regularly in order to check on my mother. So the next time I go, I take Carina with me. A mistake, as it turns out. My mother takes an instant dislike to her. Whether it is because of misplaced loyalty to Alex, or even Rosemary, I am not sure. On the other hand, my mother is now more open to coming to Barbados and entering a nursing home. So shortly after we return, I find an opening at St Joseph's hospital, and Rosemary agrees to fly over and escort my mother on the journey. In fact, as she predicted, Rosemary has formed a strong bond with my mother and she visits her almost every day at St Joseph's, while I find my maternal encounters as uncomfortable as they have ever been.

'Noel, we've got to move your mother,' Rosemary tells me one day out of the blue. 'They are not caring for her properly there. Instead of a plastic pad under the sheets, they have put newspapers down. They can stay damp for days. And nobody comes to attend to her for hours and hours.'

I find a place for her at the Seventh Day Adventist's nursing home. The care here is much better, and soon my mother is showing definite signs of improvement. She may not make a full recovery, but her spirits are much higher. I visit her often with both Carina and Rosemary, and take other friends along with whom I think she will enjoy a friendly chat. Meanwhile, my life is definitely changing. I am more settled down than ever before. I have the club working at peak efficiency and we are doing great business. Carina is running the bottle counts every morning – which is a crucial part of our inventory control system. Although Ozzie is still rough mannered and aggressive, Carina is trying to soften his manners with frequent jokes and subtle hints. She takes him on like a project, with long conversations and little lessons in the social graces. Unfortunately, I can see that Ozzie sees her intentions and his manners and vulgar swearing become, if anything, even worse.

We are deeply in love and spend as much time together as we can.

My heart sinks one afternoon when Carina tells me that her parents – Miles and Mary, as she calls the Duke and Duchess of Norfolk – are coming to the island for a visit. My suspicions about their intentions have already been aroused by an incident with an English couple, Henry and Donatella Smith. They are friends of Carina's parents, and as such we went out of our way to entertain them during their visit. On the final day, Donatella confessed to Carina that her parents had asked them to do some snooping on her and me while on the island. 'You two are so good together, and Noel is such a gentleman, it's going to be my pleasure to report back that you are in very good hands, Carina!' My reaction to this 'confession' is a heightened sense of wariness about her parents, and this is only magnified by the thought of their impending arrival.

Our first meeting, at their rental home, is cordial enough, and brief. However, Carina insists that we invite them to Sunset Lodge for dinner. She will cook, she says, although I try to protest. I sense that she is protecting me from her father's prejudice against men who cook in their own homes. On the night they are due to arrive, Carina fills the house with candles. It looks beautiful, almost like an altar, perched on its tropical hillside above the sea. Her parents arrive and I get them drinks. In the kitchen, Carina is in a frazzle, because she's overcooked the beef. Not to worry, we pull the meal together and all sit down at the beautifully laid table.

Our conversation is genial, even pleasant, everyone on their best manners, although I can feel the undercurrent of tension that runs below everything. Dessert is served, her parents compliment her on her cooking skills, and I offer coffee and brandies. Here is when it goes off the rails. We somehow launch into a conversation about British colonialism.

'It seems to me,' I say, 'that the British reaped enormous profits from all these islands, in both agriculture and industry, for centuries. The decent thing for them to have done, once the sugar cane and asphalt gravy trains came to an end, was to leave these small developing nations with proper infrastructure and management training to ensure they could make their own progress.'

'Do you think Britain should have paid for new roads and new managers once we were being asked to leave here, being asked to give back our territory?'

'Yes, of course, I think it would have been the decent thing to do.'

'I don't agree. Why should we, Britain, give anyone more money, once we've given them their freedom, which is what they demanded.'

Here is where I lost control, and veered right off the polite road onto my own personal highway. 'Miles, forgive me for being so direct, but I suspect you are not down here to talk about colonialism with me. You're here to check up on your daughter. On that issue, you should know that I doubt if we have anything to discuss. Your daughter is an adult and she is here of her own free will. If you want to discuss this with her, I am sure you will. But do remember that she is an adult and here because she wants to be. She's not tied to the bedposts.'

Carina and Noel dance in Alexandra's,
Barbados, where they had first met.
Their love affair lasted over four years.

Basil Charles, owner of the legendary
Basil's Bar on Mustique, together
with Noel.

Noel with Tom Adams at the Great Table. Tom Adams succeeded Errol Barrow
as Prime Minister of Barbados in 1976.

Singer Tom Jones and his son Mark on their boat in Barbados. Tom and his family spent their holidays in Barbados and Tom was seen at the club every night.

Alex with former West Indian cricketer, Everton Weekes and his wife.

Carina outside Barbados airport on her way back to the UK. In the end their relationship could not survive their enforced separation.

Noel with Boel Sagamak – a generous friend who helped get him back on his feet.

A pre-lunch swim at Princess Margaret's house on Mustique (from left to right): Carolina Herrera, Charles Delevine, Princess Margaret, Ned Ryan and Noel.

Noel was friends with all the members of Abba. He took these snaps while sailing the Swedish archipelago with Frida Lyngstad and Benny Andersson.

Noel has four daughters. Here he is with his second youngest daughter, Chloe, who is a talented singer/songwriter. She lives in Toronto.

Rosanna is Noel's youngest daughter who was born in 1989. She lives and works in Stockholm.

Noel and Cynthia sign the register after getting married at City Hall, Toronto on 7 June 2002. The wedding breakfast consisted of McDonald's and champagne!

As soon as the words leave my mouth, I feel a floodtide of regret. I have lost my cool with the Duke. What on earth could I gain by saying such a thing to this man?

'You could tell him that you love me,' Carina says, her eyes brimming with pain.

'He must realise that I love you, darling. That's not his concern, I think. He is concerned with other issues... which he would find difficult to talk about openly.'

'As you know, I am a devout Catholic. My daughter was raised a devout Catholic. You have been married before, and that makes it impossible for you to marry my daughter in the eyes of our church.'

I shrugged. 'I suppose you win some, you lose some. My father was a minister. I was raised a devout Christian. But not a Catholic...'

'My fears have nothing to do with your colour, if that's what you were insinuating. It's a religious issue. Divorce is not recognised by the Catholic Church.'

'Only annulments, I know. But, really, when all is said and done, this is Carina's life and her decision, don't you agree? She is not a devout Catholic now, but she is a free adult.'

Miles is too agitated to answer. He simply stares into space, seething, and I do the same, while Carina gets up to clear the dessert plates. Her mother sits beaming ahead, looking rather smug about what she has just witnessed. Perhaps, I think, she rarely has the chance to see anyone defy her husband. It certainly doesn't seem to upset her, although I have no doubt that she will not be rushing to defend me when they get back to their villa, when the Duke's outrage begins to turn the air blue.

It's clear to me that this is just the first wave of an impending disaster that could destroy all the happiness I have experienced since I met Carina. In my heart, I can almost feel the heavy chords and hear the wailing Rolling Stones singing Gimme Shelter... just like the lyrics say, it really does feel like a storm is threatening my life...

And, sure enough, within days of her parents leaving the island Carina receives a summons to return to the UK 'to sign some trust fund documents'. When I am unable to hide my anxiety, she insists, 'Please don't look so sad, darling. I promise you that I will be back very shortly. Daddy may be angry, but there is nothing he can do to stop me living with whom I want to live. And I want to live with you.'

After I drop her at the airport, wondering if I will ever see her again, I decide to drive to the nursing home and visit my mother. As soon as I enter her room, I can see something has changed. She is glowering at me and slumped way down in the bed. 'What is wrong, mother?'

'I want to go home.'

'But that would be much less comfortable for you. I am rarely home, and here you have all the nurses you like, and your other friends...'

'Not your home, Noel. I want to go back to Trinidad.'

'Hmmm... you know we would have to find you another nursing home there. You can't live in your old house by yourself.'

'I don't care about that. I want to go home and be buried beside your father.'

'I thought you were happy here?'

'I want to be beside your father. This is not my home.'

'Let's see how you feel in a few days.'

The days pass, but my mother does not change her tune. Instead of a lively conversation now all she offers is the same demand to 'be buried' on Trinidad. I find this very depressing, and my visits taper off. Then I get a phone call from the nursing home saying 'your mother won't eat unless you come see her.' As soon as I walk into her room, she shouts, 'Boy! Why won't you take me home?'

Seeing no other alternative, I agree to fly to Trinidad and look for a nursing home there. This I do, luckily finding a very nice woman who runs a nursing home in Cocorite. I call my sister Dorothy in New York and explain the situation. She agrees to fly down to Trinidad and help me get my mother settled into the new home. So it comes to pass that, a week later, when I lead my frail mother into the Port of Spain airport, my sister is waiting for us. Together Dorothy and I take her to the new home and introduce her to the friendly staff. When we return the next morning, however, we find her in bed, facing the white walls, her back turned to the world. She won't respond to any of our questions or affection. The nurses look concerned but unsurprised. 'Sometimes they get like this,' is the most anyone will say.

I can see my mother has decided to die. It makes me feel helpless, wondering if she can feel my concern, my karma and love. Later, I will blame myself for not having said, 'I love you, Mother.' I wanted to say this, but could not find a way to get the words out. I was afraid of her response, or lack of a response. Was she ready to hear these words?

'Dorothy, I can't handle this anymore,' I say when we're outside the room. 'I am going to fly back to Barbados. I'm going to write you a cheque to cover all the expenses here.'

I catch the late afternoon flight. The very next day, Dorothy calls. 'Mother died a few minutes ago.'

I pause for a long time. 'Thanks for calling. I don't think that I can face her funeral, and all the other things. I just can't.'

'Are you going to call Courtenay?'

'I am pretty sure he will not want to know. I have his number,' and I give her his number in London.

My brother had arrived in Britain about five years after I first moved there. His first love was music, stemming from his involvement in the steel band scene on our island, which he had kept secret from our parents. When he was eventually sent to London, however, it was to study music. He worked as a DJ in clubs and lived a life largely unknown to me. He could not forgive our mother and wanted nothing to do with her, I knew that, although I wasn't close to him. Not until he came to Barbados to work for me.

A few weeks later, I feel ready to fly down to Trinidad again and face my old house alone. As I walk from room to room, my head is teeming with memories, just as the rooms are stuffed with all the physical reminders of my parents, my childhood, a lost world. I pick up things – photos, china, books – and they make my head ache with pain. I need to sort through all of this stuff, and then to organise where it goes, what to sell, what to give away or toss away – and it's too much. I can't do this, and I know that my brother Courtenay will never come back here. My sister Dorothy has a family she is caring for in New York and I cannot ask her to do this.

After I return to Barbados, I call Rosemary. She and her partner Maria Eastmond have been working on a business that will mass-produce a line of Barbados clothing. They have leased some factory space, with Maria's money, but Rosemary is short of any investment capital. Most of the fabrics they will be using come from Trinidad, so I have a financial proposal for her. I will loan her the investment capital she needs – with the sale of my parents' house, if she will oversee that sale. She can then repay me later out of profits from her business. Since the law forbids the removal of money from Trinidad, she can use the house proceeds to buy fabrics. It seems like a good deal, and she agrees.

Carina has been away for months, and despite our frequent phone calls, I cannot help feeling in near despair of ever seeing her again. I don't tell her how I feel, as the last thing I want to do is 'get heavy' on the phone and possibly drive her even further away. She swears that she misses me terribly, and that she will be back on the island very soon.

The house on Trinidad is sold. All the contents have been either sold or put into storage somewhere (I think). And then the bad news starts to arrive. In the first instance, I learn from Maria – who is also a friend – that she and Rosemary have argued and dissolved their business. There will be no more Trinidadian fabrics flowing into their factory in Barbados. And Rosemary – where is Rosemary? I can't reach her on Trinidad. A rumour surfaces: she has left the island with some guy who lives in Germany. Suddenly all my own negligence, my inability to cope with my mother's estate, becomes clear to me. I am not concerned about the loan agreement, for money is just money. What sickens me is the thought that I have lost a lifetime's worth of family heirlooms: my mother's jewellery, my father's books, all the family photographs, even my old Red Circle roller skates with the lightning bolt. Everything is gone. I have not a single photograph of my beloved father.

'Darling, I've bought my ticket for next Tuesday,' Carina announces. 'And I am having my car shipped out there too.'

This unexpected, joyful news is perhaps the only thing that can lift me out of the black emotional hole that I've fallen into since word came of Rosemary's disappearance. Surely, I think, if she's bringing her car all the way to Barbados, she is coming for good.

After a passionate three-day reunion, we emerge from Sunset Lodge to resume our life together on the island. One of the first things I notice is that Ozzie is visibly annoyed by Carina's return, and his behaviour hits an all-time low. This infuriates me, and after 24 hours, I go to him and say, 'Man, this is not working. I can't work together with you anymore, so I want to buy you out.'

'No way, Noel. I like this gig and my share ain't for sale.'

'I can't work with you, Ozzie.'

'I'm not going anywhere.'

It is a stalemate, but I am sure that if I offer Ozzie the right price, he will take it. Hanging around the club with Ozzie is bringing us down. But thanks to Carina, I suddenly feel as light as a feather, and ready to float wherever the wind happens to take us. We are on a holiday island, after all, and surrounded by friends who, although serious about their work, also have the money to live out their wildest dreams. Our crowd includes, at various times, people like the Rolling Stones, Eric Idle and his wife Tania, Alan Price from the Animals, his girlfriend Jill Townsend, Mark and Fiona Cottrell, and many others.

When we meet Bill Wyman and his wife Astrid, there is an immediate connection, partly because I am already good friends with Mick and Keith, but also because Astrid is Swedish and we have lots of friends in common. So it's a lovely surprise when, after their holiday on the island, they invite us to come straight over to visit them in their house in St-Paul de Vence in the South of France.

This beautiful hillside village has been a favourite of several generations of artists, with its focal point at the Hotel la Colombe d'Or where the walls are hung with original paintings by Picasso, Matisse, Monet, Calder and Leger among others. Once upon a time these pictures were bartered for food and wine – and what a great deal that has turned out to be for the owners! Although today the village is something of a tourist trap, with dozens of shops selling cheap souvenirs and tacky bric-a-brac, its houses are far too expensive to shelter any struggling artists. Still, behind the high walls of the Colombe d'Or, celebrities and tourists alike can eat the lovely simple food and imagine that they are rubbing elbows with some of the twentieth century's greatest artists.

Bill Wyman turns out to be a table tennis fanatic, and I try to give him a run for his money every day, in between swims in the pool and visits to the village and nearby restaurants and sites of interest. Our week-long visit passes far too quickly – a wonderful idyll for Carina and I – before we are packing to return to Barbados. Unfortunately, there occurs an incident which will cast a shadow over the visit forever.

'I can't find my gold elephant hair bracelet. Have you seen it, Carina?'

'No.'

'Maybe the maid took it?'

'I'm sure not, Noel. You must have misplaced it.'

'Shit, I can't mention it to Bill. Just be on the lookout for it.'

'Darling, you have to mention it to Bill. If you don't, I will. You love your bracelet.'

Unfortunately, she does bring it up, just as we are leaving. Bill is very protective of his maid, of course, whom he trusts implicitly after all the years she has worked for him. Anyway, I try to be as casual as I can about it. I tell Bill to just forget it, however, and then am sick when at the airport I reach into my jacket pocket and feel its familiar rounded contours.

'Oh Noel, I wish I had never mentioned it to Bill. It's so embarrassing. I hope he can forgive us.'

I have to agree with her. It's a familiar feeling that I get, one that dates back to my childhood, of it being all my fault. Still, we have had a magical break and one that has taken our relationship across an invisible frontier.

Life is so good with Carina that I cannot imagine how it could be better. Then one day we are sitting on the beach at Sandy Lane with friends, enjoying the sunshine after that morning's tropical squall, when she turns to me and says, 'Darling, we have to get married.'

'Don't kid a kidder, sweetheart,' I say. She knows I am still married to Alex. The divorce proceedings haven't even begun in Stockholm.

'Noel, I am serious. We should get married. Don't you think?'

'Of course I would love to marry you, but…'

All the rest of the afternoon, Carina keeps up this litany about getting married. Finally, jokingly, I say, 'I'll tell you what. If you go kneel down in that puddle there, and ask me again, I'll say yes.'

I am shocked when she rises from the table and walks across the terrace, kneels down in the shallow puddle of rainwater, and says, 'Darling Noel, will you please marry me?'

I hate public displays of affection, but I cannot stop from rising, going to her and gently lifting her up into my arms. 'Of course I will marry you, dear Carina,' I whisper. 'I am sorry I made you ask me like that. Let's get married as soon as I can get my divorce.'

The next day I drive into Bridgetown and head straight to Coria's jewellery shop. I am looking for a diamond that will be large enough to convey the true depth of my love for her, without being so big as to look gaudy or vulgar. I find the perfect solution: a pair of diamond rings. One is the engagement ring, the other a diamond studded wedding ring. They will fit together perfectly on Carina's finger.

As if the gods were smiling down at us, shortly after our engagement, an unforeseen encounter on the beach at Sandy Lane leads to us having a kind of romantic pre-honeymoon.

There is a group of us that afternoon: Eric Clapton, Eric Idle and his wife, Alan Price and the Cottrells. Nobody pays much attention as a sailboat drops anchor a few hundred yards offshore, and then a man launches a rubber dinghy and begins to row towards us. When he arrives and pulls the boat up into the coconut trees, he turns to look at us. 'Hey guys, can you point me to the nearest restaurant?' He has a thick Australian accent.

'Where did you come from?' asks Eric Clapton.

'Oz.'

'That's fairly obvious,' Eric says, and we all laugh. 'I meant where did you just sail in from today?'

'From Europe.'

'Europe? In that?' he nods at the dinghy. We all laugh. 'Pull the other one, mate.'

'No, in *that...*' he points out at the rather beautiful yacht on the horizon, which shimmers in the light of the setting sun. 'I'm the skipper.

We sailed from the Riviera a month ago, and the food on board has been getting fairly tedious. No insult to the owner, who is a good guy. But I'm looking for a juicy big steak right now.'

'What's your name?' asks Alan Price.

'Hugh. What's yours?'

'Alan.' They shake hands and we all introduce ourselves. 'Look, Hugh, that house up there is mine. I can fix you up with a good steak. The maid's up there and she'll look after you. Just tell her what you want, and why not take a hot shower while she's cooking it.'

'That's very kind of you, Alan. Thank you very much.'

Hours later, at my invitation, Hugh the captain shows up at my club, along with the yacht's owner. I had invited them all for dinner. The owner, Jasper, is a retired British army officer, very tall, dignified and ramrod straight. His new wife, Sue, is cute and friendly, and hits it off with Carina. For weeks after this, Jasper hosts our gang on daily sailing and snorkelling excursions up and around the Barbados coast. Then Jasper announces over dinner in the club one night that he is setting sail on the following morning. 'But why don't you and Carina fly over and join us in the Grenadines, Noel? Sail with us for a week?'

Carina is keen for the adventure, and I immediately accept his generous invitation.

We fly to St Vincent and take a taxi to the dockside address that Hugh had telephoned across two days earlier. Jasper spots us as soon as the taxi arrives, and comes onto the wharf to help us with our luggage. But his big smile collapses into a scowl when he sees the huge suitcase I have brought.

'Bloody hell, Noel. You should know better to bring so much luggage onto a boat like mine. Where the hell are we going to stow this enormous bag?'

'Hold on a minute, Jasper. I think you should examine the contents before you start complaining,' I say, unable to keep the smile off my face as I reach down and unfastened the clasp.

Inside I have packed, in ice, prime sirloins and filets, California pheasants, caviar – and some bottles of vintage claret. Jasper wastes no time in apologising for his rude welcome and together we carefully lift the suitcase aboard.

When I recall those next days of sailing, I always see the dolphins. They were with us the entire journey, diving and frolicking, leaping up into the sunlight: a slew of dolphins, more than we could count sometimes, escorting us from island to island. Their playful life seems to echo the life we enjoy on the yacht. I take over the galley and every morning in port I enjoy going out to do the shopping, buying lobsters and fish from the local fishermen. I invent magical Creole dishes to match the magical atmosphere on board. But then one evening, after everyone else has gone to sleep, Jasper confronts me.

'Noel, if there's one thing I can't stand, it's being taken for a fool.'

'What? Who's been taking you for a fool?'

'We're all at close quarters on this boat. I know that you are all getting stoned, smoking pot, and you all think I don't know what's going on.'

'Jasper, I am sorry. You're right, we have smoked a bit of grass, and we've kept it a bit discreet from you. We didn't want to embarrass you, or ourselves either, I guess. It was out of respect, nothing more, I assure you.'

'I don't really understand that stuff. I've never smoked anything, and I don't want to smoke anything, including tobacco.'

'I understand that, Jasper. You are already high, so far as I can tell. A natural high.'

'I've got something far better than pot, Noel.'

'What's that?'

'I'm a spiritualist. Have you ever wondered why I bought this boat?'

'Sometimes, but that's your business, really.'

'My wife, whom I loved so dearly and who gave me two wonderful children, who accompanied me with the regiment to meet the Queen at Balmoral Castle, my perfectly normal, delightfully happy wife started to drink too much. It was a shock, and most unbecoming. From a glass of wine with dinner, she suddenly went to drinking far too much and becoming an obvious drunkard. It was terribly embarrassing, and not very helpful to my career. Within time, my embarrassment turned into a kind of repulsion. I hated... not her... but her condition. I took her to doctors and psychiatrists, but nothing could help. Then she began to have excruciating migraine headaches. I took her back to

Harley Street and this time they found a large tumour on her brain. Inoperable. She died shortly thereafter. I cannot describe how guilty I felt. Her drinking, the change in her personality, had been caused by a growth on her brain. And she died so quickly that I never had time to tell her how very sorry I was for my anger with her. She was gone, and I was submerged under a black cloud of sorrow and regret.'

'I am so sorry, Jasper. I know a bit how you feel,' I say, thinking of the recent passing of my mother, and of how I was unable to tell her that I loved her even right at the end.

'Shortly after my wife died, I met a woman who introduced me to spiritualism. Through this, I have been searching for my wife. I want to apologise to her. It's a long and difficult search, I admit.'

'I see.'

'No, you don't, that's why I am telling you. I saw an advert for this boat and something told me this is what I need to be at peace. I went to the owner's office and Susan, who was the man's secretary, asked me to wait. Eventually, I went in, did the deal, wrote him a cheque, and when I came out, Susan said, "You've bought it, haven't you?" When I replied that I had, she gathered up her belongings and left the office with me. Just like that.'

His story continued to describe how he and Susan attempted to sail to France, knowing nothing about sailing and having nothing but an instruction manual as their guide. Naturally, they almost died when they hit the first storm. Thereafter he hired a competent crew, who enabled them to reach the south of France. Later he met Hugh, who had served in the Australian navy, and hired him as captain. Another English mate was hired, and they duly set off across the Atlantic.

I am transfixed by Jasper's tale, all the while having some difficulty deciding whether he is entirely sane or not. Then he produces a new exhibit. A mysterious small white box.

'Go ahead, lift it up.'

I do so, and little bolts of static electricity flash along my fingers. It's not painful, but spooky as hell.

'Isn't this fascinating? It's called a Kirlian camera and it was invented by a Russian couple in 1939. It shows you your aura.'

'It's amazing, Jasper. I don't know what to say…'

'You need say nothing. I think it's time for bed. And, by the way, if you want to smoke pot on my boat, you needn't sneak around. I just don't want to be arrested for smuggling it.'

'Fair enough. We'll be careful.' And we bid each other goodnight.

The next morning I tell Carina all about Jasper's story, and the white box. She asks if she can see it, and later that morning Jasper brings it out. It does freak her out. Perhaps it's her Catholic upbringing, but Carina is really not into spooky or spiritualist things. We spend the day sailing to Grenada where Jasper has planned an excursion for us up into the mountains to see the volcano.

As we drive the hired car up through a nutmeg grove, Jasper shouts, 'Stop the car!' Perfectly straight rows of nutmeg trees stretch out in all directions, with their erect trunks and bushy round tops forming what seems almost to be an optical illusion. Jasper leaves the car and strikes out on his own into the trees. The rest of us get out and take some photographs, admire the weird view, and begin to wonder where he's gone. We walk up the road a bit, and pass a ramshackle cottage, a chattel house. A woman is sitting on the porch.

'Hello there,' I greet her. 'I can smell something very delicious coming out of your kitchen.'

'Are you children hungry?'

'We haven't had any lunch. We could pay you for a taste of whatever you have on the stove.'

'You don't have to pay nuthin', you know? We are hospitable people on Grenada, you hear? Where you from?'

'Trinidad, and Barbados, and England, and Australia.'

'All fine islands, but not as fine cookin' as here on Grenada. Here we always cook enough for two families, so you be very welcome.'

So we file up onto her porch where she makes us welcome, pulling some kitchen chairs out of the house so we can sit down. We each get a delicious bowl of goat stew, washed down with a fruit punch, and although she won't accept my money, I hide a wad of bills for her in a place where she's sure to find them. Then we trek back to the car, but there's still no sign of Jasper. Finally, about four hours since he's disappeared, Jasper walks out of the shady nutmeg groves with a serene look on his face.

'Jasper, are you OK? We were worried about you.'

'Of course I'm all right, man. What are you going on about?'

'Nothing, just glad you are OK.'

Later, he tells Carina and I that he had gone off in search of a place called Leapers Hill, or Le Morne de Sauteurs, which he had read about in an account of France's efforts to colonise the island in the eighteenth century. Apparently, rather than surrender, the last surviving Caribe Indians had chosen to commit suicide by jumping off a cliff in those mountains, and Jasper had wanted to find the place on his own, in search of some kind of spiritual connection.

After this, Carina takes me aside and says, 'Noel, I am not prepared to stay on this boat another minute. I don't know anything about spiritualism, and I don't care. All I know is this guy is freaking me out. We have to go.'

I manage to calm her down, and to agree to stay aboard until Sunday morning when we will sail into Mustique. In fact, when we anchor, it is just offshore from Basil's Bar. This island is under the protectorate of St Vincent, but privately owned by Colin Tennant, Lord Glenconner, since 1958. He had purchased it for a mere £58,000, and then given a house to his friend Princess Margaret. Over the years, people like Mick Jagger, David Bowie and Mary Wells had bought vacation properties on the island, along with a scattering of winter residents from wealthy Old Money families in Europe, Canada and the US.

This morning as we paddle to the shore, an eccentric scene is unfolding. A white man in a white suit and Panama hat is seated in a wicker fan-backed chair, with a beautiful, voluptuous woman dressed in a white bikini standing at his side. The pair of them are watching a congregation of black people in white robes and white headbands singing hymns, just at the water's edge. A black preacher is baptising several children.

I recognise the man in the white suit from my club. He has dined there, but I cannot recall his name. It turns out to be Colin Tennant himself. And, of course, I have met Basil before. He has been to my club on Barbados a number of times. He welcomes us all warmly and makes us some of his delicious cocktails as we make ourselves at home inside the quaint little shanty that is his world-famous oasis for the rich and celebrated. As luck has it, Basil helps arrange a plane to give us a lift to St Vincent later that afternoon. Honeymoon – or pre-honeymoon as it were – over now, much to Carina's relief, we fly back to Barbados that same evening. Come midnight, we're sitting around the Great Table telling friends all about our odyssey on the Good Ship Jasper.

Not long after our return, Carina's best friend, Cokey Dundas, arrives with her newborn baby. Of course, we put her up at Sunset Lodge. However, I am not expecting Carina's frightened phone call on the second day of her friend's visit. 'Noel, please come home right now! There is a woman screaming inside Ozzie's place, and all sorts of banging and terrible noises.'

'I'll be there in five minutes.' I promise. As I race to make the ten-minute drive in half the usual time, I keep wondering why I have not thrown Ozzie out of the guesthouse before now. He's a ticking time bomb, both at the club and at my home.

I arrive and go straight to Ozzie's door. A minute or so after banging on it, he flies open to reveal a naked Ozzie, sweating profusely, breathing hard. Behind him, on the bed, I can see a woman spread-eagled with a bloody towel in her hand. She looks up at me with unconcerned, possibly stoned eyes.

'What you want?' he demands.

'What is going on in here, man?'

'None of your damn business.'

'It's my business when you frighten my guests. We have a little child staying with us, and her mother, and Carina: they're all terrified of what they're hearing. Can you show some respect for my guests?'

He grunts and slams the door in my face. That's it, as far as I'm concerned. Later that evening when he shows up at the club, I tell him to his face that he is no longer welcome at Sunset Lodge and to clear his things out. I also tell him I don't want to be his partner and insist that we strike a deal.

'Sell my shares? Why should I sell my shares? Why don't you sell your shares, Noel, if that's how you feel?'

For an instant, I even consider the idea, but realise this is the ultimate insult. This is my business, in which I have invested years of my life, and I am not going to be driven out of it by this thug. Still, if Ozzie won't sell his shares to me, perhaps I can find someone else who will buy them from him.

Ozzie is furious, and when he's angry, there is only one way he knows to express it. His first act of revenge is to bring a can of mace into the club a few nights later and spray the room, driving everyone – customers and staff – out into the night. From then on, he begins to invite his 'friends' to stop by for visits. This is a particularly rough group of local hoodlums, who arrive drunk and stoned, and make a point of harassing the clients. They reserve their hardest scowls for me, whispering amongst themselves, threatening to 'see you outside' and giving unpleasant looks to Carina. I fear for her safety at home now. I have no choice but to hire professional security men for both the club and my house.

This is not good for my relationship with Carina, to say the least, and it is not entirely surprising when she tells me, 'I've agreed to go back to England for a couple of months, Noel. You know that Diana, the girl who is going out with Prince Charles, worked at a kindergarten in London, well the school's owner rang me yesterday to say they wonder if I could replace Diana for the rest of the year. They're really stuck, and the idea appeals to me. I love little kids, as you know.'

'I see… I guess I don't blame you. Ozzie has been making our lives hell.'

'No, it's not that. Don't worry, darling, this is just a temporary thing. I'll be back before you know it. And you'll have everything sorted out here, I'm sure.'

I don't say anything, but I am sure that her father is behind this move. Pulling strings to get her back to England, to split us up. My woman is leaving and I don't want anyone to know, but of course it won't be a secret. Just one look at my face will tell everything. We drive to the airport in silence, and I watch my beautiful Carina disappear into the crowd with a heavy heart. I know she will telephone me every night, but those calls hurt too. I cannot fight the suspicion that my life has suddenly, without warning, gone off the rails.

A few days later, there is a hopeful development. While chatting to my friend Maureen King one afternoon, and confessing my partnership problems, she suggests that she talk to a wealthy local named Dr Jordan. He is very close to the new Prime Minister, Tom Adams, and has always admired the club. In a matter of days, Dr Jordan meets with Ozzie, offers him a tidy sum that Ozzie is unable to refuse, and I have a new partner.

I take this opportunity first to ring, then fly to Toronto and meet with Robert Shad, an old friend who has a silent 40 per cent interest in the club as well. I offer to buy this back from him for a substantial amount of cash, plus several Nalivykov paintings that he's always liked. I truly want to get my house in order, now that I am rid of Ozzie, and am very pleased when Shad accepts the deal.

Unfortunately, after I return to Barbados and show David Allison, my accountant, the notarised share transfer that I've signed with Robert, he says, 'You did the [original] deal here on the island. This share transfer is perfectly valid in Canada, but worthless on Barbados. I suggest you get this sorted out at once.'

When I next meet Dr Jordan, he seems less than interested in what I am telling him about the deal with Shad. Instead, he is full of enthusiasm for his idea to turn the club into a legal casino. He has the Prime Minister's ear, he reminds me, and thinks he will be able to get a gambling permit. He says that he has made contact with one of the main distributors of slot machines in the Caribbean. 'Hold on,' I say. 'I know the casino business well, from London, but I've never considered starting a casino on this island. The club is a very different business.'

'I know the nightclub business,' Jordan says, 'and it's never going to bring us the kind of money a casino will produce.'

I bite my lip. In fact, Jordan has no idea about the nightclub business, or the casino business either, so far as I can see. I have already had problems with him and his associates, who now treat the club as if they were the management, in sole charge, arrogantly giving orders to the staff and annoying old clients.

I arrive one morning to find men in the club ripping out my expensive velvet curtains and tossing them in the garden, where they intend to burn them. I get Jordan on the telephone and he drives down. We have a fierce confrontation, in which he reveals just how duplicitous he has been. In fact, he was listening to every word I told him about my deal with Shad in Canada, and behind my back has arranged his own deal, using a Bajan document. Now he believes that he owns Shad's 40 per cent, giving him 60 per cent and total control – while I still believe I have my 80 per cent, but based on Canadian documentation. What a nightmare! When he drives off on screeching tyres, I stand there shaking, full of rage and a growing sense of dread. How I wish I had Carina here. She's the one person to whom I could talk at this moment, on whom I could depend for level-headed advice and emotional support.

Some days later, I am awakened at Sunset Lodge by the sound of cars churning up the driveway, and screeching to a halt. I wonder who the hell this could be so early in the morning. The next thing I know a policeman's head appears through the open bedroom window. 'Let us in, Mr Charles. Open the door.'

'What is going on here?' I demand, as I reach for my trousers. At the front door, someone is banging angrily. 'Hold on, hold on. I'm coming…'

'What the hell are you doing waking me up at this hour?' I demand of the crowd of policemen standing in front of my door.

'We have a warrant to search the house.' It is pressed into my hands.

'Sure, you can search away, but I don't have anything you would be interested in. What is this all about?'

'You have cocaine on the premises, don't you, Mr Charles?'

'Absolutely not, I have no drugs on the premises. Go ahead and search.' As I speak, a thought flashes through my head that one of my frequent houseguests might have left something, but otherwise I know there is nothing. I will occasionally smoke a joint or do a line with friends outside the house, but I never buy drugs, and certainly don't keep them in the house.

In horror, I watch the six large police officers completely trash my home. They slit mattresses, pull every drawer out and dump its contents on the floor, empty the closets and rifle every pocket. Lamps are knocked over; the sofas are in disarray. It goes on for more than an hour, and when it's over, it looks as if a crowd of drunken Hell's

Angels have been let loose on the place. Outside, a couple of the officers have rooted in every corner of the garden. What do they think I am, a Colombian drug boss?

'All right, Mr Charles, you are coming with us,' says the sergeant in charge.

'I have no intention of coming with you. You've utterly destroyed my home, and now I have to start putting it back in some kind of order.'

'You're under arrest, Mr Charles.'

'What on earth for?'

'This!' He hands over a small brown envelope that as far as I can see is empty. Inside there is a little bit of dust. I smell it and it does smell like marijuana, but it's nothing, not even equal to the ash you'd drop off a cigarette. Somebody must have discarded this somewhere in the house at sometime in the past, but I have never seen it before, and I almost want to laugh. 'This is nothing. It's not drugs; it's an empty envelope with a bit of residue that, I grant you, smells like pot. But I've never seen it before.'

'Handcuff him.' Someone snaps the cuffs on me from behind.

'Why are you doing this? Don't you know I work hard to promote Barbados all over the world? I employ sixty people on this island. Why are you trying to discredit me?'

'All I can say is, you're going to have to get in the car and come with us to the station.'

'This is just not proper. I own one of the island's most prestigious businesses, and I have a reputation all over Europe for promoting Barbados. And you are arresting me for a trace of dust, which I have never seen before?'

The sergeant gives me a long thoughtful look, then goes into my kitchen and dials a number on the phone. I overhear him speaking. 'Captain, what we have here is really nothing, you know. What should we do? OK, yes sir. I understand, sir.'

'Can you at least take these cuffs off?' I ask the sergeant after he hangs up.

He nods his assent, and motions for one of the officers to unlock them. 'I'm sorry, Mr Charles, but we have our instructions and we have the evidence.'

'I think I am entitled to call my lawyer, right?'

'Yes, sir. I'll sort that out for you.'

When I reach Elliot Motley, he advises me, 'Be cooperative, but keep quiet. I'll be there in one hour.'

Inside Police Headquarters in the middle of Bridgetown, I am processed as a criminal. Fingerprints are taken, then I am posed for a mugshot with a number below my face. At one point, a young constable sticks his head around the corner and addresses the sergeant who has been supervising my incarceration. 'Hey Sarge, phone call for you.'

'Who is it?'

'A Dr Jordan.'

'Tell him I'll call him back.'

At the time, my heart rose in hopeful anticipation. Surely my partner Dr Jordan, despite our recent disagreements, could help me out of this mess. I would shortly be free. Now, in retrospect, what was I thinking? I had been set up.

I am put into a cell with a boy and an old drunken man, sleeping it off. The place smells horrible and is disgustingly filthy. I truly feel degraded. What is this all about? At worst, what they found equals a very lowly misdemeanour. My mind veers away from the specifics into a tumbling free-fall depression. What has become of my life? How has everything good been transformed so quickly into this degradation and despair?

It's not too long, however, before I hear my lawyer Elliot's voice in the other room talking to the sergeant. 'I want Noel released, right now.'

'We can't do that until he sees a judge, and there's no judge until Monday.'

'That is not acceptable. He's not staying in here for the weekend.'

'I have orders to hold him…'

'Listen, use your head. You know he owns that house, and he owns a nightclub worth a great deal of money. He's not going to flee – not for a charge this ridiculous – and leave all that behind. You let him out on his own recognisance.'

The argument goes back and forth. Then Elliott says, 'When you guys want favours, you come running to me. I'm telling you right here and now, if you don't release him immediately, that stops.

No more help from me, ever again. Plus you know this is just not right. Whatever is really going on here, you know I will take this to the courts and you will all be in serious trouble. Forget your orders. They are not legal orders, I assure you.'

A couple of minutes later, a constable opens the cell and motions for me to come outside.

In Elliot's car, as he gives me a lift back to Sunset Lodge, I tell him the entire story and he listens in silence. Finally, I include the phone call from Dr Jordan that came in to the station. 'I'm grateful to him for trying to help get me out of this,' I say.

My lawyer's head turns abruptly and stares at me. Then he looks back at the road. His silence speaks eloquently.

So do the wretched island journalists later that same day. 'Noel Charles was found in possession of drugs at his home in St James,' is the refrain that evening on the local TV and radio news. From that moment onwards, rumours flood the island. Supposedly, I have been busted with ten kilos of cocaine. No, with two tons of hashish. No, make it ten tons. I hear that people are saying, 'How do you think he made his money? He's a gangster from England.' Even my staff are whispering about me in the corners of the club. Nobody mentions that the 'dope' is 0.58 of a gram of marijuana dust. It takes less than 24 hours for my reputation on Barbados to be reduced to the same weight.

Meanwhile, my relationship with Carina – daughter of one of Britain's paramount aristocrats – exposes me to a new degree of press attention back in the UK. Ever since I opened the first Alexandra's, I have become used to appearing in local gossip columns, be they Swedish or Bajan. That's part and parcel of owning a chic nightclub. Now it becomes personal, and far more titillating for the readers of journalists like the *Daily Mail*'s Nigel Dempster, and Ross Benson or 'William Hickey' in the *Daily Express*. Of course, this is all about racism, and not even in a subtle way. Here's an extract from the Hickey column of 23 June 1977:

Guess Who'll Not be at the Wedding?
My friend the Duke of Norfolk has been telling me about his 24-year-old daughter Lady Marsha Fitzalan-Howard's

wedding at Westminster Cathedral on Monday to fellow thespian Patrick Ryecart, 25. Apparently his other daughter, Lady Carina, 25, will not be bringing her Trinidadian-born boyfriend, Noel Charles, 35.

Yesterday, among the solid stone blocks and pillars of Arundel Castle, the clipped moustached duke, 61, considered Charles, a disco-owner in Barbados, and said firmly, 'He is not invited, but Carina will be there ...'

Yes, yes, but what about Charles? Could we clear this up once and for all? Would he welcome the black Noel if Carina brought him home?

The Duke smiled a brief, militarily defensive smile: 'I'm much too canny to answer that. When you've been in the army for 30 years...'

This is just one of many snide gossip items that appear throughout, and long after, my relationship with Lady Carina. Usually, as in this example, they are loaded with blatant untruths and sloppy inaccuracies. In fact, I have been invited to Marsha's wedding, because Marsha, Carina's dear younger sister, whom I have met on the island, is an extremely open-minded and lovely girl who has made a point of making me feel accepted as her sister's partner. Whatever the Duke says, or the journalist, it is my decision not to fly back to London, which I take out of respect for the Duke's own feelings.

The Duke is apparently using his daughter's wedding as a kind of rehearsal for the BIG ONE – Charles and Diana's wedding – over which he will be preside in his role as Earl Marshal of England.

In the meantime, my 'drug case' on Barbados drags on for months. Each time there is a court date, the arresting officers fail to appear, leading to yet another adjournment. This is deliberate, enabling the police to subject me to repeated searches. They stop my car and tear it apart, throw everything out onto the road, even a backgammon set, then roar off leaving me to pick up the mess. My house must be kept under constant guard, lest anyone get inside and plant some 'evidence'.

During this period, the body of a young murdered Bajan girl washes up onto a beach. The newspaper talks about a blue movie business out of Florida using locations on the island. Then a second body is found. The next morning the same six policemen show up at my house and loudly search for cameras or filmmaking equipment. It's so horrible, yet I try to keep a sense of humour about it. Still, it is eroding my personality, making me suspicious of new people, whom I used to always see as potential new friends. This paranoia is not exactly the right attitude to have if you are operating a nightclub on a tourist island.

One day when the police arrive at my house again they order me into one of the squad cars and drive me to the club. 'Show us your safe,' they demand.

I have to open it for them. Inside is a Patek Philippe watch. It's mine; I bought it for myself, I explain over their accusations and reminders that there has been a string of jewellery burglaries on the island. 'Listen, I know. My own Rolex, which I left at a friend's house, was stolen a couple of months ago, and I reported it to you lot after the burglary.'

They just laugh at me. As far as they are now concerned, I am a big-time drug smuggler, a pornographer, a cat burglar, and insurance scam artist – whatever suits their fantasy of the moment. How else could I, this uppity nobody from Trinidad, ever have raised the money to open the most glamorous nightclub in the history of their island? It drags on and on, and I even get word that my name will not appear in the next edition of *Who's Who*. Well, I can live with that, but how long can everybody else watch the harassment and read the newspapers and not begin to wonder, 'Isn't there an element of truth in this, or why would it be happening?'

One example of this occurs when I meet a charming young Englishman who starts to come to my club every night during his holiday. I see him first waiting patiently at the crowded bar, money in hand, trying to get noticed so he can order a drink. I walk up and introduce myself, then go and get his drink myself. 'No, keep your money. If you have to wait that long for a drink, you deserve to drink for free,' I tell him. A few days later someone tells me that this young man is actually Viscount Linley, the son of Princess Margaret and Lord Snowdon. Over the next couple of weeks, we become better and better friends. I suggest we go to the Harbour Lights Club one night, just for a change of scene. We have a few drinks there, and I, regrettably, confide in him about all the police harassment I have been subjected to and how I am desperate to get a fair hearing in court. Unfortunately, that is the last time I ever see him. I hardly blame him, for he can't risk his own reputation by associating with someone in my position. It is a valuable lesson.

Which is why I am very surprised sometime later to receive a phone call from Ned Ryan and Charles Delevine, good friends who have a house on the island of Mustique. Apparently, Princess Margaret – who has her own house on the island – would like me to come to lunch. She has heard about me from Carina, and would like to meet me. She's sending me an invitation.

'Listen, that's flattering, but I have to decline. She must not realise what's happening here right now. Things aren't going very well, and I don't want to embarrass her in any way by association.'

'Noel, you don't get it, do you? This is a royal command. The Princess has invited you and you must attend.'

'I wonder what Carina's been saying about me?'

'You know, Noel, how women chatter away at all these parties. Carina adores you, and so PM's curiosity has been aroused. You can stay with us, of course. It's next Saturday, so just fly into Mustique and we'll come and meet you at the airport.'

As soon as I hang up, I panic. The way things are going, how can I trust anyone to look after the club and the house while I am gone? I fear that all sorts of damage could be done. It's already got to the point where I have had to fire my security people when they became obnoxious and disrespectful. I don't want my clients bothered, or my house trashed, or bogus 'evidence' planted on my property.

Then I have a brainwave. During the past year, since our mother died, I have got closer to my brother Courtenay, who is living in London. If there is anyone I can trust, and who is tough enough to stand up to any threat, it's my brother. I ring him and offer to fly him over in return for the favour of living in my house and keeping an eye on the club while I am gone. Truth is, I very much need to clear my head with a few nights away from Barbados. Courtenay agrees to come.

The following Friday, I fly to Mustique to stay with my friends the Cottrells. Ironically, our landing is delayed because the Princess is flying out of the airport on her way to Barbados to attend a military tattoo! We are not allowed inside the 'purple zone' of airspace until she is well on her way. Of course, she will be back in plenty of time to play hostess the next day.

We are greeted the following day by the young – and now famous – 'companion' to the Princess called Roddy Llewellyn. He's a pleasant enough 'Hooray' who had visited my club some time ago. In fact, he behaved somewhat disrespectfully that night. After he and his friends had consumed masses of fine champagne, wine and spirits, along with dinner, he had waved away the bill at the end of the night, saying, 'No, no, just send that to London.'

Carina was in the club and overheard. She had marched straight up and said, 'Who do you think you are? Send it to London? Where in London? It's not being sent to London, you are going to pay for it right now, here.' Recognising her, Roddy and his friends had finally come up with the cash to settle their substantial bill.

Now, of course, Roddy doesn't mention this, nor do I, as we shake hands beside the large salt-water swimming pool behind PM's house. (She likes to be called 'PM', I am told, by her close friends. Otherwise she insists on being addressed with strict formality, as the Queen's sister demands.) 'Noel Charles, how do you do? I have heard so much about you,' she says when I am introduced. She holds my hand for longer than necessary, with a distinct twinkle of mischief in her eyes.

We join a good-sized group of people being served drinks by the staff. Among this group are a couple of prominent Venezuelans, including a well-known fashion designer.

'I hope you've all brought your bathing costumes,' PM says. In fact, this had been noted on the invitation. Then she takes me by the arm. 'Noel, let me show you where to change.' The next thing I know she is escorting me to her house, and continuing to talk as she leads me inside. I look at her, and she pretends nothing is amiss, motioning for me to go ahead and get changed. Somewhat nonplussed, I obey the royal command and proceed to strip off and don my suit. This is, so to speak, a truly personal touch. I am not so much flattered, as quizzical about what exactly Carina has told PM back in London. In any case, if she was curious, she no longer needs to be.

As we return to the pool, we draw a number of stares, but PM chats away as if we are alone. 'I do say, that is a remarkable costume you are wearing, Noel.' In truth, without thinking, when packing for the trip, I had grabbed one of my tightest Speedo bathing suits without thinking. I suppose it doesn't leave much to the imagination.

So I dive into the pool. PM, in her own rather revealing but definitely proper bathing costume, mixes with the other guests, a large whiskey in her hand. I splash about for a while, before clambering out to refresh myself with another cocktail. I am clearly the main attraction for PM this afternoon, who devotes herself almost exclusively to chatting and flirting with me. Frankly, it makes me self-conscious and uncomfortable, particularly the undertone of being patronised, indeed 'toyed' with.

About 2 p.m., the butler announces that lunch will be served down on the beach. There is a palm-frond shelter there with a long table immaculately set. Roddy, who has been noticeably absent for the first stage of this social event, is waiting at the head of the table, directing us all to our seats.

'Noel, you're here on my right,' Roddy says.

'No, no, MY right, Noel. You sit here,' PM says. She glares at Roddy with an intensity that leads me to believe she is annoyed at more than just his clumsy placement. True enough, I will learn after lunch, for Roddy has earlier that week told PM that he has another love interest and will soon be returning to the UK. This has obviously not gone down well. This explains, I think, my trip to the changing cabana earlier, and now the blatant games of 'footsie' under the table. At one point, she even says, 'Have some more chicken, Noel. Let me find you a nice big juicy piece.' Whereupon she reaches out and grabs a cold chicken breast with her bare hand and plunks it down on my plate. A flashing smile at Roddy. It's all I can do to contain my laughter. At the same time, I have to feel sorry for the obvious unhappiness (although I don't yet understand it) behind such a loss of composure. She is drinking more than anyone else at the table – although I am doing my best to keep up.

After pudding has been consumed, she announces, 'Right. Walkies.' Everyone's chair is pushed back and she leads the group, men guests, followed by women, up the beach for a post-prandial constitutional. All except me and Mark Cottrell, who has come along to the lunch with me.

'Perhaps you ought to go too, Noel,' Mark says. 'And I'll come with you, of course. There may be "repercussions" if we don't.'

'The hell with that. Let's go. I've had enough of whatever is going on here. Let's walk over to Basil's Bar.'

I plan on spending a week with the Cottrells, but a couple of days pass and my brother Courtenay rings to say that Ozzie Cox was in the club the previous night and created a terrible scene: pissing on the dance floor, insulting clients. I tell him I will fly back straight away. When I discuss my awful situation on Barbados with Basil, he says, 'Maybe you should close down for a while. Come over here and you can stay with me. Look after this place while I am away.'

'I appreciate the offer. In fact, it sounds like good advice.'

So I call Courtenay and ask him to close the club and shut up my house. For the next couple of months, I am resident on Mustique, flying back a couple of times for court dates, which are invariably adjourned. Then, lo and behold, after months, the judge in the case insists on holding the hearing. He listens to the prosecution's evidence – and immediately throws out the case. Not only this, but he reprimands the police and the prosecution for wasting the court's time.

I am vindicated at last, and ready to re-open the club, moving back into Sunset Lodge, when a couple of weeks after the trial, the same police goon squad make another raid on my home.

'Well, well, what have we here?' announces the cop who has walked straight into the kitchen, reached into a basket full of crumpled plastic bags, and pulled out a chunk of hashish and an ounce of grass.

'What? That's not mine, and you know it!'

'You can tell that to the judge. You're under arrest!'

I cannot begin to describe the despair I feel at this moment, as handcuffs are fastened to my wrists, and the smirking sergeant pushes me outside towards the waiting patrol car.

Naturally, this unleashes another round of harmful radio and television reports later that day. But at least my lawyer has no trouble getting me before a judge. And something has gone terribly wrong with their frame-up this time. For when the Crown attorney requests a postponement, even though all the police officers are present in the courtroom, it is 'to locate the evidence.'

'You mean you can't find the evidence?' asks the judge in disbelief.

'Not yet, Your Honour, but we will, I am sure. Unless the rats ate it.'

'Must be some stoned old rats down at the police station,' calls a voice from the back of the public gallery, causing a wave of laughter to crash around the court.

Once the judge stops laughing, he is definitely not amused. He dismisses the case on the spot, and issues another reprimand to police and prosecution.

That night I fall into bed exhausted and sleep without nightmares. Surely they won't dare to try another one of these fraudulent drug raids on me, at least not for a long time. They have made themselves look like bumbling idiots, which they clearly are.

Suddenly the phone is ringing. I reach for it. 'Hey, Noel.'

'Who is this?'

'Never you mind. Know them bodies we keep finding? Next one gonna be found on your land. You know we do hang people here…'

Click. I put down the receiver. I am one hundred per cent freaked out, wide-awake and paranoid. I lie there almost twitching with anxiety, hearing the voice over and over in my head. Then the unmistakable sound of tyres crunching on my gravel driveway brings me to my feet. Hell, they've come back. I throw on a pair of trousers and a shirt, and go to the front door. But it's not a squad of coppers, rather two middle-aged men, sweating in the morning heat, are walking towards me.

'This is private property. What do you want here?'

'Excuse us, are you Noel Charles? We're from the *Sun* newspaper.

We've heard about your problems with the police, and we wonder if you might be willing to give us an interview?'

I am so freaked out that I am willing to grasp at the most unlikely straws. Perhaps if I get my true story into the press, whoever is persecuting me will be afraid to continue. 'Yes, well, I might give you an interview. Why don't you gentlemen come inside and I'll get us all some coffee, and we'll talk about it.'

For the next two hours, including the time they spend taking photographs of me and the house, I am a willing participant in my own public humiliation. Of course, I think that I can dictate the story to them: my life as a successful and law-abiding businessman, all the notable clients I've entertained over the years, my contribution to the Bajan tourism miracle – and the true facts about the police harassment that I've suffered for more than a year now. It's only after they've gone, their notebooks full, their cameras satisfied, that I get a nauseating flash of doubt. How can I believe that they will not tell the story in the most sensationalist way?

Carina has been separated from me for many months, and I cannot abide her absence any longer, so I call her. I tell her about the threatening phone call, and then confess that I have just spilled my guts to a couple of hack journalists. She seems concerned by the threat, but absolutely unconcerned about the press. 'You just have to ignore the rubbish they write, Noel. It's not worth thinking about for two seconds.' I am pleased that she is unconcerned, so supportive.

'I miss you, Carina.'

'Then why don't you come here, Noel? I'm buying a house here, and you can come live with me. Forget that ungrateful island where they are trying to ruin you.'

'I have property here, Carina. I can't just move to London. But, yes, I think I will come to see you as soon as I can get a ticket. Do you still love me?'

'I love you very much, Noel. But do *you* still love me?'

'You know that I do.'

This visit to London is a whirlwind of social activity: lunches, dinners, gallery openings, fashion shows. I catch up with many friends: Dot and Barry, Johnny Gold, David Bailey and Penelope

Tree, Robert Chan, Nick Frye, Lord and Lady Dundas, Ronny Drier and Charles de Lavigne. We dine out at hot spots like the White Elephant, Langan's Brasserie, and San Lorenzo. We go to the theatre, and to casinos, and, of course, Tramp and Annabel's nightclubs.

We also mix with Carina's family. Her newlywed sister, Marsha is incredibly friendly and warm. Her brother Eddie cooks us a memorable Sunday lunch. However, during a visit with her older sister Tessa, something truly nasty suddenly reveals its hideous face. Over dinner in her home, Tessa suddenly turns to Carina and makes a spiteful, vulgar jibe about what our children would look like.

I say nothing. While a shocked Carina rages back at her sister, I fold my napkin, rise and walk out of the door. The reality of who I am, who Carina is, and the always-present undercurrent of prejudice in England converge at this moment to give me a sobering glimpse of the odds against our relationship ever being accepted and celebrated. Yet I am in love, and so is Carina, and nothing will divert us from love's all-powerful embrace at this point. We're thrilled to be back in each other's arms.

However, after some weeks, there are pressing issues that I have to face back on Barbados. Carina urges me to stay. 'I'm afraid for us, if you go back, Noel… afraid for you, and what might happen. Look, I have enough money to support both of us. Don't worry about that. Just sell your house and the club as soon as possible.'

'Darling, I've never lived off anyone in my whole life. I have millions of dollars at stake back on the island. Why don't you come back there with me, until I can get this settled? They won't harass me if you are there. They are too afraid of your family connections, I am sure.'

'I'm sorry, Noel, but I can't go back there. I don't want to get in the middle of all that horrible corruption and whatever they are doing to you. Stay.'

'I can't. But I do understand. Once I get things straight there, I promise that I will move back here to London and we will get married.'

'I want to believe you, Noel. I really do.'

So I fly southwards a few days later, across the Atlantic, into the heart of my native Caribbean, and lurking inside me is a phantom of unhappiness and dread. Over the next months, that phantom will become as real and sharp as a steel blade. It is honed by a series of articles that appear in the English press, in the gossip columns. There is an item in Nigel Dempster's column, complete with photo, of Carina arm in arm with the actor Al Pacino. What hurts even more is the information that the 'couple' have been out on the town with Dot and Barry. If anyone knew how much I had suffered over Alex's betrayal, it was Dot. Now this item in the *Daily Mail*.

Then a few weeks later there is an item about Carina with another actor. Then another. And another. Then I read in William Hickey:

David and the Duke's Daughter

The ambitions of David Frost have gone too far this time. The zealous Frostie, who has curried favour with the likes of the exiled Shah of Iran, the shamed Richard Nixon and the narked Henry Kissinger, has found a new dynasty to mix himself up in.

It is the Duke of Norfolk's.

Frostie's most recent escort is the beautiful Lady Carina Fitzalan-Howard, 28, the Duke's eldest daughter. At the weekend he could be seen weak-kneed and currying favour with the grand old Duke himself. Says Carina – known to friends as Keeks – 'It's a stop-start sort of relationship. It's very hard for it to be on a regular basis when we're in different parts of the world. I've known David for about five years.'

Despite their differences – Frost was born to a modest Methodist family and the Duke is the head of the Roman Catholic Church as well as our premier peer – David is definitely approved of by His Grace. After all, Keeks' former lover was a Barbadian – divorced nightclub owner Noel Charles, 39. The Duke did not approve. And – as proved last week in the Education Bill – the Duke will not allow even a prime minister to come in his way.

I cannot let on just how I feel – I feel crushed – but I do not say anything. The only thing that has sustained me since I started going through the nightmares on Barbados has been Carina. I truly believe that she is waiting for me to sort out my problems and move back to London, to marry me and live together happily ever after. Still, when I do ring her as usual, and casually mention the article, she says, 'Oh, that, I know darling. I read all that rubbish. Don't worry. You know how horrible the press can be.'

Eventually, after months with the newspapers full of Carina's romantic adventures, I start dating on Barbados. Nothing serious, but not a deep secret either. I take a girl, a Swedish model named Ann Sophie, along on a visit to Mustique where we stay with Mark and Fiona. At breakfast one morning, Ann blurts out some remark about missing her period, wondering if she is pregnant. I don't have any evidence that Fiona reported this back to London. (The girl's not pregnant it turns out.) But within a week of our visit, the London newspapers are full of news about Carina's marriage to David Frost. I feel like I have been slammed against a wall, or hit with a knockout punch. There has been no warning, not a word. And there never will be an apology.

Lost and Found

My life is all loose ends. Of course, some knots take longer to unravel, but others fly loose in the blink of an eye. What I once thought was solid – my business, my home, my friends – have now become so insubstantial that I wonder if it was all a dream. The actual events of this period – of these years – are difficult to recall in exact sequence. At times I feel as if my house is made of pain and tears. At other times, I remember that my house is only as real as my life. My house is wherever I live in the world. The point is to live. Funny how the older I get and the more experience I gain the living never gets any easier.

After Carina, my days on Barbados are numbered. It takes me a long time to realise this, but it's a fact. I have begun living in the spare room of a friend's house in order to avoid the police harassment, the telephoned threats. I keep the club open. My brother Courtenay and I have become close again. He offers to look after the club while I escort his wife Marion and her friend Lorraine to Trinidad for Carnival. Also attending this year will be Mick and Jerry Jagger, who love the event. I get us all backstage passes to the competitions and we put up in the Hilton.

The weirdness starts at a moment of great joy. My friend Sparrow is crowned the King of Calypso. Marion, Lorraine and I are caught up on a wave of euphoric happiness, dancing through the streets. Suddenly, Marion freezes in place, terror knocking the smile off her face.

'What is it?'

'I just saw the most awful man, absolutely terrifying, his face all painted red. If looks could kill, Noel, you would be dead. The way he was staring at you was so hateful!'

I turn and scan the crowd, but there's no sign of this man. 'Well, he's gone. Forget about him, Marion.' But as we continue through the crowded streets, neither woman can relax, and keep looking back over their shoulders fearfully.

'Noel, look out!' Marion screams.

It's too late but enough of a warning to make me dodge the full force of the large Coke bottle the madman swings onto my head. It glances off, and I am staggered, but I see the red glare of murder in those eyes – eyes that look deeply familiar. The bottle shatters. Without thinking, I take off running. I weave and push my way through the crowd, aware of the blood pouring down my face and neck. I run until I turn a corner and head up a narrow alley, full of rubbish. I run to the end, where I am trapped. I do not hear any footsteps behind me. Good thing, because he would surely kill me in this dead end. Who is trying to kill me? I have a strong feeling I know who this is, but the laws of libel (since he is never caught or charged) forbid me from naming him in this book.

In any case, after waiting ten minutes or so, I leave the alley and make straight for the hotel, fearing I will be ambushed the entire way back. Once I'm through the lobby, I head up to Mick and Jerry's suite.

'Noel, what happened to you?' Mick asks. I tell him. 'You are bleeding everywhere, man.'

'Mick, you've got to take him to a hospital,' insists Jerry. And within minutes, we grab a taxi in front of the hotel.

In the ER, Mick causes quite a stir among the staff and patients, but he ensures that I soon get treatment. I am sitting on a table having my head stitched up by a young doctor when a vaguely familiar face pushes around the corner. It's Janice, a girl from my childhood, the girl upon whom I had the biggest crush of my boyhood, now the hospital's in-house pharmacist. 'My God, it is you Noel. I haven't seen you in so many years. And what have they done to you?' She takes my face in her soft hands and stares at the wound.

I explain the sudden and terrifying assault to her. She listens and then says, 'Did you know my father is Minister of State for Trinidad, Noel. You wait right here. I am going to call him.'

When she comes back a few minutes later, she says, 'They are going to manhunt him and catch him. And when we do, that man is gone. You rest easy, because he's gone, honey.'

But I could not rest easy, not for a very long time, as I kept recalling those murderous eyes in the red-painted face, those familiar eyes that wanted to kill me on that first morning of Carnival. As it is, I spend the rest of the festival in a very dark mood and am pleased when I can take Marion and Lorraine back to Barbados.

During these painful months after Carina's marriage, one of the people I become closest to is a wonderful woman named Maxie Kindersely. We're just friends, but our friendship is based on a mutual unhappiness about the current state of our personal lives. (Maxie is going through an unwelcome separation from her husband.) We spend many evenings sitting and drinking together at the Great Table, trying to figure out what went awry in our love lives. I often have dinner at her Oliver Messel-designed colonial home on the island, and I become good friends with her two sons: Robin and Kim. Just before they return to London, we agree a plan for me to meet them in England soon.

A few weeks later in London, we spend an evening at my friend Johnny Gold's nightclub Tramp. When Kim arranges to meet his friend Julian Lennon in the club, I brace myself for a weird evening. It's less than a year since John Lennon's murder, and Julian is only 18 years old. I can't imagine how he is coping with his grief, but Kim has told me that Julian is under a lot of pressure from various sources to exploit his legacy and that is the last thing he wants to do. I steel myself as we head down the stairs into the competitive spotlight that I know Tramp can be for any celebrity, a place that is often full of recording industry executives.

Julian joins us at our table. He's a modest, intelligent and sensitive young man who is keenly aware of his surroundings at all times. His physical resemblance to his father is uncanny.

I can't help thinking about that afternoon almost a year earlier at Sandy Lane on Barbados. I had been having a drink with Paul Simon and Art Garfunkel on the terrace above the beach, when a waiter approached and told Paul there was a call for him at the front desk. When he returned, Paul's face was ashen white. 'We have to get back to New York right away,' he told Art.

'What's wrong?'

'John Lennon's been killed, shot right outside the Dakota. I live there too, Noel.'

'My God, that's terrible. Who shot him?'

'Some kid. A crazy kid. Art, let's finish these drinks and see about getting the first flight back north.'

Now, here is Lennon's son, the visible survivor of that horrible tragedy, pulling his chair closer to our table.

Sure enough, as soon as he is recognised around the room, I start to have visitors, table-hopping big shots who whisper in my ear. 'Hey man, if you can get me connected with the kid, I guarantee you'll make half a million.' One after the other, they approach me, bidding on Julian as if he was a prime steer at a livestock auction. I am disgusted, and start to shake my head as people try to approach our table, waving them away.

We manage to have a good time, however, joking around the table and doing a fair share of drinking. Before we part, I say, 'Julian, I'm sorry about all the sharks in here tonight. I can imagine how it must be for you right now. If you ever feel like getting away, I've got a house in Barbados where you can stay, and a nightclub to party in. You're very welcome to come down at any time.'

My visit passes all too quickly as I do the rounds of restaurants and clubs in the London I love, and I fly back to Barbados feeling much more cheerful than when I left it. A week passes and I get a call from Kim. 'Look, Noel, you remember what you said to Julian? He wonders if you were serious.'

'Of course I was.'

'OK, good. Is there room for me and Julian's friend Reg to stay as well?'

'You know there is always room for you guys.'

'Well, the three of us were thinking of flying down rather soon.'

'Tomorrow won't be soon enough.'

'A couple of days actually.'

So it was that I pick the three chums up from the airport a few days later and drive them back to my house. When we arrive, I ask Julian if he needs anything.

'You know it would be great if you had a piano here.'

'That's no problem at all. I'll hire one in for you and get it delivered down here this afternoon.'

We all change and head down to the beach for some serious sun and relaxation. A few hours pass, and we head back to Sunset Lodge. The piano is installed in my sitting room, but instead of playing it, Julian offers to play us a tape he's recorded of four of his own songs. I am more than impressed. He has a major talent. The songs are fantastic and he sings them in a powerful voice that echoes his father's in a way that is both inspiring and almost spiritual.

That evening in the club, I ask Julian if he has any desire to seriously pursue a musical career. He says that he does, but I sense his reservations about not wanting to appear to be 'cashing in' on his father's life, and tragedy.

'I am not a music industry expert, but I have some good friends who I trust with my life who could help you. Not like those guys in Tramp. I am thinking of my old friend Lee Hazlewood. He's been around the block, knows everyone, and is completely honest. He would make sure that you could control your own destiny. If you want to talk to him, I can give him a ring and he might fly down. You two could talk. I don't want to be involved as a middleman or anything, not in any way. I am your friend and that's all I want to be, ever. Do you want me to give him a call?'

Julian says that yes he would like to meet Lee. So the next day I give Hazlewood a ring at his home in LA. I tell him that Julian is very shy, and very talented, and doesn't want to be exploited in any way. 'I understand, Noel. I would love to meet him and hear his songs. In the meantime, do you mind if I make a couple of calls to see what the level of interest is out there in the shark pool?'

'No, go ahead, but be discreet. I don't want any of those people showing up down here.'

'Absolutely. I'll ring you later.'

Some hours later, Lee rings me. 'Wow, it's a feeding frenzy. I have a solid offer on the table from someone whom I trust. And there are lots of others, whom I don't trust, who might offer the same money or more. Should I come down and meet Julian, talk it over with him?'

'Yes, now's a good time. He's relaxing and coming out of himself down here, and I trust you to give him good advice.'

When Lee arrives with his girlfriend Linda a few days later, I put them in the guestroom next to the one Julian is sharing with Reg, his oldest friend. I decide to make no effort to introduce the subject of business, but just to let nature take its course while we're all enjoying this house party. I assume that Lee and Julian will get a chance to talk at some point. Ten days pass, and Lee informs me that he has hardly spoken a word with Julian.

'He is very shy, and he is just 18 years old, and has had a very rough time,' I tell Lee. 'If he doesn't want to talk, that's his gut telling him to be cautious. He's a very intelligent kid and, by the way, a great waterskier. Did you see him today?'

Soon afterwards Lee and his girlfriend head off to Stockholm. Julian, Kim and Reg end up staying for almost two months. They learn to waterski and have lots of great days and nights out all around the island. I am pleased to see that Julian looks far happier when I drop them off at the airport than he did when I collected him.

It's been a wonderful visit, and the start of a friendship that I will cherish for the rest of my life.

Still, I am getting harassment from the police. The club seems more trouble than it is worth now that my brother Courtenay has returned to London. When I get another out-of-the-blue phone threat reminding me that 'we do hang people on this island', plus an encounter with a psychotic German who invades my house one morning with a gun, accusing me of sleeping with his girlfriend (true enough I had, years before, long before she met him), I close the club and put Sunset Lodge on the market. Before very long, I have sold it, so eager to sell that I accept a ridiculously low price. The money is very welcome, but I have failed to realise an important fact. I cannot take any of the money off the island. I take off for Mustique where I have been told I can stay in Mick's Jagger's cabin anytime I want. Basil and I work a temporary deal whereby he uses my money to buy supplies on Barbados, then reimburses me on Mustique with money I can bank.

My relationship with Mick and the other Rolling Stones goes back more than a decade now. Mick has been a long-standing regular at the Great Table on Barbados. The Stones 'bad boy' image has been contrived, to some extent, but it isn't entirely fictitious. In particular, I recall one night out on the town with Mick on Barbados. This was the night I introduced him to Richard Pryor, who was 'visiting' the island, in the same sense that hurricanes 'visit' you. It was late, but not that late. Richard was doing his usual money and poker riffs, and keeping us all laughing uproariously. I suggested that we head down to Slim's, an after-hours club where some of the best local musicians put on late night jams.

'What the hell is Slim's?' Richard demanded.

'It's a club called the Belair down on Bay Street, owned by a guy called Slim,' said Mick. 'There's a great trumpet player named Ernie Small who will blow you away.'

'Hell, yes, let's go to Slim's. What are we wasting time for in a dive like this?' Richard declared, leaping to his feet. 'Right, Noel?'

'Hey, I am the one who suggested we go to Slim's, right?'

The joint was jumping when we arrived, literally, with the old wooden floorboards rattling up and down as a sea of dancing bodies work out their troubles and passions to the sounds of the tight calypso-jazz band. We took our drinks up into the rickety balcony so we could watch the action. 'Hey, what's that across the street?' Richard asked. 'Mick, just look at all those pretty women. How come we aren't over there with them?'

'That's the Coco Cabana,' I told Richard.

'Is that what I think it is?'

'Come on then, you'll see,' Mick said.

We crossed the street, with Richard waving and smiling at all the girls who were laughing at him from the front porch and the windows. Inside, Richard immediately ordered drinks for everybody. He flashed his usual huge roll of dollars and it took about two minutes before he was surrounded by women. Within 15 minutes, Richard and Mick both disappeared into the 'henhouse' out back.

I had no intention of following them, but ordered another drink at the bar. Then I felt small arms grasp me around the waist from behind. I turned to discover Rosita, a sweet little Dominican girl whom I had first met five years ago in Trinidad. Like many pretty girls from her impoverished island, Rosita had become a whore in order to support her family. I had met her in a restaurant one morning after a night of partying in Port of Spain, and had ended up buying her breakfast. Our relationship was never sexual, but more like older brother – little sister. I had no idea that she was on Barbados. So I bought her a drink to keep the management happy, and we sat down to talk. After an hour of catching up, I was feeling exhausted and didn't want to interfere with Rosita's commercial prospects any longer, so I gave her my phone number and told her to ring soon. Then I walked out to the back and shouted into the henhouse 'I don't know where you guys are, but if you aren't here in five minutes, you can find your own way home.'

To my surprise, both Mick and Richard appeared in less than five minutes. 'Let's stop for breakfast at my place,' Mick suggested.

'Where's your place, man?' Richard asked.

'On the beach next to Sandy Lane. Come on, it's got everything. Noel, you're driving, I presume.'

It didn't take us very long to reach Mick's – the Warner's house at Jane's Harbour. Soon we were in the kitchen putting together all the necessary components of a great tropical breakfast, when Richard came back from a prowl around the house.

'You weren't kidding, Mick. You sure got *everything* you need in this place. Including that pretty maid.'

'What are you talking about?' Mick asked.

'Well, I took a peek in one of the bedrooms and there was a real beautiful motherfucker of a woman sleeping in there, man. I just assumed she was your maid.'

Mick stared at him, then said, 'That's no maid, that's Bianca!' He threw the eggs he was cooking right up in the air and they landed on the floor. 'Now look what you made me do. I have to crack some more eggs, you lunatic.' What more could he say to Richard Pryor, a man who always saw the world from his own hilarious perspective?

'You got any freshly squeezed vodka to go with this freshly squeezed juice?' was all Richard had to say.

It was just one of many memories of good times from the past, but it was one of my favourites.

The first person I seek out on Mustique is Basil, of course. And this time I find him in a foul mood, perhaps the worst mood I have ever seen in a man whom I know so well and often think of as a kind of brother. He tells me that his girlfriend, Lady Virginia Royston, with whom he has been for nine years, has suddenly left him for another man.

The romance between Basil and Lady Royston – who had married Philip Viscount Royston, the heir to the Earl of Hardwicke, after herself being Debutant of the Year in 1959, only to be widowed after just three years – was one of the British tabloid's favourite romances during the 1960s. A great beauty with a fearless streak of independence, she had moved her two young children to live on Mustique. Her exploits were as legendary as the life of the perpetual party inside Basil's Bar. Indeed, Basil was so close to her two children that he escorted the elder son back to England for his first day at prep school. Later, once British society had accepted their liaison, the couple danced together at a ball given in the Queen's honour, but of course there was always a hidden racist condescension towards Basil. For my part, I had also become very fond of her two children, and the four of them had often been guests at Sunset Lodge over the years. On one of these occasions, in fact, after Basil had quarrelled with Colin Tennant, I had put together the strategy by which Basil eventually bought control of his bar. Before this he had been operating without any real rights, and was threatening to quit the island. I had convinced him to go back and fight for his rights. So, too, Basil had often given me emotional support over these difficult years.

Now he tells me that Virginia has fallen for a local man named Eddie Boom, an employee of Basil's. The two have gone off to live in a tenement on Mustique. Her two children are off at boarding school in England. Basil is distraught. I tell him to get away from the whole scene, take a long vacation, and I will run the bar while he's gone. He thinks it over for an hour or so, then comes and thanks me. Yes, he agrees that the best thing to do will be to get away from this island for a while.

My life settles down over the next few months. Mustique is only five miles long and three miles wide: you can walk around it in a few hours. The handful of residents are very wealthy, very private people like Princess Margaret, Sir Mick Jagger, Contessa Idana Pucci of the Italian design house and lingerie designer Janet Reger. Above all, of course, there is the island's owner: Lord Glenconner, Colin Tennant.

There are no nightclubs on the island, and I am usually in bed far earlier than in my old life. I open the bar as the morning sun warms the beach. Sometimes in the mornings I open the door of Mick's small, pink two-bedroom cottage straight onto the beach, wearing my dressing gown, to confront a gang of tourists off some yacht who are hoping for a glimpse of the rock star.

In fact, after a month or so, Mick, Jerry and his parents do arrive for a visit. Basil returns from his holiday, and I move in with him. I decide to throw a lunch party for them at Macaroni Bay, with the guest of honour being Princess Margaret, whom I gather is still miffed at me for refusing to go 'walkies'. I'm hoping this will pour some oil on the waters, and she does turn up, the last guest to arrive.

She is seated directly across from me, but refuses to speak a single word during the entire meal. Oh well, despite her frosty demeanour, I have made the effort and she has met me halfway.

One of the other guests at this party is a handsome French aristocrat named Arnaud de Rosnay, who has been brought along by Janet Reger. As well as being a *Vogue* photographer and the heir to a Mauritian sugar fortune, Arnaud is one of the world's foremost windsurfers. He was the first man to have windsurfed across the Bering Strait between Alaska and Siberia, and he tells me about how a Soviet submarine had followed him most of the way across the freezing cold straits, dodging ice floes, on a specially modified board. When he reached the Chukchi Peninsular, he saw a large contingent of the Red Army waiting for his arrival on the shore. He was, of course, frightened out of his wits as he dragged his sail and board to shore. Then he saw they were all holding cameras and taking snapshots. That night he had to drink endless toasts in vodka with his new Russian friends. (Sadly, Arnaud would die a couple of years later, lost at sea, attempting to windsurf from Taiwan to China.) Listening to his stories makes me yearn to try the sport for myself.

I know just the guy to teach me: David Greison, a Canadian who is staying on the island and who goes out on his board every day. He agrees, and so I spend three days falling into the water, going to bed with aching shoulders and arms, before I finally get the hang of it. It is more strenuous than it looks, and two hours of windsurfing is about all I can manage. However, it is more fun than it looks too, and makes all the exertion worthwhile.

On my fourth day, having mastered the board (ha ha), David tells me that he will leave me to my own devices. He'll alert Eddie Boom – Lady Royston's new lover – who drives the speedboat at the beach, to keep an eye out for me in case I get into trouble. 'You see where those ripples are out there?' he says pointing down across the beach. 'That's where the wind really picks up strong. Avoid that area. If you do get out there and get into trouble, just sit down and wave at Eddie. He'll come out and pick you up.'

Naturally, as soon as I am alone, I head straight out to the ripples. The wind fills the sail and suddenly it sends me flying, right into the drink. No big deal. I haul myself up and try to pull up the sail. This time it's different, however, as the wind is much stronger. I try and try, and all the while I am being carried further out. I give up and sit down and wave in the direction of Basil's Bar, but it is just a dot on the white ribbon of sand. Within a few minutes, the island itself has grown miniscule. Within an hour, all I can see is water, in every direction.

I simply have to sit there and wait. Too bored to be scared, I begin examining with distaste all the rubbish floating in the supposedly 'empty' sea. I have no idea that I am now riding the Gulf Stream, on my way to South America. However, I do notice that the swells begin to rise. Soon I am straddling the board, coasting up and down the sides of huge waves, unafraid, but increasingly uneasy. Surely by now Eddie will have noticed that I have gone missing and soon I will hear the outboard motor and see him racing to my rescue.

Another hour, perhaps more, passes. Then I do hear something besides the wind. It is the low thud-thud of an inboard diesel engine. I catch sight of a mast with a black flag on the top, then a wave blocks it. Another minute, and suddenly the fishing boat is alongside me. 'What you doin out here, man?' shouts a guy.

'Windsurfing.'

'Windsurfing, man? We does catch the big man eatin fish out here, you know? You want a lift back?'

'Yes, please.'

It is only during the long journey back to the island that I begin to fully comprehend what danger I faced, how very far out to sea I have been. When I tell them to drop me at their fishing village, which is just a few hundred yards from Basil's bar, they agree.

Eddie Boom is standing near the speedboat when we arrive back, and one look at his face brings the gravity of the situation home. He looks terrified. I have left my sunglasses, cigarettes and a wallet with two hundred dollars in the boat. I go to retrieve it.

'Noel, I just heard what happened. So sorry, man. I was keeping an eye, but then I got a call and had to go meet Lady Royston at the airport. I am really sorry, Noel.'

I just nod, knowing that Eddie really doesn't like me since he considers me one of Basil's best friends. I go out to the fishing boat and empty my wallet for them – two hundred dollars – that's what my life is worth now. 'If I had more, I would give it to you. Thank you, gentlemen, for saving my life.'

They seem pleased with their 'catch' now, and after cautioning me to keep my windsurfing a lot closer to shore, they chug off towards the fishing harbour.

One of my best friends on Mustique and St Vincent is Danny the Cowboy Pilot. We play lots of backgammon, and Danny allows me to tag along as his 'co-pilot' on his frequent circuits around the islands: from St Vincent to Grenada, or St Lucia, sometimes stopping by Barbados, or all the way up to St Barts. Danny brings in the supplies for Basil's Bar, and other little businesses that Basil has working. He is a born pilot, whose dramatic take-offs and landings are legendary. He knows how to skim just above the tops of the coconut trees, and start banking towards his destination with the wheels barely off the runway.

One day he takes Basil and me north to Martinique to meet Isabel, a model whom I first met on Barbados some years earlier. We are planning to spend the night on the French island, with an excursion to the casino. Basil needs to purchase more wine and French cheese for the bar. Isabel will accompany us back to Mustique the next morning. We have a very good dinner and then head off to the gambling tables. I start with roulette, but begin to lose steadily. Out of restlessness and frustration, I turn my back on the table and put down some chips on the nearby blackjack layout. After about 20 minutes, I notice there is a huge commotion on the roulette table.

'Look at this. They don't know whose chips they are on black – but black keeps hitting!'

There is a huge pile of chips on black. Jesus, it's mine! I forgot that I had left that little pile on black, and now it's doubled up into a small fortune. Before they can spin the wheel another time, I scoop up all the chips. Good thing too, because the ball falls on a red number!

The next day we all do some clothes shopping thanks to my roulette windfall. Once we board the small plane and are aloft and on course, Danny asks Basil if he would sit in the co-pilot's seat, while he gets into a backgammon game with me. He's already deep in debt to me, and constantly wants to play to see if he can't recoup some of his losses. He never thinks of calling it quits.

'Look at this, Danny!' shouts Basil. Straight in front of us is a massive black thunderhead, a huge tropical storm with a white spot in the middle.

'Just steer us into the white part of it,' Danny says, rolling the dice, lost in the game.

'What is this, the eye of a hurricane or something?' I say. And the next thing we know the plane is out of control, juddering violently, feeling like it is coming apart at the seams. Danny lunges for the throttle and pulls Basil aside, then throws us into a power dive, dropping thousands of feet in seconds until, just above the water, he pulls the nose up and level. The rest of us are on the ceiling. I think we must be upside-down. I can see the flesh on Isabel's cover-girl face stretched into a G-force contortion. The rain is like a solid wall on every side; visibility is zero. How the hell is he going to get out of this storm, let alone find our way back to the island?

Of course, Danny the Cowboy Pilot gets us home safely.

Basil and I share the same last name: Charles. I really think we are brothers, with a bond thick as blood, brothers of the spirit. We have a relationship based on mutual respect and the same zest for life, I think at the time. Years later, I hear that Basil has said a number of unpleasant things about me, and that he was even jealous of me, but certainly at the time he was a great friend to me.

It's a small island and I spend a lot of time feeling lonely. Isabel's visit is a great respite, but she is one of the world's busiest models and soon must fly back to Europe and New York. One day I have an unprovoked flash of memory about a Canadian girl I spent some lovely times with, years before I ever met Carina, on Barbados. Her name is Victoria, and we had first been introduced by Courtenay Devenish, who married her sister Lee. We've kept in touch a bit over the years, and seen one another a couple of times, and her mother even came down one winter for a visit. So this afternoon, on impulse, I call her number in Toronto. I invite her to come down to Mustique.

'Noel, I was just thinking about you! And wondering how I was going to get out of this dreary Toronto weather. I would love to come down and see you.'

We have a fairy-tale fling when she comes, in such an idyllic setting that it would be impossible not to get along. She stays for two weeks. All my real problems disappear while she is there, so that within a day after she's gone I am feeling very low indeed, with the problems in my life starting to rush back to fill the void. The truth is, I am like a man who is stuck on a desert island. Mustique is a little paradise, but it is a very, very small island, and I feel trapped on it. I want to get my life moving, and yet I see no clear direction in which to move. So I do what I have always done – which is to follow my gut – and I make a telephone call that, in retrospect, is more of a reaction to my present circumstances than it is a genuine response to the feelings in my heart. I telephone Victoria in Toronto.

'Do you think you would ever want to marry me?'

'Noel, what are you asking?'

'Will you marry me?'

'Oh, Noel, of course I will marry you. I never, ever thought you would ask me this. I mean I never dreamed you would want to get married again. But, yes, I do love you and I would love to marry you.'

Thing is, even as I hear her words, I know that I am not in love with Victoria. I know what I am yearning for is a change, any change almost. I want to find a new safe harbour – a place to feel secure from which to launch a new life.

'It feels right to me,' I tell her.

Of course, I cannot get married until I obtain a legal divorce from Alexandra, whom I call straight away in Stockholm. We are on friendly terms again, as enough time has passed to allow us to talk openly and directly. She is still running 'our' nightclub, with a new partner, and doing very well, although the venue has moved to a new location at the Stockholm Plaza. When I tell her that I want to get a divorce because I am engaged to someone else, she reacts calmly, and promises to help. Within a week of first calling, I realise that she has far more on her mind than getting a divorce, and that if I want to expedite this, I will have to fly to Sweden. When I suggest it, Alexandra cheerfully agrees that it is probably the best plan, and invites me to stay with her.

It's not long before I am back in the city where I first made a real name for myself – glorious Stockholm, so full of people I like, food I love to eat, memories I will always cherish. Within a few hours of my arrival, I find myself working in Alexandra's again, at my ex-wife's invitation. Although no longer mine in any legal sense, I will always feel it's my creation and a part of my destiny. As often happens with married couples who share a lot of history, Alex and I now find that we get along better than we did for years when we were married. During my stay, while I am busy pushing through the legal papers that will result in our divorce, I spend my nights mixing with the guests in the club, and helping to oversee the operations.

When Rod Stewart cancels a big party in the club at the last minute, his people call back to reserve the piano bar for later that evening. Can we make sure that the bar is staffed with beautiful blondes, as Rod will very much appreciate this? I let them know that I am not a model agency or a pimp, but Alex doesn't blink an eye and ensures that some of Stockholm's prettiest girls will be working that night. As it turns out, Ronnie Wood is one of the guests, and we make a deal to host an exhibition of Ronnie's paintings in the club a few weeks later. That, too, is a success. However, I can't keep my old managerial curiosity completely under control and ask Alex if the bills for these parties have been paid on time and in full. She gives me a vague answer, so later I check the books in the office and see that both parties have been hosted gratis. Well, it's all very familiar stuff, and used to drive Tom and me insane, but now it's not my worry. It's Alex's new partner's worry.

As soon as the divorce decree comes through, without any major hassles, I am off to Toronto, where Victoria is waiting for me at the airport. After a kind of passionate pre-marital 'honeymoon' in the early spring of 1984, we are officially married at the City Hall in Toronto, with a reception held at her aunt's house.

I am going to compress the months of my marriage to Victoria into the next few pages, for I don't believe there is any point in putting a failed relationship, that probably was never meant to happen, under the microscope. Let me hasten to say that I accept my full share of responsibility for this failure.

I married knowing that I was not really in love. I was at a very difficult point in my life, with very little money, and no real wish to suddenly take an 'ordinary' job as a salesman or bartender (although I was willing to work at that level when financially necessary). What I desperately wanted was to get back into the nightclub business, but Toronto was a long way from my friends and contacts in Stockholm and Barbados. Right from the start I was unable to provide the financial security that Victoria had assumed she would gain from marriage to me. On the other hand, her reaction was not what I would have ever predicted, not from the sweet and reasonable girl I had known in the islands. She had a very sharp tongue, and a weak head for alcohol, which soon combined with my own stubborn, confident nature to turn our lives into a nasty domestic battleground. The fights never became physical, but they were extremely unpleasant.

I had married someone I hardly knew, except for a few scattered weeks of blissful holiday romance. In many ways, our marriage was a disaster, but something very good and precious did come from it. Our daughter Chloe was conceived a few months after we were married. The pregnancy period became increasingly acrimonious, with Victoria's resentment towards me extending to all the men in her life. She was determined to have a natural birth and I duly accompanied her to regular Lamaze classes. I was trying to get various nightclub and entertainment projects together but all to no avail.

The birth of our daughter on 24 May 1985 lifted both Victoria and I into a blissful period, bringing out the best in both of us. The bickering and fighting ended and I really lost myself in the joyous exhaustion of new fatherhood. Even changing nappies and walking the baby after her 2 a.m. feed seemed a wonderful change from what had gone on before in our marriage. This period lasted for about six months. Then, inevitably, we were back on the same domestic battlefield. Above all, we were desperately short of cash. Victoria's job had ended with the birth and, while I was receiving occasional funds from Basil as he restocked his bar in Barbados, this was not enough to keep us secure and happy.

Out of the blue, I was the subject of a profile in the Toronto Star. *The reporter was, he soon confessed, also representing a London tabloid which had offered big bucks if I would dish the dirt on the Royals, Carina, and other celebrities I had known over the years. He mentioned a very substantial sum. I refused, without any hesitation. He was stunned, and wondered why I wouldn't talk in return for enough money to turn my life around at that point. 'Because my life is my house, and I still have to live in it – long after this article is published.'*

Seeing his vision of a huge payday vanish in a second, the journalist decided, at least, to write an article for the same newspaper which would justify the time spent in our meeting. In fact, he must have liked me, for he wrote a very flattering profile. Two days after it was published, an editor from the paper rang and said, 'Our switchboard has been taking dozens of calls about you. People are trying to reach you and want to talk about your business plans, want to see if you can help them promote their own. A lot of these calls are from people who say they know you. You've just arrived in Toronto, so how do you know so many Canadians?'

I explained that I had hosted many Canadians at my club in Barbados. I had also worked with Air Canada, Fiesta Tours and Sunquest Tours. 'OK, can you give us a telephone number where we can tell these people they'll be able to reach you?'

I gave him my number, and was soon having conversations with many old acquaintances and with people who had ideas for new projects with which they thought I might be able to help. I also was invited to do a TV interview on a morning programme on CBLT. I accepted, with the condition that no questions would be asked about Carina or Princess Margaret. As it turned out, the woman who interviewed me on live TV was a notorious sourpuss, who opened her questioning with, 'What makes you think you can come to Toronto and open the best nightclub? Who do you think you are?'

I must have gone into a trance, for I have no memory of what I said after that, but apparently I remained calm and handled myself reasonably well. The consensus of opinion was that I had done just fine with 'the Dragon Lady' and, since I really had blacked out the whole experience, I had to take people's word for it.

At this point, I found myself in a very frustrating position. The publicity that I had just gained was worth thousands of dollars, and I was being deluged with questions about 'when is your new club opening?' Sitting in the bank in Barbados, I had more than enough start-up capital. There were now several people keen to go into partnership with me Unfortunately, I just couldn't get my hands on that money in the Caribbean. Or could I? The more I thought about it, the more I wanted to believe that there must be a way.

I told Victoria that I needed to go down and meet with Basil in Mustique and see if we couldn't work a deal that would allow me to access my money. She didn't seem pleased, but she didn't protest. Not at that time, but a couple of nights after I arrived on Mustique, the phone rang in Basil's bar (very odd, since the phone system was usually shut down after 10 p.m. on the island) and it was an operator on St Vincent saying she had an urgent call for Noel Charles.

Victoria was in the worst rage I'd ever known (which is saying something – no doubt she'd been drinking). She never wanted to see me again. I would never see my daughter again. She was going to throw all my clothes down the incinerator chute the moment after she hung up. She hung up. I turned to my friends in the bar, who had been able to hear every word she'd shouted down the phone line. 'It sounds like my marriage is over'. Without telling me, she had also contacted the immigration authorities and withdrawn her sponsorship of my visa application. Without that I would not be able to work in Canada.

I flew back to Toronto shortly afterwards, but stayed with friends. When I went by the apartment to salvage what was left of my belongings, taking a friend along as a buffer, my daughter Chloe was not there, having been sent to Victoria's mother's house. I was desperately sad but, I suppose, at least I was spared the agony of a tearful farewell. It would be a long time before I saw my daughter again.

What was I going to do? Where was my next destination? My life had gone from bad to worse, and now there were more people – like Chloe – who were suffering as a direct result. The guilt I felt did not help, nor did my feelings of loneliness, anger and isolation.

While I had been in Sweden arranging my divorce, I had renewed an old friendship with a Swedish woman named Boel, whom I hadn't seen since my early days on Barbados. When we first met, she had been working as a Pan Am stewardess and used to come to Alexandra's during its first months. However, during one of her stays on the island, she suddenly announced that she was engaged to marry a wealthy New Yorker, and probably wouldn't be coming to the island again for a long time. I didn't see her again until I ran into her on a Stockholm street, and we had exchanged numbers. Shortly thereafter, she had rung me to say that her husband had just been diagnosed with a very serious illness, and needed a liver transplant.

Over the next year or so, Boel and I kept in touch via the telephone as we each went through our own versions of emotional hell: me in Toronto, her in New York City. We had become confidants, so when I next talked to her and explained my dire situation in Toronto, she said, 'Noel, why don't you come down to New York for a while. We've got plenty of money, but that's all we've got. I would be happy to help you start getting your career back on track. Maybe New York is the city you have been destined for all along? I mean this. Keep it in mind, please.'

I was working on one last possible deal in Toronto, with a railway entrepreneur, but when he abruptly changed the terms in his favour (thanks to an intervention by Victoria behind my back) I knew that I was finished in that city.

I called Boel and she immediately offered to buy a ticket for me and to have a place for me to stay waiting in New York. Three days later, I was picked up at La Guardia Airport by her car and driver, handed an envelope full of cash and driven to the Barbizon Hotel on the Upper East Side where a suite was reserved in my name. 'OK, Lady Liberty,' I thought to myself, 'here is another one of the tired, poor, huddled masses yearning to breathe free. Please smile down on me in your tough city.'

Wow, what a change in lifestyle. While Boel was usually occupied caring for her very ill husband, she introduced me to her friends – and I already had a number of friends in the city. The envelopes full of cash kept coming. I tried to discuss this with her, but she said, 'These are gifts, so please just accept them gracefully. I know you need to get out and move around until you find the right opportunity. You can't do that in New York unless you have some cash.' I wasn't comfortable with this, but in the past I had done the same kind of thing for many of my friends. I vowed to repay Boel in some special way once I was back in business.

I was living the high life again: eating in fine restaurants, going to plays on Broadway and discos to dance until dawn. One of my frequent companions was Kitty Shields, a theatrical agent and Brooke Shields' aunt, who would get us front row seats at most Broadway opening nights. We'd meet at the Zulu bar, catch a show and have a late supper. Kitty wasn't into late nights, so I would drop her off and afterwards head downtown to Nell's on 14th street.

Although from a distance, my life at the time would have appeared to be totally random hedonism, in fact I was working hard – networking, scouting, on the hunt for an opportunity.

The first real prospect that I encountered was just a couple of minutes stroll from the Barbizon Hotel. A block on East 58th Street, between Madison and Park, was being completely gentrified, with many chic European boutiques leasing space there. On the block was a bar with a tiny dance floor owned by a guy named Rudy, whom I liked to chat with when I dropped by for a casual drink. Rudy was hurting badly – one of his partners had run off with all his money. He was one step away from being evicted by his landlords. I could see the potential to turn the place into something special. It turned out that Kitty's sister knew the landlords, who owned most of the block. She arranged a meeting. I talked it over with Rudy, and he liked the idea of going ahead and re-launching his club, with me as his partner. However, when I met with the landlords, after they heard about my credentials and my plans, they said they had given Rudy all the breaks they could. If I wanted to proceed, they'd be happy to talk to me alone. Maybe, I sensed, there was something else going on, but couldn't quite understand it.

Then Rudy introduced me to a couple of his 'friends' and I understood immediately who their 'connections' were. They said they liked what they heard of my plans for the club, and that they could deal with the landlords, 'no problem'. These guys were tough, no nonsense, neighbourhood New Yorkers. They were offering to put up some money to finance us. I thought it over, and decided I had to pass. I remembered my days in the London clubs, when the Krays started muscling into the scene, and the subsequent disappearance of my friend Tony Michel. It might have been a sweet deal, but it was not the kind of foundation upon which I wanted to base my new life.

I had a number of good friends in New York, including Caroline Stewart and Wendy Sonnenberg, but one of the new friends I made during this period stands out in my mind. This was Joe Runner, a small, immaculately groomed man who had once dreamed of becoming an actor, but had ended up working for decades as a floor salesman in Brooks Brothers, the legendary menswear store on Madison Avenue. I was first introduced to him by my friend Chris from Toronto, and we had gone to Brooks Brothers to meet him at the end of the working day. From there, we went straight to Sardi's, the famous Broadway theatrical hangout. I was astonished when we entered. Almost every head in the place turned, hands waved and the non-stop chorus of 'Hi Joes' echoed in my ears long after we moved on to the next bar. I soon learned that Joe knew everybody in New York's theatrical district. He lived there, of course, and walking the Times Square area with him was literally taking a lap of honour through every bar, restaurant and theatre foyer. I began to hang out with him several times a week and was fascinated by his unique New York attitude, his dapper attire and his incredible energy. It was thanks to Joe that I met one of the most elusive and sought-after celebrities in the world, who happened to be Swedish.

'By the way, Noel, I mentioned your name to Greta Garbo and she said that she knows you,' Joe announced one evening when we were drinking in Sardi's.

'But I've never met her!' I said. 'How do you know Greta Garbo, Joe? Isn't she a recluse?'

'Yeah, sure, but she likes to buy her clothes at Brooks Brothers. I've been serving her for years. She won't speak to any of the other salesmen. If I'm with a customer, she waits until I'm free.'

'Why, does she wear men's clothes?'

Joe just shrugged.

Sure enough, a few months later, I went round late one afternoon to meet Joe, who was going to take me to the Hotel Algonquin and show me what was left of the old Round Table, where once the famous wits – Dorothy Parker, Robert Benchley, Thurber – of New Yorker magazine fame – had congregated nightly. I found him busy at the cash register. He nodded, finished the sale, and nodded me closer. 'Don't stare, but that woman by the neckties is Greta. You should go say hello.'

I was unconvinced, but decided to give it a try. I went to the table where hundreds of silk neckties were laid out on display and worked my way in the direction of the woman who was dressed in a wide brimmed hat, dark glasses and very tailored coat. How was I going to break the silence without being rude?

'Did Joe send you over here?' she asked suddenly. Her voice did have a discernable Swedish accent.

'No… er, yes.'

'You are the man who started Alexandra's nightclub in Stockholm, aren't you? I read the Swedish press and the articles about you and your club have always been interesting.'

'Thank you. I wish you had visited us. But it's not my club anymore.'

'Yes, it's a pity I never came to your club,' she said. Then Joe arrived on the scene and she turned her back to speak with him. That was the end of my acquaintance with Greta Garbo.

I was told later – typically not by Joe – about how this unique character had organised his own personal charity. Every summer he would round up a dozen or so kids from Hell's Kitchen on the west side of the theatre district and pay for them to take a two-week excursion to Algonquin Park in northern Ontario. Out of his own pocket, he would buy them all sleeping bags, camping gear, fishing equipment as well as their rail tickets. He also paid a couple of out-of-work actors to accompany the kids as their camp councillors. It wasn't something he ever talked about with me, but I guessed it wasn't a secret either.

After a time, Boel suggested that I move out of the Barbizon Hotel and into her and her husband's apartment on the East Side. 'We almost never use it now, since we are stuck in the Connecticut house where everything is set up like a hospital,' she told me. This naturally made my life even more comfortable, and I wished there was some way I could repay her and her husband for all their generosity and kindness. As it turned out, there was something I could do.

Although she was very loyal to her ill husband, by nature Boel was someone who liked to travel and to shop, especially since she had the money to do both in style. She asked me if I would occasionally accompany her and her great friend Kathleen Stewart on their shopping excursions to places like Milan, Paris, Rome and Stockholm. She said the two of them got tired of being stared at like a couple of 'wallflowers' and would really like to have some male company on these trips, particularly since men usually could get more respect and better service in foreign countries than a couple of ladies on their own. If this was one way I could start to repay her, I was happy to go along for the ride.

In general, as the weeks in New York stretched into months, and then a year had passed, I was less than happy with my daily existence. My deal with Rudy was no longer of interest. Other exciting opportunities suddenly appeared, and then disappeared just as suddenly. New York is always fizzing with chances for success, but intoxicating as this may be, a lot of these chances end up like the bubbles in champagne. They disappear into thin air. In truth, I was mostly walking on air in New York, and it didn't make me very happy. I needed to find my own business, but where once everything had seemed to fall into place naturally, this was no longer true for me.

When I look back at those years, I sometimes feel like I am staring at something like the swirl of water you see in your bath as it empties. I felt trapped in a downward spiral. That is how my life seemed to flow from the time I left Barbados for Mustique. I had moved to Canada, got married, had a daughter, watched the marriage fail, and then escaped to New York. Next, after a year or so, I found myself in Stockholm. And from there to London. Then back, of all places, to Barbados.

The swirl moved around and round, and I fought a daily battle to escape the pull of its gravity. I was fighting so hard to get my house settled on firm ground again, yet this spiral of energy was constantly turning on itself. It was a battle, and anyone who has ever been in a battle knows that you do not, if you survive, come away with detailed memories of exactly what happened. What I can recall is the general shape of events, and the way I felt, and where I was – but it's all slightly out of focus. Thankfully, I guess. Here's the drift of those days.

One evening, during a trip to Stockholm with Boel and Kathleen, we found ourselves sitting around the Great Table in Alex's new club. An old friend of mine from Mallorca, Max Gazala, walked through the door and soon we got talking.

'Noel, are you by any chance thinking of getting back into the nightclub business here in Stockholm?'

'At the moment I'm based in New York, but I'm not sure where my next club is going to be. I'm open to suggestions.'

'Well, you could do a lot worse than coming back here to Stockholm. Aside from the fact of your fantastic track record, and all your friends here, let me tell you why…'

He explained that he was in the process of organising a huge two-week long equestrian event, sponsored by the King of Sweden, that was attracting interest from tens of thousands of rich 'horsey' people from all across Europe. It would be a great platform on which to launch a new club. I started to make enquiries, and soon found a place that looked perfect – owned by an Iranian, located near the original Alexandra's, and losing money at a furious pace. So I arranged to meet the owner, and he expressed strong interest in selling. With his permission, I met with Berg Architects and asked them to put their ideas together with mine to produce a proposal for redesigning the club.

At this point, Boel gave me her blessing and returned to New York, leaving me to get on with what I did best. Months passed, but negotiations with the Iranian owner dragged along painfully slowly. Berg delivered some wonderful drawn projections for the new interiors, but now the Iranian had decided that he wanted to retain a percentage of the shares. I had a fling with Ulla, the ex-wife of Quincy Jones, *and I took a side-trip to escort Boel and Kathleen around Italy, but finally I saw there was no chance I would ever get a new club up and ready in time for the equestrian festival. I told the Iranian to keep his club, and flew to London.*

What happened to me in Stockholm became a kind of paradigm for what would happen to me, again and again, in London, then Marbella, and finally back in Barbados. It's not that I didn't come close to achieving my goal – my own nightclub – but as W.C. Fields might say, 'close, but no cigar'. During the next years, I made some wonderful new friends. I had a couple of intense love affairs. For a time, I worked as a consultant at the Limelight, a converted landmark church on the corner of Chinatown at Cambridge Circus in London, and helped its owners to renovate and upgrade its magnificent interior, as well as to organise many private functions and memorable evenings.

When the chance came to lease a new club on the site of the old Wellington club in Knightsbridge from a man named Les Moore, who had launched the old Valbonne back in the 1960s, I jumped at it. The problem was that I didn't have the kind of money necessary to buy the lease. Les proposed that I work as manager, until I could save or find the money to buy ownership. He even suggested that I should brand this as the new Alexandra's, and make a special promotion aimed at the many Swedes who lived in or visited London. Suddenly everything began to look very promising again, until I was told by a friend that Les had been arrested for a major tax fraud.

If that wasn't bad enough, during my stay in London I had rented a dank, dark basement flat in Chelsea. I poured tens of thousands of pounds into the place, and in time it was as elegant as any apartment in Mayfair. No sooner had I finished, than my landlord started sending me eviction notices. It turned out that he had sold the place out from under me, despite all the work and money I had invested. In the end, this went to court, and while I avoided immediate eviction, eventually I had to find a new place to live. That was the end of my London dream.

There's a lot of material that I have left out, but you can see the clear shape of my downward spiral from these details. Life was turning around on itself, over and over.

Now, of all the places in the world, I was back on Barbados, the island whose very name, when mentioned during the past decade, would bring me out in an ice-cold sweat. I had been living high in New York, top of the ladder in Stockholm, almost back to my real self in London. Now here I was on the island where my own Caribbean people had betrayed me: fucked with my marriage, fucked with my livelihood and fucked with my karma. And why had they done this? Nothing more or less than jealousy.

However, somehow, I managed to get to grips with my own head. Instead of bitterness, instead of feeling like a victim, I came to an important realisation. Everything I had been doing for these past difficult years was a kind of education. I had been learning how to pass the most difficult tests life can throw at you. Here, then, was Barbados: my final examination. Could I face my old enemies and rivals, forget the old nightmares, and put my house in order?

I got a job. It had been a long time. It felt good, pure and honest to be working as a bartender at Crocodile's Den, a hodgepodge of bric-a-brac and alcohol, the 'fun bar of Barbados', a world away from Alexandra's elegance or refinement, but vastly popular with both locals and tourists. Its owner, my boss, was Harry Hinds, a kind man, compulsive collector and true island character. Harry was enormously loyal to me, as was I to him. When he wasn't re-arranging all the junk in his yard, or inside the bar, he'd be off attending a yard sale or auction in pursuit of another miracle 'prize find', be it a tacky painting of Elvis Presley on velvet, a thousand dried up ballpoint pens, or the occasional genuine antique chest, table or chair.

Of course, all the mess, the rotting furniture in the yard, the constant moving and shifting of the 'décor', drove me a bit mad. In a way, we were like the Odd Couple, with me constantly nagging Harry to tidy the place, to stop letting pretty girls help themselves to drinks behind the bar, to run a more professional operation. Harry was only the leaseholder, and the landlord was a local judge who also didn't appreciate the mess. I knew he was threatening Harry with eviction if he didn't clean up his joint.

Still, thanks to Harry, I quickly furnished the little chattel house that I had rented. And thanks to the outrageously generous tips of my friends when they came by the bar, I was soon making enough money to allow me to start paying back some loans and to keep my head held high.

Of course, my decision to stay and work for Harry received mixed reactions from my old friends. 'Noel, what are you doing? This isn't you,' some of them told me. Well, I thought, how well had they ever known me in the first place? Others, like William and Phillipa, were much more supportive. 'If ever I lost everything,' William said once, 'I don't know if I would have the guts to do what you're doing. Especially right here on this island. We're very proud of you, Noel.'

Then came the day when my former accountant David Allison rang me and asked if I had seen the day's newspaper. 'The government has published a list of companies that owe land tax, and Alexandra's is on the list. That means the property still belongs to you. All you have to do is pay those back taxes, and you could be back in business.'

With some difficulty, I found a lawyer willing to represent me (most did not want to cross my old 'partner' and adversary Oscar Jordan) and write letters to the bank, the receiver, the registry and even Jordan himself. I just had to sit and wait.

And wait. Not a single person answered my lawyer's letters.

But someone had been paying attention. One day, without any notice, Erin Hall Great House – a truly historical building on the island – was condemned for rats and bulldozed to the ground. It was not as if every old building on the island didn't have its fair share of 'rats'. All my lawyer could find out from visiting the registry was that the land had been 'sold' by some other rats, for a song, to a new owner. I went to look at the devastated site. So much of my life had simply disappeared without a trace on this wasteland spot. It was almost incomprehensible. How could people be so cruel, so destructive? I think it was at that moment that I knew one day I would have to write this book.

However, I was not going to stand around in a depression, nursing my 'victimhood'. I was going to continue to live on my own terms, working part-time at the Crocodile, seeing my friends, starting to take notes for a memoir. Living comfortably and quietly, for the most part, until one day a face from the past suddenly arrived back in my life unannounced. It was Julian Lennon, back for a winter holiday, and keen to share my company. It had been years since I had last seen him, when he was an 18-year-old visitor at Sunset Lounge and I had tried to help him get his musical career rolling with Lee Hazlewood.

Now we became close friends, hanging out almost every day he was on the island. There is no question that I had felt a paternal affection for Julian ever since I had first met him in London. He was older now, more confident, and had brought a few of his friends along on his holiday. Together we had many memorable evenings of good food, fine drink and magnificent music. When he left a month later, we were solid friends.

The months passed slowly, sometimes not so enjoyably, but other times – as when I visited England and stayed with William and Phillipa in Hampshire – very agreeably indeed. It was while I was in England that I was contacted about managing the Baku disco on the west coast of Barbados. I flew back and eventually met with Mark O'Hara, and was offered a management job. After I had supervised a major renovation, Baku re-opened and soon became the most popular club on that side of the island, with cars parked all over the area and a huge line of people waiting to get inside. However, it wasn't really my scene, particularly when I realised that locals were being discouraged in a way I suspected was racism, while young white kids were allowed ready access. I began to spend as little time in the club as possible. I would open up the doors, spend the evening supervising the staff, and then leave right after closing. No more socialising with my friends and clients at a Great Table all night until dawn. I did most of my paperwork at home. I was happy for the money, but not thrilled by the job.

When Julian Lennon arrives for another month's holiday, I am very pleased to see his smiling, familiar face standing in the doorway of my tiny cottage. This time he is accompanied by his mother Cynthia, whom I have not met before, and her best friend Phyllis. It's wonderful to have Julian back, and great to have some charming and attractive ladies my own age with whom to hang out. I enjoy showing them around the island, and we have many delightful lunches and dinners over the next few weeks.

Watching Julian with his mother fills me with emotion. They are so close, and devoted to one another, it cannot fail to remind me of the painful relationship I had with my own mother. It also evokes for me the terrible pain that Julian and Cynthia must have suffered as a result of the hugely public separation, then divorce from their father/husband John Lennon. How did they manage to cope with the unspeakable tragedy of his murder? It isn't something they talk about very much, and certainly I am not going to broach the subject. Without being told, I know that the key to their survival is their strong love and trust for one another. Somehow, this gives me comfort, and makes me feel even closer to them. Perhaps too close...

Late one evening, Cynthia and I are having a last drink in Harry's bar, watching Julian talking to some friends across the room. 'You know, I really love your son. I've known him all these years and I couldn't bear it if anything bad ever happened to him. Did he ever tell you how we first met at Tramp?'

'No, he never mentioned it,' she says, a sudden coldness in her voice. 'Do you know how many people in Julian's life have said that kind of thing to me? "I love Julian. He's like my surrogate son." Or even "I'm his surrogate mother". Do any of you people ever stop to think how insulting this is to me – as if I don't exist. I am his mother. And the truth is that all these "surrogates" want is to get something from my son, not to give him something.'

'But that's not how it is with me...'

'Oh sure, you're different. You only want to help him, right? Piss off. If you had gone through three days of agony like I did to bring him into this world, then you might understand what real parental love is all about. I am his mother. There are no surrogates in our family. His father is not with us anymore. So don't go there. I'm not interested.'

'I am really very sorry. I mean it,' I say. At that moment, more than ever before, I can see what these two people have endured over the years. I see the 'first Lennon family' fending for themselves while the 'second Lennon family' shines in the floodlights of the world's monstrous publicity machine. I can see Cynthia and Julian trying to fend off every con artist on the planet who has a plan to cash in on their names. I can see how Cynthia has fought to protect her son, to respect his legacy, and to hold her own head aloft in the face of tragedy and exploitation. For the first time, I have seen the tiger's strength that lives within this beautiful lady.

The next day everything is back to normal, and nothing is said about our previous evening's conversation. We have more pleasant, informal lunches and dinners, and when the time comes for them to fly back to London, I am truly sorry to see them go. Cynthia and I are friends, of course, but I have learned not to let my own emotions cross an unspoken boundary between casual friendship and family.

The months pass without much incident, until one morning a nightmare leaps out of the past and is back with a vengeance. I am startled by a hammering on the cottage door, rise and confront 14 police officers, some with sniffer dogs.

'What do you want?'

'We got a warrant to search for drugs here.'

'Go right ahead and search. You won't find anything, not unless you've brought it here yourselves.'

Two hours later, after completely trashing my home, they tell me they're taking me down to Baku to continue the search. I slowly get the drift. Someone from the club has been busted for drugs, and they are using that as an excuse to focus on me again. The same powers of darkness on the island that have almost ruined my life are still in force, and still want to destroy me.

We go to the club and their search of the premises turns up nothing. Of course, their raid has consequences. Tongues will wag, and heads will turn, and within a week, the owners of Baku decide they no longer need my services, despite my contract. When I go to my lawyer, he tells me that he cannot help me. Yes, my contract has been breached, but the owners are also clients. It would be a terrible conflict of interest – for him. (They have the big money; I am just an old friend down on his luck who needs his lawyer to help him fight for what's right.) There's nothing I can do but head down to Harry's to get my old part-time bartending job back, while continuing to work on my memoir.

It's not too long after that, a whole year gone already, that Julian and Cynthia, together with a batch of friends, turn up on the island for Christmas 1999. They have rented Buttsbury House and plan on celebrating the millennium with a great party.

Over the next week or two, Cynthia and I go out to lunch several times and begin talking more about our lives than we had during her first visit. This time I know where the boundaries are, and I can see that gradually Cynthia is less distrustful. She talks about her past, and I am full of my own stories since I have been dredging up my memories while doing my memoir.

'Yes, I think I am going to write another book too,' she says. 'How is yours going, Noel?'

'I don't know. I find it very hard to remember the correct sequence of events when they span so many years. And it's difficult to concentrate when you're wondering what your enemies are likely to accuse you of next.'

'You know I'm living in Normandy now. It's very quiet, with no distractions, and I have two bedrooms in my house. Why don't you come and visit me and try to do some concentrated work, without any worries, no pressure? It's a serious invitation.'

'Thank you. It's a very generous invitation. I will think about it seriously.'

The day before New Year's Eve, our whole group goes out on a catamaran for a buffet lunch, music – a mini-tropical cruise. There must be forty people on board, most of them much younger than me. A sudden squall blows up, and everyone races for the confined cabins to wait out the rains. I end up sitting opposite Cynthia, scrunched down in the swaying claustrophobic shadows. We mouth 'Are you all right?' at one another. That's all the conversation we have, but somehow I sense that there is unspoken communication taking place. Nothing I can, or want, to put into words.

The next night is the end of the twentieth century and the start of the new millennium. Cynthia and I spend the night together. We fall in love. These are all the words I want to say about this most blessed night of my life.

More than ten years have gone by since then, and Cynthia and I have been together in Normandy, and now Mallorca, ever since that morning of 1 January 2000. I'll never forget how sheepish we two adults felt as we arrived, late in the afternoon, back at Buttsbury House. Of course, the place was rocking with lots of Julian's young friends, but everyone went silent when we turned up.

'Mother, what have you got to say for yourself – coming home at this hour?' Julian's voice bristled with mock-outrage. 'I've been worried sick about you.'

Then everybody started to clap and cheer. Cynthia's face turned bright red. So did mine! We were like two adolescents at that moment.

Today we are husband and wife, a married couple. I understand now why it took me so long to put my house in order. As I wandered from island to island, continent to continent, project to project: I was searching for a number of things, including money, respect, independence, security. I was searching for good things, the kind of things we all search for in our lives.

A familiar quest, yes, but not really the ultimate destination I think. In truth, all those years, all my life, I have been searching for my own heart. I now understand that my heart is not something I could ever find on my own. Cynthia's love – and my love for Cynthia – these together have revealed my heart to me. My life is my home, and home is where the heart lives. Welcome, readers, to my house.

Afterword

by Cynthia Lennon

When we first met on the island of Barbados, Noel mentioned that he was writing a book – the book which you have just finished reading. I asked him how the work was proceeding. 'Slowly,' he said.

That was December 1998. Thirteen wonderful years have passed. It is difficult to express just how pleased, amazed and enlightened I felt after reading these final pages. Slowly, but surely, it was worth waiting for this book about my husband's extraordinary life. I've learned so much from it. When we met and fell in love more than a decade ago, we were both almost strangers, although Noel and Julian had been close friends for years. In this book, the tale ends happily with our meeting and falling in love. Of course, for me, that was just the beginning of our happiness. I thought most readers would like to know a bit more about what happened next.

Perhaps it would be helpful if I explain some of the background to our first meeting – from my point of view. During the 18 years prior to our first encounter in Barbados, I had been living with a man who had been my partner in various undertakings, including three restaurants, many Beatle-related events and, finally, a move to a small village in Normandy. At that time, I was keen to 'retire' and return to the full-time painting career that I loved. Unfortunately, my partner felt this left him without his job 'as my manager'. He was not as comfortable in the quiet French countryside as I was, far from any cosmopolitan city. He felt, he told me, a bit redundant.

We quickly made friends with a group of local British ex-pats living in the area. Amongst them was a woman in her forties, wealthy, rather lonely, who was visibly suffering from a scandal involving her parents back in the UK that was then very much in the newspapers. We had taken her under our wings, and soon she was showing signs of blossoming: she lost weight, dyed her grey hair red, and became much more active. She even taught my husband how to play golf. One night before a total eclipse of the sun, we threw a dinner party. In the middle of dinner, my partner and she announced their love for each other in front of our closest local friends. Needless to say, that ended the party fast. When the other guests had all gone, the couple declared their continuing love for me, and their hope that we could all stay friends. I asked them both to leave.

I was in total shock. My future had been stolen from me in the space of five minutes. ('Lost in France' comes to mind). It took me a while to compose myself, and then I was on the phone to friends. I longed to call my son Julian, but he was just about to go on tour to promote his new album *Photograph Smile* and the last thing I wanted was to make his life difficult at that moment. My friends insisted that I must tell him. Despite myself, I couldn't hold back the tears when I heard his voice down the line. I told him everything.

'Mum, stay where you are. I'll be with you in a heartbeat. I'll fly to Paris, hire a car and drive straight to Normandy. You can help me with directions when I get close.'

It was 3 a.m. when Julian finally arrived, after many phone calls for directions from the maze of rural roads leading to my cottage. The chicken I had cooked for him was well and truly past its best. His car was stuffed with enormous suitcases full of the clothes he would need for his first tour in seven years. He was supposed to be on his way to Hong Kong to meet his band. I was overjoyed to see him. He insisted that he would stay with me, if I wished, and delay his tour, but as happy as I was to have Julian there, I was adamant that under no circumstances should my personal dilemma interfere with his life and future.

So, as intense as our reunion was, we had to say goodbye almost immediately, as the sun was rising. He didn't look very happy about driving away that dawn but, in fact, in just a couple of hours he had given me the heart to go on with my life.

The fact was that Julian and my former partner never had had much time for one another. It had made life 'complicated'. While Julian was busy exploring the world, creating his own music and forging his career, my partner and I had been busy earning a living.

During the next few weeks, I realised that I had lost a companion, but that I had gained real freedom. Above all, now I could have my son back, and he could have his mother back. My plans evolved over the next weeks and I decided that I would sell my house and move to the nearby seaside village of Port Bail, where I would rent a fisherman's cottage and dedicate my time to writing and painting.

During those previous 18 years, Julian had formed a deep affection for Barbados, as Noel describes in his book, and taken to renting a villa over the Christmas holidays, to which he would invite his closest friends. Due to the tension between my partner and Julian, I had never been able to accept an invitation before. When one door closes, another opens, and the blinkers do come off. This year, when Julian insisted that I come down to Barbados for Christmas and New Year 1998, inviting along my dearest friend from Liverpool, Phyl, I was free to accept.

In the days before we left, Phyl and I were like little kids, constantly singing, 'Whoa, we're going to Barbados.' And soon enough, although the flight was very long, suddenly we were at the airport and there was Julian waiting for us. The villa was magical, tropical, sumptuous. There were monkeys playing in the garden trees, friendly maids waiting to help us in any way, and it was a short walk to the white beach and the bright turquoise sea. Julian's friends welcomed us with open arms and we were up for anything: restaurants, nightlife, sailing excursions. It was heaven for me, a far cry from the grey skies and solitude of a Normandy winter.

It wasn't long before I noticed a tall, mysterious black man who seemed to pop in and out of the house as if he belonged there, who chatted to Julian as if they had known each other forever. Soon, I was introduced to Noel. He kindly offered to show Phyl and me around the island. Because we were closer in age than I was with Julian's other friends, it was natural to fall into easy conversations. In truth, we became friends, but nothing more than friends during that first visit. When the time came to catch our flight back to Europe, Phyl and I agreed that it had been a marvellous holiday. I was returning to Normandy where I felt strong enough to tackle life's challenges alone – to get on with my painting – to let my heart mend.

Jump forward one year. It was the dawning of a new millennium, and Julian had insisted that we both return to celebrate this with him on Barbados. This time (perhaps he was worried that I might not accept?) Julian had booked us tickets on Concorde! I had always wanted to fly on that amazing aeroplane and, of course, the idea of making the long journey in only three and a half hours also appealed. Most of all, I was delighted to spend another Christmas holiday with my son.

That second visit was even more revelatory than the first. Undoubtedly, I had put another year between me and the emotional stress of my break-up. From the moment I arrived on Barbados, it felt as if the dark clouds of the past had finally all gone away. I experienced a creative surge and began to write poems every day. Noel was a frequent visitor and, as before, we three 'oldies' found plenty to talk about sitting around the pool and sharing stories about our lives. It turned out that Noel and I had lots in common, so much so that it struck me as quite bizarre. Our lives seemed to run on parallel tracks; we knew so many of the same people. His contacts through the two nightclubs he'd owned were often people that I had met via my own journey through the Beatle extravaganza. Now that I was emotionally independent, I was able to connect more easily with this gentle, intelligent, charismatic man. I knew without a doubt that he loved my son and had protected him, without my knowledge, over many years.

Over a few days, we became closer. It was a meeting of minds, and eventually bodies. We all went out for dinner on New Year's

Eve, and then off to Harry's 'Crocodile Den' bar afterwards. Instead of heading home, the two of us ended up back at Noel's little chattel house. I had no questions in my mind. It felt so right. What a fantastic beginning to a new millennium – and a brand new life at the age of sixty.

The following day we both were very nervous about returning to the villa. We waited until two thirty in the afternoon, hoping everyone would have gone to the beach. No such luck! We found ourselves walking into a lion's den: everyone was gathered out by the pool. As soon as we arrived, there was thunderous applause, wolf whistles and laughter. Julian stood up and approached us with a serious frown. How worried he had been! Where had I spent the night? Was this a decent hour to be coming home? The tables of authority were turned on me so that, for a few moments, I felt like a naughty schoolgirl. Then I got the joke and joined in the laughter. Noel and I had finally made a leap into commitment, in public, and it wasn't long before Julian started calling him 'Dad' with a sincere and humorous affection.

Even before we became lovers, I had suggested that Noel come to Normandy to work on his book. He had so many friends on Barbados, and so many frenetic distractions (both welcome and unwelcome, as he makes clear), that it was difficult to make sustained progress with his writing. I thought my little house would offer him the peace he needed to concentrate and create. Now we made a decision that Noel would, in fact, return to France with me. Over the next two weeks, he packed up his entire life into a few suitcases. We went to many parties where his friends cried openly at the thought of losing him. This made an impression on me, of course, but it would be years, and several drafts of his book, before I would fully understand the struggles and the successes that Noel had experienced.

I let my friends back in Normandy know that I would be returning with a new man in my life. This provoked some fascinating responses. One friend actually phoned me to recount her nightmare. She had imagined me in a wrought iron bed with a thirty-year-old Rastafarian. I was dressed in black tights, stiletto heels and nothing else. 'Are you sure that you're all right?' she asked me over the phone. 'I mean, are you sure you know what you are doing?' I assured her that I was very happy and knew exactly what I was doing.

Our departure from Barbados was chaotic, with a great deal of luggage. In the melee, I lifted a large case that was far too heavy. My back suddenly went into a spasm of pain. I was in agony. Thank God the Concorde flight was so short. We couldn't stay at Julian's flat for the first two nights, as there were other guests staying, so we checked into the Kensington Palace hotel. Our first morning in London dawned and I was completely paralysed by the pain in my back. We were on the seventh floor, and while Noel was in the bathroom, the fire alarm suddenly began to blare. He rushed to try and help me out of bed. I told him I couldn't walk. 'Don't worry, I'll carry you down the stairs,' he promised. Seven flights! Somehow we tried to dress, gather our valuables and head towards the door, with the alarm making a horrendous, incessant klaxon wail. Then suddenly it went silent. Noel stuck his head out of the door. It was a false alarm, just testing, he was told. I managed to make it back into bed.

The pain was excruciating and, when the time came to make the move to Julian's flat, we had so many suitcases that Noel hired a 'people mover' through the concierge. It was just a ten-minute drive to the flat, but I was dreading it as I hobbled through reception, and was so stressed out that I walked straight into the closed glass doors of the hotel lobby. When I had recovered from that stunning blow to my forehead, it was only to discover that the 'people mover' was actually a large furniture van. It took a while to sort this out, until we agreed that I would ride up in front and Noel would go in the back with the 'furniture'. In the end, it took three weeks of strong painkillers and rest before I was fit enough to continue our journey to Normandy. I might have stayed in London longer, but I had an appointment which I had agreed to months earlier and which I couldn't break.

A popular TV show at the time was *Through the Keyhole*, hosted by David Frost, which involved filming people's homes, then having a celebrity panel guess whose home it was, and finally bringing the owner onto the stage to be interviewed live in a London studio.

I had agreed to participate long before I knew that David Frost was married to Carina, of whom you will have read much in Noel's book. In any case, the TV film crew would soon be arriving on my Normandy doorstep, with Loyd Grossman as the location presenter. My neighbours were all excited about this, and about meeting Grossman, but my feelings were decidedly mixed, since my back was not really healed, and I knew the house was in desperate need of a spring clean. However, whatever history he might have had with Frost, Noel rose to the challenge after we arrived. On went the pinafore and rubber gloves, and an amazing whirlwind of cleanliness swept through my home. I was basically confined to bed, where I kept thinking about something Noel had told me in Barbados. 'Life is all about luck and timing.' Lying there, listening to him working on the house, I feared that the timing of our arrival couldn't be worse and that my luck was running out. Fortunately, I was very wrong.

When the crew arrived, Noel and I kept a low profile, delegating Grossman's reception to two of my best local friends. We went off to lunch while they filmed the interior of the house. Noel had, of course, explained to me his unhappy associations with David Frost, and there was no tension between us at all. When, some weeks later, I had to journey back to London to go on the TV stage, it was my friend Phyl who accompanied me to the studio. I had actually met David Frost some years earlier, with my friend the singer Lulu, and so was quite relaxed about the whole deal. One amusing moment came backstage when Phyl met another guest, Bernard Matthews (the turkey man), who had arrived in his own helicopter. 'So what do you do for a living then?' she asked him. A perfect 'Golden Girls' moment. I had a brief chat with David Frost after the show, and kept thinking, 'He wouldn't be so smug if he knew who I was sharing my house with now.'

Our first months in Normandy were memorable, a true adventure. Suddenly I was receiving more visitors per week than I was used to having in a month. Everybody seemed to want to take a look at my new 'guest'. Amongst the first to call were a couple of English ex-pats who had moved to Normandy after sojourning in South Africa (where things were changing a little too fast for their comfort).

He was a Lord Lucan lookalike, she a classic English Rose. One of their conversational mantras was about how British television was being taken over by ethnic minorities. They had a beautiful house and plummy accents, and when they turned up, unannounced, at our door one afternoon, their jaws both dropped in astonishment.

Noel had opened the door. He was dressed in a beautiful Harris tweed suit, brogues, the full monty: a perfect English country gentleman. His speaking voice is impeccable. His colour is Black. I was standing behind him. We greeted them and invited them inside. They were so astounded and confused by what they had not expected that they refused to come inside, and hastily retreated to their car. We watched them drive away down the lane, sharing a laugh between ourselves. There was no need to say anything.

In fact, all my friends in Normandy were bowled over by this man from the Caribbean with class, style and gracious humour. All preconceived ideas soon went out the window. Being social animals, we both loved to entertain. Coming to terms with my chequered past and my title as the first wife of John Lennon must have been bewildering to him. In truth, following our whirlwind romance, we were still in relative ignorance of each other's past lives. I had named my Normandy cottage Détente – an appropriate site for coming to terms with each other. Space was limited. There were two small bedrooms, one bathroom, a kitchen with open shelves that led into the lounge with its lovely Normandy fireplace. In there, I had two pieces of antique furniture, dating back to my mother's saleroom days, and a black leather three-piece suite. When Noel lay down on the couch, I couldn't see him unless he opened his eyes or smiled. I used to walk past him frequently, utterly surprised when he spoke up.

My Irish friend who had dreamed about me with a young Rastafarian used to call on us often, usually with her girlfriend. She loved her liquid refreshment. On one occasion, Noel offered to drive her into our local hamlet (a butcher and a grocery/post office) where she needed to do some last minute shopping. Her French was far from fluent, and on this occasion failed her completely. So she asked the butcher, 'Do you have any *baaah*?' He looked at her in amazement. 'I need some *baaah* for dinner.

Do you have any?' It took a while before he understood she wanted to purchase some lamb.

We loved to cook on the open log fire. Lamb cutlets were our favourite. Television reception was poor. However, we were on everybody's guest list, and we often felt as if we were living a series of 'judgment days' as our new love was put on display at dining tables across the region. It wasn't long before the women in our circle were flirting outrageously with Mr Noel Charles, the new man on the block. So much for my 'protective' friends. We both found this turn of events rather blatant but very funny.

My first introduction to Noel's past life and his friends in England was fantastic fun, as well as enlightening. We planned to take the ferry from Cherbourg to Portsmouth. At the port, the French officials informed Noel that he had no visa to enter Europe. But he was already here! Thus began a continuing saga of his Bajan passport and lack of visa that would take ages to sort out. Pleading honest ignorance, we were waved onto the boat. We took the train up to London, where we would stay at Julian's flat. Because of my continual back pain, our first stop was going to be the office of Noel's friend Chris, a noted chiropractor, and a Canadian by birth. Larger than life, Chris had suffered a stroke a couple of years previously.

We arrived at his office on time, only to learn that he would be late. This was quite unlike him. When Chris did arrive, both Noel and I were taken aback. The poor man looked very ill indeed. We told him to go straight home and we would come back when he was feeling better. There was no way Chris would let us down, however, and as he began to work on my back, adjusting my spine with his skilled hands, I really feared that he might die on the job. In fact, this was not far from the truth, for shortly after that appointment he was taken to hospital.

We went to visit him a couple of days later. He still looked very poorly, but he was determined to finish the job, and we had to stop him from climbing out of his bed to deal with me there and then. He explained to me that my back problem was not the result of lifting Noel's heavy suitcase (the butt of many a friendly joke), but the result of years of stress. We went to visit him several more times in hospital, and on one occasion met Mel, his friendly sister-in-law. She lived in Toronto and, unbeknownst to us at the time, would play a pivotal role in our lives in the future. Sadly, Chris died shortly afterwards. A lovely man who would be much missed by all his friends: I had the terribly sad honour of being his very last patient.

Noel was adamant that we visit his dear friends William and Phillipa at their stately home in Hampshire. I come from Liverpool and, before we visited, I felt as if I knew nothing of the world they represented. I was trained as an artist, but this was truly a blank canvas for me, not unlike my new relationship with Noel. Everything was fresh, new and exciting. Although Noel came from Trinidad, he had easy access to an upper class British world that even the Beatles would only encounter on rare, organised occasions. (I had met Princess Margaret once, briefly, without any warmth, at the premiere for one of the Beatles' films.)

When we arrived at their grand house in Hampshire, my stress levels were so high that my back was really giving me gyp. I was immediately welcomed by Phillipa and William with so much love and concern that I was almost overwhelmed. They escorted me to a beautiful bedroom where an electric blanket was quickly brought for my back. Apparently, Phillipa also suffered from back pain and was incredibly sympathetic to my plight. While I rested and chatted with my gracious hostess, Noel and William caught up on old times: Barbados, Ascot, the life they had shared over many years. By the time I went to sleep that night, I was feeling completely at home. I knew that I had fallen in love with a wonderful human being, a man who was loved and admired by so many people from all over the world, who was proud to introduce me to his very special friends.

We happily returned to Normandy at the end of that visit, but it was not long before we crossed the Channel again. In fact, twice during that year we came back to Blighty for weddings of old friends of Noel's. The first of these was between Brigitte Hill (daughter of racing driver Graham, sister of Damon) and Anthony Haas. This was held at the House of Commons, and all the guests were given a brilliant tour of Westminster Palace. After a while, many of the guests, including me, while impressed with all the 'historical' sights, were also gasping for a drink. Shortly thereafter, we all noticed a sign pointing to the Bar of the House. Our spirits rose, and we all headed in that direction. However, this 'bar' was not one of the 19 bars and restaurants that operate inside the Palace, but was a ceremonial landmark just inside the House of Lords which marks the official boundary separating Commons members from the Lords during official events. Lots of history, but not a drink in sight! Soon enough, we were guided out onto the magnificent terrace that overlooked the Thames where the champagne began to flow faster than that famous river ever has.

The second wedding couldn't have been more different. The groom, Noel's friend, was Scottish. His bride held a range of advanced New Age views on life and love. So the ceremony itself was rather extraordinary, especially considering that all the groom's male relatives were dressed in full Hibernian outfits. Noel had borrowed, with my encouragement, a kilt and the rest of the classic outfit from my Scottish friend Gordon, who was just 5 foot 6 inches tall. This made for a tight fit. Still, I thought that Noel's presence – the only Black Trinidadian in a black mini kilt – actually raised the tone of what I found a rather bizarre wedding.

These were wonderful shared experiences for us both. I felt that I was truly alive again in a way I hadn't felt for many years. At one point in Normandy, Noel's daughter Chloe came to visit us from her home in Toronto. She was 16 years old. It was a great change for me, aged sixty and used to living with men all my adult life, to suddenly have a lively, charming young woman in my familial life. It was a bit challenging, yes, but yet another fantastic part of the new winds of change that were blowing us into the future that year.

We continued to see Julian frequently. At this time, he was dating Lucy, a young lady who lived on the Spanish island of Mallorca, with her ex-pat parents, whom Noel had met often during their winter holidays in Barbados. As the relationship became more serious, Julian decided that he wanted to buy a holiday home in Spain. He insisted that Noel and I accompany him around Mallorca as he looked for a suitable property. Noel, of course, had lots of friends on the island where he had once lived, so we were happy to come along. After a week of house hunting, instead of buying one house for Julian, we ended up buying two, with the other for Noel and I. It all felt right, part of this new 'magical mystery tour'.

Although we hadn't really spoken about it, life in Normandy was not quite right for either of us. Unless you wanted to run a B&B, or work an agricultural smallholding, it really wasn't all that stimulating. Noel was used to having many different kinds of friends in his daily life, and since I had fallen in love with him, my previous dream of living alone as a solitary artist had obviously been replaced by a much more exciting reality. So our move to the villa outside Palma de Mallorca was brilliant. The weather was heavenly; we quickly had a social life full of vibrant, fascinating friends, both old and new; the island itself was a gorgeous mix of many cultures, breathtaking landscapes and delicious food. It was here on Mallorca that I accepted Noel's proposal of marriage.

It wasn't his first, for he had made several others before we left Normandy, but I had demurred, thinking that, after three previous marriages, I ought to recognise when enough's enough. In Spain, I realised that I should never say 'never again' because, in my heart, I must be the marrying kind. When we told Julian of our matrimonial plans, he was a bit surprised at first. He made sure to take me aside, ever the protective son. He felt he must be honest and point out that his dear friend, Noel Charles, did have a history that included many ladies in his life. 'Well, darling, I haven't done so badly myself,' I told him. In truth, with three marriages apiece, I felt Noel and I balanced one another 'even stevens'. With a wry smile, Julian told me that obviously I knew what was best.

We were planning to visit Toronto for Chloe's 17th birthday in May. Why not get married there, once we had sorted out Noel's divorce papers? We thought that we would keep it a big secret. Unfortunately, Julian's career commitments would keep him from attending, but we agreed to hold a big celebration when we returned to Mallorca. Toronto would be very low-key, we decided, and we enlisted Mel, the sister-in-law of Chris, Noel's now deceased chiropractor friend, to help us. She not only insisted that we stay with her, but also promised to get all the paperwork together. 'Don't you worry about a thing.

I'll get it all organised,' she promised. That took a load off our shoulders. Or so we thought.

Our first priority in Toronto was to surprise Chloe on her birthday. We hired a limousine with darkened windows to drive us to her college, where we waited for classes to end. When she emerged, surrounded by friends and clutching a bunch of balloons, Noel and I emerged from the car. Chloe caught sight of us and her face broke into a huge smile. I have never seen anyone, before or since, leap so high into the air! As it happened, this would be the highlight of our trip. It made everything worthwhile.

Mel's apartment was rather eccentric, and thus set the tone for the rest of our visit. Her walls, every shelf, the entire place was decorated with ornamental angels! She had a real obsession with them, which may have been linked (I'm still not sure) with her religious beliefs. She belonged to a sect who spoke in tongues (although her native tongue was German) and she kept up a non-stop monologue of 'tongues' throughout the day. Meanwhile, she was on a permanent diet, and hence there was no food in the house. Naturally, she did not smoke, while both Noel and I are smokers. Her tiny white Persian cat had been declawed and 'de-meowed', the poor thing. Mel's frequent mood swings did not make it any easier to relax as our wedding day approached.

Still the paperwork took days to arrange. In the meantime, Noel and I managed to organise a trip to the supermarket. We were introduced to Mel's boyfriend Nick, who would 'give me away'. Mel also insisted that we spend our wedding night at a country house hotel outside Toronto, and booked a room for us.

Finally, the papers were complete, and our wedding day – 7 June 2002 – was at hand. It was a beautiful sunny day. Chloe and her friend arrived, looking lovely, but they were a little bemused by the ornamental angels. That made four of us. We drove off to City Hall together. Mel was to join us there, with Nick. On arrival, we were ushered into a tiny chapel with loud piped music. No sign of Mel or her boyfriend. Both Noel and I were very nervous. What else could go wrong? Then they arrived in a tizzy, and Mel shoved a bouquet of flowers into my hands. Chloe and her friend couldn't stop giggling.

Then something went right! The 'preacher man' arrived and he was from Barbados! Very tall and black, he towered over us and put us instantly at ease, despite the loud music. He conducted the service with real dignity. Nick, a relative stranger, gave me away and we exchanged rings, signed the wedding register and breathed two deep sighs of relief. We were both thinking: 'Now we can leave Toronto!' Well, not quite yet. First we all trooped back to Mel's flat where the reception consisted of champagne and a McDonald's takeaway. This was unique, and truly memorable. Then we were off to the country house hotel: Noel and I, Chloe and her friend. Julian rang us while we were in the car, and sent his love and congratulations.

The hotel itself was located on a large and beautiful Canadian estate. Unfortunately, on arrival at reception, we were informed that the hotel was fully booked and there was no room for the girls. We had asked Mel to book an extra room for them, but she obviously had had other ideas. Moreover, the whole place was non-smoking. Eventually Noel managed to arrange for us all to occupy a cabin on the grounds. We were allowed to smoke outside on the porch. There seemed to be a security guard posted nearby to ensure that we broke no regulations. Exhausted, and putting the whole experience down to experience, we all promptly went to sleep. Years later, I can look back and laugh. It was hysterical, and historical.

Given that one of my first conversations with Noel was about this book, and my subsequent desire to help him to finish it, you can imagine how very pleased this publication makes me. What happened after we first met – two lost souls in search of their equal mates – was genuine Kismet, I believe. Having read these pages that describe Noel's life so honestly and vividly, I again feel so fortunate that we met when we did. The many rivers he's crossed, the mountains and valleys that he has known: Noel is one of life's genuine explorers and, for so many different people over the years, an amazingly loyal and generous friend. Finally, if Noel can survive me, and being called 'Mr Lennon' in every hotel we stay in, he can survive anything.

"You are my knight, I am your day."

Noel

It wasn't as if I'd had a dull or boring life before we met but I can only thank you for our time together.

What is lovely for me is your generosity, your loyalty, your sensitivity - I even find your temper tantrums quite fascinating and your shopping - well what can I say?....

We have, I believe the closest we can get to soul mates.

What do we have in common?
We love to cook
We care about the ones we love
We even care about the ones we dislike

I think the basis of our understanding is our friendship, our individual history. We have both endured the pain and bathed in the pleasure.

Neither of us will ever be "middle of the road"

Darling, as long as I am on the same road as you

I will be forever grateful   ♡
                              Love Cynthia x

Acknowledgements

With heartfelt gratitude to all my dear friends for their constant support and encouragement in helping me fulfil my dream of writing my memoirs. It took a while but we finally made it! Thank you.

Thank you to Celia Quantrill for her energy, ability and belief in this project. You are a very special person and your work on the book has been much appreciated.

A special thank you to Paul Spike. Without his compassion, integrity, determination and professional skill *In My House* may still have remained in my house!